Political Cohesion
in a Fragile Mosaic

Westview Replica Editions

The concept of Westview Replica Editions is a response to the continuing crisis in academic and informational publishing. Library budgets for books have been severely curtailed. Ever larger portions of general library budgets are being diverted from the purchase of books and used for data banks, computers, micromedia, and other methods of information retrieval. Interlibrary loan structures further reduce the edition sizes required to satisfy the needs of the scholarly community. Economic pressures on the university presses and the few private scholarly publishing companies have severely limited the capacity of the industry to properly serve the academic and research communities. As a result, many manuscripts dealing with important subjects, often representing the highest level of scholarship, are no longer economically viable publishing projects--or, if accepted for publication, are typically subject to lead times ranging from one to three years.

Westview Replica Editions are our practical solution to the problem. We accept a manuscript in camera-ready form, typed according to our specifications, and move it immediately into the production process. As always, the selection criteria include the importance of the subject, the work's contribution to scholarship, and its insight, originality of thought, and excellence of exposition. The responsibility for editing and proofreading lies with the author or sponsoring institution. We prepare chapter headings and display pages, file for copyright, and obtain Library of Congress Cataloging in Publication Data. A detailed manual contains simple instructions for preparing the final typescript, and our editorial staff is always available to answer questions.

The end result is a book printed on acid-free paper and bound in sturdy library-quality soft covers. We manufacture these books ourselves using equipment that does not require a lengthy make-ready process and that allows us to publish first editions of 300 to 600 copies and to reprint even smaller quantities as needed. Thus, we can produce Replica Editions quickly and can keep even very specialized books in print as long as there is a demand for them.

About the Book and Authors

Political Cohesion in a Fragile Mosaic: The Yugoslav Experience
Lenard Cohen and Paul Warwick

This book represents the first comprehensive empirical investigation of political cohesion in the multi-ethnic state of Yugoslavia, covering the entire period from the nation's independence to the present. The authors base their analysis on an extensive body of aggregate voting data from elections during both the precommunist and communist periods and on their own field research in Yugoslavia. Drs. Cohen and Warwick categorize the country's sixty-year course of political development into distinct periods to assess the influence of each regime's policies and strategies for managing cultural diversity. Using census data on ethnic composition and on economic development, they demonstrate how cultural identity and modernization affect political behavior and incorporation. Beyond offering a general evaluation of Yugoslavia's past and present experience with political cohesion, the book's sophisticated methodological approach may prove useful for the study of other political systems.

Dr. Cohen is co-editor of *Communist Systems in Comparative Perspective* and Dr. Warwick is the author of *The French Popular Front: A Legislative Analysis*. Both authors are associate professors of political science at Simon Fraser University, British Columbia.

FOR OUR PARENTS
FANNIE AND LOUIS COHEN
JEAN AND SIDNEY WARWICK

Political Cohesion in a Fragile Mosaic
The Yugoslav Experience

Lenard Cohen
and Paul Warwick

Westview Press / Boulder, Colorado

81-8796

Copyright © 1983 by Westview Press, Inc.

Published in 1983 in the United States of America by
   Westview Press, Inc.
   5500 Central Avenue
   Boulder, Colorado 80301
   Frederick A. Praeger, President and Publisher

Library of Congress Cataloging in Publication Data
Cohen, Lenard J.
   Political cohesion in a fragile mosaic.
   (A Westview replica edition)
   Bibliography: p.
   1. Elections--Yugoslavia--History. 2. Yugoslavia--Politics and
government--1918-1945. 3. Yugoslavia--Politics and government--
1945-   . 4. Minorities--Yugoslavia--Political activity--
History. 5. Political stability--Yugoslavia--History. I. Warwick,
Paul. II. Title.
JN9679.A15C63   1983   320.9497   83-6585
ISBN 0-86531-967-7

Printed and bound in the United States of America
10 9 8 7 6 5 4 3 2

Contents

Tables

Figures

Preface

Several years ago, when Yugoslavia was still in the twilight of the Tito era, we began a research project to explore the critical issue of political cohesion in that highly diverse multi-ethnic state. Rather than following the example of most books on Yugoslavia (or other communist states) which offer a snapshot of the country's divisions and bonds at one particular time, or during the span of one regime, we decided to examine the changing levels of political cohesiveness revealed during each historical stage since the creation of the country as an independent state following World War I.

To accomplish this ambitious task we focused our analysis on a rich and largely neglected body of evidence -- aggregate voting data for elections during both the pre-communist and communist periods. While some scholars had already recognized that elections in Tito's unique type of communist regime were different from those which took place in other East European states, the potential of this evidence for making comparisons between the non-communist and communist periods had apparently gone unnoticed, or at least untapped. This may have been due to the awesome methodological obstacles involved: frequent changes in the boundaries of electoral units, constant political reorganizations, and difficulties in data collection (especially for the prewar and early communist periods) compounded the task of analyzing empirical data on such a large number of elections and over such diverse regime-types. This book is testimony to our conviction that these obstacles could be surmounted with considerable effort and that the effort was worth undertaking.

The findings provide, we believe, a fresh perspective on the Yugoslav experience in state-building and conflict management. Categorizing the fascinating 60-year course of political development into distinct periods, we examine the differential impact which a wide repertoire of changing policies or strategies have had on the level of political incorporation and political cohesion. Each so-called "regime-strategy" for managing the country's extreme cultural diversity is discussed, and then assessed in terms of its influence on the incorporation of different nationalities and regions. Using census data on ethnic composition and economic development, the study also explores the contrasting effect of cultural identities and modernization as determinants of political behavior and incorporation. The objectives of the study are to offer the reader a general evaluation of Yugoslavia's past and present cohesion (and therefore a more systematic basis to speculate about the regime's further evolution) and also to allow for

xii

comparisons and projections regarding other political systems which may have already utilized similar strategies, or may wish to do so in the future.

The authors wish to express their appreciation to Simon Fraser University for a President's Research Grant to support our study, and to Terri Sussel for her diligent help as a research assistant. We are also grateful to Barbara Barnett, Linda Manheim, Pamela Nori, and Margaret Paine for their help in the completion of the manuscript. Finally, we owe a special thanks to our families, friends, and those of our colleagues who contributed to our "personal cohesion" throughout the course of the study.

Lenard Cohen and Paul Warwick
Burnaby Mountain, British Columbia

1
The Study of Political Cohesion: A Neglected Issue

The cohesion and survival of political systems have been central concerns of rulers, citizens, and political analysts throughout history. These concerns have assumed a special and very practical urgency in societies composed of highly diverse and conflicting cultural groups, where centrifugal pressures constantly test the merits of political structures, policies, and leaders. In such divided or "segmented" societies, the difficulties of ensuring the regime's continued existence often comprise a good deal of the political process.

Among contemporary states, there is no better example than Yugoslavia of the problems that extreme cultural diversity present for the attainment of political cohesion. The cultural complexity of that polity is legendary and has made the very survival of a single Yugoslav state from 1918 to the present day something of a minor miracle.[1] But the achievement has been a troubled one at best. Failure, or the risk of failure, to maintain the state has been an ever-present possibility to Yugoslav leaders throughout the six decades of the country's existence. Even today, after thirty-eight years of communist rule, the problems of cohesion and regime survival still occupy the attentions of the country's rulers and strongly influence their policies. Yugoslavia remains a volatile and uncertain experiment.

That the Yugoslav state continues to exist as a single entity is due in part to the ceaseless quest for solutions by her various political leaderships. As diverse as the country's cultural makeup is the array of institutions, policies, and actions that have been devised and introduced to enhance the political cohesiveness of the polity. Indeed, as we shall elaborate in the next chapter, every major regime-type -- from right-wing authoritarian dictatorship to liberal democracy to socialist one-party rule -- and, more importantly, virtually every extant strategy for coping with cultural diversity has been tried at one time or another in Yugoslavia's brief history. Yugoslavia has not wanted for political innovation. But with what success?

Oddly, this question, so central to the Yugoslav experience and potentially so instructive concerning the problems of many other new states, has not received comprehensive and systematic treatment to date. It is true that considerable attention has been devoted to the exposition of the various culturally-derived centrifugal forces that have manifested themselves during each distinct historical period in Yugoslavia, and some of these studies of the "national problem" do offer exceptionally useful treatments of the historical literature (Shoup, 1968; Hondius, 1967; Rusinow;

1977). Most, however, have been restricted in scope to a short period of time or to the analysis of one event or personality (Tito, Djilas, etc.), and/or have lacked a solid empirical basis for generalizations and conclusions of a broader nature. Regrettably, these studies have occasionally been marred by extreme value commitments on the part of ex-participants in the specific issues and events under consideration (Popovic, 1968; Djilas, 1969; Tudjman, 1981).

It is also true that information of a more systematic sort on political attitudes and behavior has been provided by public opinion surveys conducted, for the most part, during the 1960s (Zaninovich, 1970; Jacob and Teune, 1971; Verba et al., 1971, 1978). Although these studies have been quite valuable in themselves, they, too, lack the scope to address larger issues such as the influence of changing institutional structures and strategies on levels of political cohesion throughout the course of Yugoslav political history. Moreover, the survey studies and the voluminous workers' council literature in particular have had the inevitable effect of focusing attention almost exclusively on individual orientations, leaving the reader with the impression that properties such as political cohesion and regime durability emanate directly from the political attitudes elicited from the man in the street or the factory. But this is patently not the case, for these properties are properties of the system, not of its components taken individually, and as such have meaning only at the level of the system. Even if survey researchers were free to ask their respondents questions in such sensitive areas as system support and legitimacy, and even if the responses were frank and accurate, their individual-level focus would condemn the evidence they provided to at best an indirect and supportive role in dealing with such questions. Elite studies, which also offer important insights on the political process, are equally inappropriate for our central concern. Political cohesiveness, although not an individual-level concept, is not an elite phenomenon either: it is a property of the system, not of its leadership.

How, then, can the issue of political cohesion in Yugoslavia be addressed? Cohesion, which in ordinary usage refers to the process of sticking together or agglutination of parts, can be indicated empirically by a variety of phenomena that point to its absence: acts or statements of dissent on the part of intellectuals or political leaders who reject, for nationalistic or ideological reasons, the state as presently constituted; the emergence of nationalist or separatist movements, politically-motivated strikes and demonstrations, or widespread evasion of citizen duties such as payment of taxes or military service; violent confrontations between subcommunities or subcultural groups within the society; and the like. Yugoslavia has experienced no shortfall in these types of non-cohesive behaviors. However, to concentrate solely on activities of this sort, which usually involve minorities and are sporadic and haphazard in their occurrence, would be to neglect the general state of cohesiveness in the polity in favor of occasional, more overt manifestations at its fringes. It would, moreover, involve establishing the existence of political cohesion in an exclusively negative fashion, i.e., by the dearth of indications to the contrary.

Accordingly, in this study the principal indicator of political cohesiveness shall be the extent of mass political incorporation that exists in the polity. By political incorporation we mean the degree to which various components (territorial units, cultural groups, social classes, or other sub-societal collectivities), especially those which have been excluded from, peripheral to, or even outside the boundaries of the state, function as parts of a single political entity. This conceptualization of political incorporation relates to "the generalized problem of holding a system together" which Weiner (1965:55) has suggested as the core meaning of the term "integration." We prefer to avoid this latter term, however, because it has been associated definitionally with a variety of political processes, including national identity formation, elite-mass integration, central control over peripheral units, and societal capacity to organize for common purposes, that are outside the focus of this study. Our concern is more simply with the degree to which mass political behavior is manifested in ways that are consistent with the sustained existence of a single political system.

This study focusses upon the degree of political incorporation, so defined, that has existed at various stages in Yugoslav history, and its consequences and implications for the future of the state. As the empirical source for evidence of incorporation, we shall rely upon the one political activity that has engaged the participation of most adult Yugoslav males (and, since 1945, females) at fairly frequent if irregular points over the course of Yugoslavia's existence; namely, general elections. Specifically, this study undertakes the quantitative analysis of twelve legislative elections[2] spanning three regimes and sixty-odd years of Yugoslav history, with a view to determining the effect of regimes, strategies and events upon the state of political incorporation in the polity.

In order to proceed in this direction, we require a theory that can indicate which kinds of voting behaviors can be considered as indicative of incorporation, and which can not. Such a theory should also have as its main focus the political system itself, since it is not our goal to use aggregate voting data simply to make inferences about individual voting behavior and motivations. Finally, the theory must permit the comparison of results across different elections, even if the particular parties and issues involved are not the same, and, given the scope of this study, across different institutional frameworks (i.e., regimes) as well.

These are demanding assumptions, for the usual tendency in aggregate data analyses of national elections is to generalize "downward" to subgroups of the electorate, rather than upward towards the state of the political system. Even when the concern is with the system itself, the generalizations tend to be specific to a particular election, or, at most, to the regime which sponsored it. Fortunately, there is one theoretical approach in the literature that attempts to break out of these restrictions. This approach was presented by Stephen Coleman in his book, The Measurement and Analysis of Political Systems (1975). Coleman's theory is mathematical and abstract, and at first glance may seem rather removed from the problems of incorporation in a multi-cultural state. A brief discussion of its nature and implications at this point, however, can suggest the manner in which the theory links aggregate data on voting behavior to the state of political incorporation in the system.[3]

Coleman's (1975:22) basic premise is that in the analysis of social (and political) systems, "we are concerned with the predictability of social events and their rate of occurrence." By "events," Coleman means the alternative outcomes or choices that are possible in a given situation. To measure the predictability associated with a situation, Coleman borrows from information theory the concept of "entropy," a measure that ranges in value from zero (i.e., minimal uncertainty) when one event or outcome is inevitable to the logarithm of the number of events, which occurs when all of the events are equally probable and predictability is at a minimum for that situation.[4]

One important advantage of the entropy measure for comparative purposes is that it is a function, not of what the various events or alternatives in the situation or "event-set" are, but simply of their number and their relative sizes. This property of being content-free suggests Coleman's main hypothesis:

> The entropy measurement gives the average social uncertainty about what will happen for events in event-sets in the social system. The entropy measurement is independent of whatever the content of the event is. Therefore, we must assume that we would find approximately the same entropy value in different event-sets within the system (Coleman, 1975:37).

Elections provide a suitable forum to analyze the validity of this hypothesis because they provide two separate, measurable event-sets. One event-set is constituted of the choice among the various parties or candidates; the other is the two-choice event-set of voting or abstaining. According to Coleman's reasoning, the entropy measurements of these two event-sets, referred to as party-choice entropy and turnout entropy respectively, should be equal once differences in their ranges have been controlled for. This constitutes the entropy hypothesis.

The importance of the entropy hypothesis for our purposes lies in its use of electoral data to make inferences, not about voters, but about the political system itself. For Coleman, an election is not just the aggregation of a large number of individual choices that can be analyzed best by means of public opinion surveys or other individual-level techniques, but rather a collective act expressing a community level of social complexity or uncertainty. It is this assumption that allows Coleman to postulate conditions for system survival or breakdown, which are of prime importance to us.

The entropy level of a society, since it reflects average social uncertainty, ideally should be uniform not only for all event-sets in the social system, but across the territory occupied by the social system as well. In practice, this is a rather unlikely situation. For instance, since processes associated with economic development, such as urbanization and industrialization, increase social complexity and thus uncertainty, one would expect to find that entropy levels are higher in more developed regions of any country. Therefore Coleman (1975:127-143) argues that in a well-integrated or cohesive political system, there should be, if not a uniform entropy level, at least a smooth, "harmonic" distribution of entropy values over the various electoral units such that the minimum and maximum values occur at the geographic boundaries of the system and other districts display patterns of graduated departure from these extreme values towards values that lie in-between. By way of contrast, systems which contain sharp internal discontinuities, such as a ridge of high (party-choice) entropy values adjoining a low entropy region, exhibit weak cohesion and are inherently unstable. Unless this pattern substantially changes, systems of this sort cannot be expected to survive.

The value of Coleman's approach to our objectives should now be clear: Coleman proposes the use of electoral data to assess the degree of political incorporation of the various geographical units of the political system and its likelihood of survival. Nonincorporation is related to survivability because in poorly incorporated polities, certain territorial units will display voting patterns distinct enough to be regarded as separate political subsystems for which secession becomes an attractive option. In this study, the entropy hypothesis will be employed to best effect in Chapter 3, which contains the analysis of the elections of the interwar era. The elections of the 1920s, the first two of which were basically "free" in the liberal-democratic sense, provide the most accurate measurement of the natural propensities of the political system. Our analysis of these elections will demonstrate a very high and increasing level of political non-cohesiveness in this period, a non-cohesiveness which grew to the point of system breakdown in the latter 1920s, despite the policies and electoral manipulations the authorities introduced to check it. The paralysis and threatened collapse of the system provided the context for the first major structural manipulation by the country's leaders: the introduction of a conservative, authoritarian political system in 1929. In the remainder of Chapter 3, we shall explore the efficacy of that regime's strategy by examining its effect upon mass electoral behavior in the 1935 election. The brief and often overlooked experiment in the late 1930s with aspects of what today would be known as a "consociational" strategy, which was doomed by the international developments of that period, will also be examined.

The quest for political cohesion took a radically different turn with the accession to power of the Communists under Marshall Tito. In Chapter 4 we shall discuss the evolution of the party's thinking on cultural diversity up to 1950, and the ways in which the party's own unbalanced ethnic and regional support affected the implementation of this thinking. This discussion of the party's approach to ethnic relations will set the stage for the empirical analysis, in Chapters 5 and 6, of the regime's postwar efforts to foster political incorporation.

The means by which we assess political incorporation must be altered to take account of the constrained context of Communist-sponsored elections. The Communist regime has gone to extreme lengths to avoid any possibility of ethnic considerations, which formed the basis for the politics of the interwar period, becoming a factor in postwar elections. With the divisive tendencies of inter-ethnic relations eliminated from the electoral process by structural means, they had hoped that elections would function as a legitimating and incorporating force, demonstrating and encouraging the alignment of the masses behind the leadership and goals of the party. Accordingly, the principal means by which non-incorporation in the political system is manifested in this period is through patterned dissent. Electoral manifestations of dissent take two forms: electoral abstention and deliberate ballot invalidation. There can, of course, be many idiosyncratic reasons for voters to exhibit either of these behaviors; therefore the crucial element in assessing dissent is the degree to which it is patterned along ethnic lines. In Chapter 5, we analyze the results of every federal election from 1950 to 1969 looking for patterns that can be related to ethnic and developmental variables derived from census data, and, by means of a complex process of matching of electoral units which were changed with almost every election, examining the evolution of these patterns over time.

We are not confined in the Communist period to examining dissent alone. In the late 1960s when the regime experimented with a more liberal form of one-party rule, a new strategy for syphoning off discontent was adopted: electoral choice without opposition. Constituencies were encouraged to allow more than one candidate to compete in national and republic-level elections provided that there was (a) no inter-ethnic competition, and (b) no anti-communist candidates. This experiment in a limited form of electoral pluralism is not nearly as hollow as it might appear. There is strong circumstantial evidence to indicate that the mass response to it was a prime motivating factor in the subsequent decision to eliminate electoral choice, and in fact to eliminate direct elections to national and republican assemblies entirely. What could have happened in such a highly controlled electoral setting to have so disturbed and threatened the regime? Very little empirical work has been done to answer this question, in part because the experiment was more extensively undertaken at the republican than at the national level. Accordingly, we have gathered the results of the republican elections held during the 1960s for those republics and provinces for which the data are available. For the election of 1969, which marked the apex of the experiment, the republics (and province) in question contain over 500 electoral constituencies out of a total of 780; of these constituencies, about 58 percent had more than one candidate. To these constituency-level electoral statistics, data on ethnic composition and levels of economic development from the 1971 census have been matched. Chapter 6 presents the analysis of this very interesting body of data.

Finally, in Chapter 7, we attempt to draw the threads of the book together by relating the findings and conclusions that emerge from the data covering 60 years of Yugoslav elections to the issue of the effect and success of the various regime-strategies for achieving political incorporation and cohesion. We shall also discuss the less participatory 1970s and the problems facing post-Tito Yugoslavia, which include the recrudescence of demands for greater ethnic equality and electoral choice, and the dangers that political changes of this sort would pose for a party elite as concerned as ever with avoiding any steps that might expose or encourage political non-cohesiveness in Yugoslav society -- the perennial problem.

NOTES

1. A detailed breakdown and discussion of Yugoslavia's ethnic composition, taken from information in the 1981 Yugoslav census, is given in Appendix A. A discussion of the ethnic composition at earlier points in Yugoslav history figures in Chapter 2.

2. The following elections were analyzed in this study: for central legislative bodies, 1920, 1923, 1925, 1927, 1935, 1950, 1953, 1958, 1963, 1965, 1967, 1969 (Yugoslavia, 1921, 1924, 1926, 1928, 1935, 1938; Službeni list-Jugoslavija, 1945:994-1006, 1950:554-574, 1953:585-602, 1958:403-420, 1963:545-553, 1965:930-934, 1967:534-539, 1969:614-623); and for regional legislative bodies 1963, 1965, 1967, and 1969 (Službeni list-Bosna i Hercegovina, 1963:375-376, 1965:324-325, 1967:276-277, 1969:223-225, Službeni list-Vojvodina, 1969:234-240; Narodne Novine-Hrvatska, 1963: 269-279, 1965:227-230, 1967:187-189, 1969:334-341; Službeni Vesnik-Makedonija, 1963:489-496, 1965:479-482, 1967:274-277, 1969:371-376; Uradni list-Slovenija, 1963:253-254, 1965:252-254, 1967:304-307, 1969:340-342). Three elections are discussed but omitted from our detailed empirical analysis: the 1931 election because of its totally non-competitive structure; the 1938 election because of a complete absence of official voting data as a result of World War II; and the 1945 election due to incomplete data in the

official sources. Related problems also limited the analysis of republican-provincial elections in the communist period.

3. Coleman's theory is elaborated in much greater detail in Chapter 3.

4. The entropy measure is defined as:

$$H(s) = - \sum_{i=1}^{k} p_i \log_2 p_i$$

where p_i is the probability associated with alternative or event 'i', and $\Sigma p_i = 1$. Entropy may also be interpreted as a measure of fragmentation, e.g., the fragmentation of the vote among the 'k' parties. This interpretation is used in Chapter 2 where the religious fragmentation of census districts is presented in entropy terms. The units of entropy, incidentally, are known as "bits."

2
The Management of Cultural Diversity: Theory and Case Study

The degree of political cohesion or incorporation that exists in a polity is not simply a function of the number, saliency, or patterning of social cleavages, nor is it just a matter of the length of time that a state has been in existence. Rather, cohesion is a property of the system that, like many others, can be affected both by the policies adopted by central decision-makers and by the specific institutional framework of the regime. Among multi-cultural states where problems of cohesion are likely to exist, efforts to "manage" inter-group hostility and accommodate divergent group interests have differed markedly by regime-type, and have involved a varied repertoire of organizational managements, public policies, and guiding normative formulas (Esman, 1973; Lijphart, 1977; Gladdish, 1979; Rothschild, 1981; Van den Berge, 1981; Rothchild and Olorunsola, 1982). In order to bring some degree of conceptual order to the considerable variety of means employed for the management of cultural diversity, a general typology of such strategies is developed in the first part of this chapter. This discussion is followed by an application of the typology to the case of Yugoslavia, a country which has adopted over the years a very substantial number of the available strategies in order to cope with the extremely difficult nature of its ethnic problems.

THE CONCEPTUAL FRAMEWORK

The conceptual framework of strategies for managing cultural diversity is presented in schematic form in Figure 2.1. The framework is formed according to two criteria: the type of regime and the management strategy. Across the top of the figure, three broad categories of regime-types are distinguished: left-wing, centrist, and right-wing. Left-wing regimes are defined as those which are officially "Marxist-Leninist" or "Socialist" in ideological orientation and have one dominant party in power that does not genuinely share control and has not alternated in power with any other parties which may legally exist. By centrist regimes we mean regimes usually termed liberal democracies, including those occasionally governed by social-democratic parties. Lastly, right-wing regimes refer to anti-marxian and at least theoretically non-socialist political systems of the authoritarian or fascist type, irrespective of the number, or even presence, of political parties. Along the left-hand column of the figure, management strategies for confronting cultural diversity are also grouped into three categories: syncretic amalgamation, pluralistic accommodation, and group domination. The three

FIGURE 2.1
The Regime Management of Cultural Diversity: A General Typology with Yugoslav Examples.

MANAGEMENT STRATEGIES	REGIME TYPES					
	Left-Wing		Centrist		Right-Wing	
	Extreme	Moderate	Liberal	Conservative	Moderate	Extreme
Syncretic Amalgamation	Revolutionary Fusion (1945–1950)	Evolutionary Merger (1951–1960)		Melting-Pot Assimilation		
Pluralistic Accommodation		Pluralist Socialism (1963–1970)	Cultural Pluralism	Consociationalism (1938–1941)		
Group Domination				Charter-Group Hegemony (1918–1928)	Authoritarian Exclusion (1929–1938)	Ultra-Nationalistic Purification (1941–1945)

strategies emphasize, respectively, the replacement of all traditional cultural groups through the creation of a singular and completely new form of group consciousness, the recognition and accommodation of existing group differences, and the political hegemony of one or more groups over the other groups in society.

The cross-classification of different regime-types with various general management strategies generates a typology consisting of nine distinct approaches or regime-strategies for the management of cultural diversity. The rough alignment of these regime-strategies along a diagonal in Figure 2.1, is a reflection of the degree of association between regime-types and strategies that gives the typology its rationale. Thus, syncretic approaches are connected, at least in principle, with left-wing regimes, group domination strategies tend to be preferred by right-wing regimes, while the more "liberal" centrist regimes, although much more eclectic in their use of strategies, show a tendency to adopt more pluralistic approaches.

The typology is intended to provide a theoretically significant categorization that will prove to be of assistance in comparative research on political cohesion in a variety of culturally divided societies. For the purposes of this book, it is of particular utility because the political history of Yugoslavia has exemplified not only all three regime-types, but fully seven of the nine regime-strategies that we have identified (as indicated by the dates given in parentheses in Figure 2.1). Accordingly, we shall present a brief description of the essential characteristics of each regime-strategy type before going on to indicate the particular features of Yugoslavia that have provoked their utilization.

Syncretic Amalgamation

The general strategy of syncretic amalgamation represents an attempt to dilute or eradicate existing cultural identities through the creation of completely new bonds or cases of collective solidarity. The establishment of such new bonds -- usually ideological or biological -- involves relatively high levels of governmental intervention in societal relations as a means to transcend existing group loyalties. The approach also implies extensive contact among the members of the different cultural groups which the leaders of the regime have scheduled for eventual amalgamation. Three variants of this approach to the phenomenon of cultural diversity can be identified according to the regime-type.

Revolutionary Fusion. Used primarily by Marxist-Leninist regimes during the early "mobilization" phases of their political development, this strategy seeks to utilize or engender bonds deriving from class consciousness to supplant existing group loyalties which the regime's ideology alleges to be parochial and retrograde in terms of the "inexorable laws" of historical development. This strategy is based upon the elite expectation that a combination of rapid politically-induced economic development and energetic social engineering can supercede pre-revolutionary group loyalties relatively quickly. As Lenin put it: "the aim of socialism is not only to abolish the present division of mankind into small states and all national isolation, not only to bring nations closer to each other, but also to merge them." "Economics," he points out elsewhere, "will amalgamate the different nationalities." (Low, 1958:116-117)

In practice, fusionist policy generally makes allowances for the existence and even temporary cultivation of traditional cultural practices, provided such activities are essentially of a folkloric and pro-regime character (as exemplified in the Soviet formulation "national in form, socialist in content"). The governmental structure is usually constituted on the basis of federalism, although in practice political power remains highly centralized and concentrated in the unitary party organization. Moreover, although the strategy of revolutionary fusion theoretically aims at forging working-class consciousness on a global basis (as expressed in the phrase, "proletarian internationalism"), efforts to actually transcend traditional cultural bonds have typically begun with single country ("national") policies to create a new "Soviet man," "Chinese Socialist man," "Czechoslovak communist citizen," etc. Thus, while left-wing amalgamationist regimes have sought to replace group nationalism with internationalism, they have often consciously or unconsciously contributed to a strengthening of nationalism at the state level. The continued vitality of individual ethnic group chauvinism and the persistence of "national antipathies" (see below) have considerably weakened the grandiose claims on behalf of the Marxist-Leninist strategy of "amalgamation." The evidence indicates that enthusiasm for fusionist strategies generally diminishes as revolutionary regimes become more institutionalized and resistant to rapid and experimental modes of social change, and also as the citizens of such regimes become less amenable to elite appeals based on normative incentives and coercive sanctions (Allworth, 1971; Simmonds, 1977; Azrael, 1978; Goldhagen, 1968).

Evolutionary Merger. This strategy also owes its ideological inspiration to Marxist-Leninist thought, and includes a basic regime commitment to the replacement of existing cultural identities through the creation of class consciousness. It differs from the previous variant of amalgamation primarily with respect to the scope of regime involvement in the process of societal transformation. Generally this approach is characteristic of post-revolutionary leftist regimes which cannot, or no longer wish to maintain the rapid tempo and costs of change borne during the mobilization stage of political development. Having failed to fundamentally alter the pattern of traditional group loyalties (ethnic, religious, sectional, etc.) despite tremendous material and human costs, the leadership now adopts an evolutionary strategy to achieve the same "revolutionary" goals. The most blatantly coercive sanctions and "utopian" normative appeals are replaced by more persuasive appeals and material incentives. The expectation still remains that traditional cultural ties will eventually decay as a result of modernization, but it is acknowledged that this will be a very extended and gradual process. Moreover, although the merging of long established identities can be encouraged and guided, this process requires methods more mild and subtle than those utilized by the earlier fusionist approach. The cultivation and even "flowering" of old cultural forms and practices is tolerated, although the overt politicization of such cultural bonds is still frowned upon and often sharply repressed by the central agencies of the party and the state. Soviet nationality policy in the post-Stalinist period, and the policies of several other multi-ethnic communist states since the early 1950s, have manifested such an evolutionary approach to the syncretic amalgamation of cultural groups.

"Melting-Pot" Assimilation. This approach to cultural diversity is an outgrowth of the view put forth by various American (Gordon, 1964), and Canadian (Palmer, 1976) writers during the 19th and early 20th century regarding the absorption and transformation of immigrants to North America. Depending on the particular advocates, the approach may range from a desire that all immigrants adopt a common set of values, to a much more ambitious vision urging the biological amalgamation of distinct cultural groups into a new culture, i.e., physical as well as value integration. Whether individual writers envisioned only the normative indoctrination of immigrants or the fusion of ethnic groups into a "new national stock," all proponents of melting-pot assimilation shared a disdain for the retention of beliefs and behavior patterns imported from outside of North America. Theodore Roosevelt's suggestion that there was "no room" in the United States for "hyphenated Americanism" and John Diefenbaker's campaign for "unhyphenated Canadianism" expressed the views of many of their countrymen. As Woodrow Wilson put it in 1915, "a man who thinks of himself as belonging to a particular national group in America has not yet become an American" (Gordon, 1964:101). Wilson's fear was that the attraction of ethnic loyalties brought from abroad was incompatible with being a "thorough American."

Wilson's outlook, and that of other melting-pot supporters, thus had certain similarities (allowing for the enormous differences in other basic goals and in the environment) with the fusionist strategy of Marxist revolutionaries. Lenin, for example, although willing to use cultural "self-determination" as a revolutionary tactic, also feared that nationalism might become a rival to the socialist movement. Writing at just about the same time as Wilson, Lenin's solution was the "unconditional unity" and complete "amalgamation" of all nationalities in what he called a "higher unity" (Low, 1958:116). For Lenin, the "higher unity" was Marxism, for Wilson it was "Americanism."

Although American and Canadian supporters of melting-pot assimilation assumed a much less extensive and centralized framework of government intervention to encourage their schemes of cultural transformation than did either advocates of revolutionary fusion or evolutionary merger, all three strategies of syncretic amalgamation share a similar problem. While each variant of the strategy theoretically assumes that all of the cultural groups amalgamated would make an equal contribution to the new cultural or class collectivity, or at least not endure further subordination from any other group, such equity proved difficult to obtain in practice. Thus, in the "Americanization" and "Canadianization" versions of amalgamation, circumstances have tended to give the Anglo-Saxon cultural group a disporportionately greater influence in the process of cultural intermixture, while in the Marxian version one or another large and traditionally influential ethnic group (Great Russian, Han Chinese, ethnic Romanian, etc.) usually has a dominant position in the political system. Such a deviation from the theory of syncretic amalgamation may bring these strategies much closer to the group domination strategies (discussed below) in practice than our conceptualization would imply.

Pluralistic Accommodation

Pluralist strategies are characterized by regime toleration and even encouragement of cultural diversity. The rulers of the political system seek to provide adequate procedures for the resolution or adjustment of inter-group conflicts and the accommodation of divergent group interests rather than government-sponsored programs for the transformation or standardization of cultural values. Although this strategy is mainly employed in liberal democracies of the parliamentary and presidential types, other variants or "pluralist recipes" (Gladdish, 1979:168) can be identified in "liberal" regimes on the left- and right-wings of the ideological spectrum.

Pluralist Socialism. This strategy is revealed in "liberalizing" state socialist regimes which attempt to combine the preservation of an "oppositionless" and mono-ideological political system with toleration for cultural diversity. Unlike the model of evolutionary merger in which a centralized and interventionist party apparatus modernizes (de-Stalinizes) its assault on existing cultural identities, pluralist socialism presupposes a more decentralized socialist state in which the single party, although still having a monopoly over the adoption of all significant public policies, plays a less direct role in the operational management of social and economic activity. Mass socio-political institutions other than the party function in a semi-autonomous manner rather than as pliant "transmission belts" of the party leadership, a situation which allows for a type of institutional or organizational pluralism not found in a more centralized one-party state.

Deep cultural diversity and the conflicts which it engenders are not considered incompatible with socialist development in this pluralist mode, and there is little expectation that anything can or should be done in the immediate future to eliminate sub-cultural differentiation. Stress is placed on the development of institutions for the "harmonization" and "coordination" of divergent group interests through a more open expression and confrontation of differences than under Soviet-type regimes. Ethnic conflict is no longer a taboo subject to be suppressed or resolved behind the closed doors of central party organizations. The federal structure which is usually present in multi-ethnic socialist states becomes a more vital and genuine framework for the division of power between the central and sectional components of the political system. Aspects of such pluralist socialism were found in their most developed form in Yugoslavia during the late 1960s (see Chapters 5 and 6 below), in a less fully crystallized and very short-lived version in Czechoslovakia during the "thaw" of 1967-1968 (Barnard, 1972, 1977; Skilling, 1976), and can also be seen with respect to religious expression in the incipient Polish liberalization of 1980-1981 (Wjatr, 1981, Erlich, 1982).

Cultural Pluralism (Multi-culturalism). This approach to cultural diversity is manifest in liberal democracies and is the principal strategy utilized in such regimes during the post-World War II period. It postulates the recognition and preservation of existing cultural differences in society and also of newly arriving immigrant cultures. The minimum requirement for members of all cultural groups is affiliation with and loyalty to a common state citizenship or state-nationality, and also the fulfillment of routine civic responsibilities. It combines, in brief, minimal group integration with support for group diversity, and even "divided-loyalty."

As a rule, theorists of cultural pluralism advocate enough separation between cultural groups to ensure the preservation of distinct communal traditions (for example, only a moderate amount of cross-cultural intermarriage, and some retention of ancestral languages), while promoting enough cross-cultural communication and interaction in other areas of socio-economic and civic life to maintain a cohesive society. The amount of inter-group linkages and group segmentation encouraged differs from one proponent of cultural pluralism to another, and from one particular pluralistic regime to another, as is well illustrated in the recent outpouring of literature on cultural diversity by Canadian and American writers (Gordon, 1981; Anderson and Frideres, 1981; Reitz, 1980; Dahlie and Fernando, 1981; Liebman, 1982).

Although all members of society are expected to share a common core of political values (the "rules of the game") in a regime endorsing the precepts of cultural pluralism, it is also quite legitimate for cultural interests to become politicized. It is expected, for example, that ethnic groups will organize and lobby to achieve their interests and redress their grievances in the political system. "Politics must follow ethnicity," writes one exponent of such pluralism, "recognizing and supporting communal structures" (Walzer, 1980:785). The strategy of cultural pluralism assumes that the existence of a multi-party system and a framework of civil liberties along with the principles of majoritarian rule -- of either the Westminster or Madisonian variety -- will allow for organized minorities to peacefully coexist in a single state.

<u>Consociational</u> <u>Democracy</u>. Another pluralist approach which has recently challenged the ability of majoritarian democracy to successfully cope with the political strains exhibited in multi-national societies is that of consociational democracy. Briefly, this view contends that democracy and majority rule are incompatible in deeply divided or plural societies. In place of majority rule, consociational thought emphasizes four principles: grand coalition government, mutual veto, proportionality, and segmental autonomy. The first principle refers to the need for consensual decision-making by elite political representatives of the various communal groups in society. Instead of social and political interaction among citizens of diverse cultural backgrounds, which is encouraged by the strategy of cultural pluralism (as an end in itself) and by the syncretic amalgamation approach (as a means to an end), consociationalists prefer that members of potentially antagonistic groups remain relatively isolated from one another, while deferentially allowing their respective elite spokesmen (interest group and party leaders) to negotiate on their behalf with other groups. Secondly, each cultural group or segment in the society is accorded the right of veto over decisions taken so that minorities are protected from being outvoted by majorities. Third, political positions and funds are allocated according to the principle of group proportionality rather than by the winner-take-all principle of majority rule. In some cases of allocation, parity representation is advocated so that the smallest group segments reach a level of equality with the largest or majority group. Finally, consociational democracy devolves as much decision-making authority as possible to the individual (minoritarian) segments of the society (Lijphart, 1975 and 1977; McRae, 1974; Nordlinger, 1972).

While advocates of consociationalism feel that their brand of democracy offers a better chance for political stability under conditions of extreme cultural diversity than the majoritarian model, critics claim that among other things, the elite-centered and consensual consociational practices seriously detract from the quality of democracy (Barry, 1975). Supporters of consociationalism respond that while the grand coalition principle of their model may preclude a government-versus-opposition pattern of politics, the latter feature of majoritarian democracies often leads to the permanent exclusion of minorities from power (Lijphart, 1978:38). They also point to the use of consociational practices in a number of liberal democracies such as Switzerland, the Netherlands, Austria (from 1945 to 1966), Belgium (since the First World War with respect to language issues), Lebanon from 1943 to 1975, and on a lesser scale in Canada and Israel ("semi-consociational democracies"). Leaving aside the democratic credentials of the strategy, there is evidence that consociationalism has had a serious appeal to writers interested in justification for practices which allow a formerly dominant group to preserve the basic separation of distinct cultural communities and oligarchic modes of decision-making. Thus, one occasionally finds "consociational practices" adopted piecemeal by regimes that are clearly not liberal democracies (Rhoodie, 1978; Adam and Giliomee, 1979) and causes us to locate consociationalism midway between centrist and right-wing regimes.

Group Domination

This class of strategies exists whenever members of one or more cultural groups assign themselves superior status in society and through their control of political and economic resources attempt to mold, transform, or eliminate other less privileged cultural groups. Three different variants of this strategy can be distinguished, according to the treatment of the subordinated group members by those in positions of dominance.

Charter-Group Hegemony. Regimes which utilize this strategy are generally located in the centre or right positions on the ideological continuum. The strategy is characterized by a situation in which the values and customs of a politically dominant group ("charter-group," "core" group, "people of the state," etc.) are considered to be a model which members of other cultural groups must accept and emulate through a process of acculturation or assimilation. This may or may not involve biological assimilation to the dominant group, although it usually does not when the members of the subordinate group are racially different. It always differs from melting-pot assimilation, however, in that cultural intermixture is not intended to create a new amalgamated cultural "blend," but rather to dilute the characteristics of subordinate groups.

Occasionally this approach to cultural diversity will involve a group coalition whereby several cultural groups sharing some common features or values enjoy a special status vis-à-vis all other cultural groups in the society. This type of charter-group hegemony often involves the earliest immigrants in a "settler-state," who expect that their values and modes of behavior will be adopted by later immigrants, or even the indigenous population (native peoples). Aspects of this strategy can be seen in American and Canadian views expressed throughout the 19th and 20th centuries that all cultural groups in society should adopt the values and behavior of the early Anglo-Saxon immigrants, an approach referred to as the policy of "Anglo-conformity" (Gordon, 1964; Palmer, 1976). What distinguishes charter-group hegemony from other variants of group domination is the eligibility of all non-charter cultural groups for incorporation into the dominant grouping, provided they renounce their ancestral culture and are of an acceptable racial composition.

Authoritarian Exclusion. When one dominant cultural group or an alliance of groups simply excludes all other members of society from legitimate or meaningful participation in the political system, authoritarian exclusionism may be said to exist. The elite in such regimes discourages any substantial political mobilization, even on the part of members of the dominant group, and refrains from any schemes of fundamental social transformation. In such regimes there is no pretense of acculturating or assimilating the oppressed groups. If the members of subordinate groups are not physically segregated from contact with the dominant group members, they are legally or informally unable to obtain significant political and economic influence. The ideological or "philosophic" justification for such a strategy is rarely fully elaborated, and public policies are often very eclectic and arbitrary combinations of different autocratic practices which are frequently changed to perpetuate the survival of the dominant group (Linz, 1976). Regimes that refrain from systematic genocide such as Franco's Spain and Mussolini's Italy, as well as various exclusionary one-party states in the Third World (Huntington, 1970), illustrate this type of group domination with regard to cultural relations.

Pierre Van den Berghe's (1967:18, 29) description of racism in South Africa and the United States before World War II (especially in the Southern States), which he calls "Herrenvolk democracies," illustrates aspects of the authoritarian exclusionary strategy, as well as the hegemonic charter group approach discussed above. According to Van den Berghe (1967:18) such regimes "are democratic for the master race, but tyrannical for the subordinate groups. The desire to preserve both the profitable forms of discrimination and exploitation and the democratic ideology made it necessary to deny humanity to oppressed groups." In "Herrenvolk democracies" all members of the dominant racial group, irrespective of what cultural sub-group they belong to, enjoy a parliamentary or presidential system of majority rule, but the exercise of political power and the suffrage is denied de facto, and sometimes de jure, to the subordinate racial group or groups. Although the dominant charter group (whether Anglo-Saxon in the United States or Afrikaner in South Africa) may practice a type of "liberal" group hegemony vis-à-vis other cultural groups of similar racial composition, they completely exclude members of allegedly inferior racial groups in an authoritarian fashion.

Ultra-nationalistic Purification. Under this most brutal approach to cultural diversity, a dominant group either liquidates, enslaves, or deports members of all groups that it views as inferior. (Sometimes, however, certain subordinated groups are given a protected "honorary" status or exemption as temporary allies of the dominant group.) While such purification may be used as an official strategy systematically employed by a right-wing regime over a considerable period, it is often employed in a more selective manner by other types of regimes in association with the various strategies described above. The most notable systematic cases of the approach include the Nazi genocide or enslavement of non-Aryan "races," and the emulation of Nazi policy by their (ironically) non-Aryan European allies. Examples of more selective cases would include the Turkish massacre of the Armenians, Soviet policy toward a number of small nationalities in the U.S.S.R. during the Stalinist period, Idi Amin's treatment of Uganda's East Indian population, and particular actions taken against native people in North American history.

The preceding survey of regime strategies for managing cultural diversity raises a number of additional issues which must be mentioned at the outset of this study. First, in practice very few of the strategies are expressed by a coherent, philosophically-grounded, and officially justified set of public policies. Even in the more goal-oriented left-wing regimes, it is rare for the analyst to find a codified statement of intent or a program of action concerning the treatment of cultural diversity. In fact, a fully-developed body of thought on the "national question" is one of the most neglected components of the Marxist-Leninist literature. Most regime-strategies include a relatively loose collection of elite statements and policies (e.g., on the treatment of immigrants, education, intermarriage, and other aspects of group relations) which are frequently modified, and may even be contradictory. To that extent the different regime-strategies found in the typology presented here, although resembling real state policies, are also ideal types abstracted (and perhaps overly systemized) for analytical purposes from the experiences of a large number of different states at different periods.

It is also important to bear in mind that the specific strategies utilized by a particular regime at any given time may be quite eclectic, and include elements which overlap a number of strategies. This eclecticism or incoherence may, for example, result from the simultaneous and pragmatic experimentation with various methods of conflict regulation, from a genuine dissensus in a regime about how to cope with cultural diversity, or from an officially maintained divergence between theory and practice. Nevertheless, the regime-strategies designated in the typology do encompass remarkably well the general thrust of the various Yugoslav efforts at managing cultural diversity, as we will discuss below.

Secondly, despite the very different intentions and methods of the strategies employed by regimes to manage cultural diversity and establish political cohesion -- a new blending of cultures, peaceful co-existence, or exclusionary status quo, etc. -- in practice all of the approaches have resulted in a good deal of oppression and discrimination for at least some of the cultural groups in the societies affected. It seems that regimes at all points on the ideological spectrum have a low tolerance for those cultural groups who wish to change the basic rules of the game, or who are seen as intractable opponents of the regime's fundamental goals. As Tom Farer (1981:13) has recently observed:

> Honest scholarship would have to ask what is the difference between a revolutionary state that decides to eliminate a group with bayonets and one that proceeds to do so by indirection. Both claim that they are promoting modernization and advancing national interests as defined by those who rule. . . . Minorities standing in the way of progress are generally despised whether the regime is democratic, as in nineteenth century America, conservative authoritarian or authoritarian socialist. We should at least recognize moral parallels where they exist.

Finally, and closely related, most multi-cultural societies, irrespective of the regime-strategies to which they have been subjected, have recently been faced, to at least some extent, with political unrest and instability resulting from the conflict of cultural groups. Thus, the expectation of both Marxists and liberals that modernization and growing economic interdependence would eventually erode primordial bonds and traditional group commitments has been disconfirmed by the growing politicization of cultural diversity, not only in the economically less-developed countries, but also in "modern" or industrially advanced societies previously thought to have achieved a high level of cultural integration. Even the liberal-democratic strategy of cultural pluralism, which recognizes such politicization as a normal and positive feature, has been unable in all cases to prevent disruption caused by the confrontation of different cultural and racial groups. In a major revision of conventional wisdom, social scientists have now largely concluded that economic modernization is a double-edged phenomenon, both standardizing ("leveling") values across cultural lines and also exacerbating antipathies derived from cultural differences (Enloe, 1973; Bell, 1975; Hechter, 1976).

This is not to say, however, that all regime-strategies are equally oppressive, or equally ineffective. Much of this book is devoted, at least implicitly, to the comparative evaluation of the efficacy of the various strategies attempted by Yugoslav governments to cope with their particularly pronounced ethnic problems. We shall entertain the expectation that the analysis of Yugoslav politics from 1920 to the present will reveal that some strategies have proved more valuable than others in enhancing political cohesiveness (or at least in limiting manifestations of non-cohesiveness).

THE FRAMEWORK APPLIED

The experience of Yugoslavia over the last sixty years offers a fascinating and theoretically promising setting in which to explore and assess different strategies for the enhancement of political cohesiveness. The reason for the richness of the Yugoslav case lies both in the extremely high levels of ethnic and regional differentiation and in the unusually broad range of regime-strategies which have been successively employed to cope with that differentiation. Let us first consider the ethnic complexity of the country.

Yugoslavia's unique ethnic composition derives from the territorial concentration and interspersion of several major and minor (in demographic terms) nationality groups, many of which have distinct religious affiliations and languages, not to mention historical traditions and levels of socio-economic development. Although information on ethnicity itself was not recorded in the country's first census taken in 1921, it is possible to derive from information on language and religion the following ethnic categorization of the country's approximately 12 million inhabitants at the time of its creation: Serbs (with Montenegrins), 43 percent; Croats, 23 percent; Slovenes, 8.5 percent; Macedonians, 5 percent; Bosnian Moslems, 6 percent; non-Slavs, including Albanian and Turkish Moslems, Germans, Hungarians, Romanians and Jews, 4.5 percent (Rothschild, 1974:202-203). Although the country is notable for the territorial concentration of the major ethnic groups, there is a considerable degree of ethnic heterogeneity in certain areas as well. This is illustrated in Figure 2.2, which presents a mapping of the degree of religious fragmentation[1] for the fifty-nine census districts of the country in 1921. In the figure, the levels of religious heterogeneity by district correspond reasonably well to the pattern of ethnic complexity in the society if certain factors are taken into account. For example, virtually all of the Slovenes and Croats are represented as "Catholic" in the census although they constitute two distinct ethnic groups. Nevertheless, Figure 2.2 does reflect the fact that Slovenia has a very low level of cultural diversity while Croatia-Slavonia and Dalmatia are much more fragmented because of the presence of ethnic Serbs who are Orthodox by religion. Similarly, Serbs and Macedonians are both heavily Orthodox but are two ethnically distinct peoples. Again, what is important in terms of societal complexity is that "old Serbia" (or what is today termed Serbia proper) has a low level of cultural heterogeneity, while Macedonia (called "South Serbia" in the interwar years) is highly fragmented due to the presence of a large Moslem community made up of Turks and Albanians. Montenegro, which is Orthodox and ethnically Serbian but with concentrated minorities, is a mixed case. The two most fragmented areas of the country are Bosnia and Vojvodina. Bosnia's multi-religious composition (Moslems, Catholic Croats, and Orthodox Serbs) closely

20

FIGURE 2.2
Religious Fragmentation (in bits of entropy) by Census District, 1920

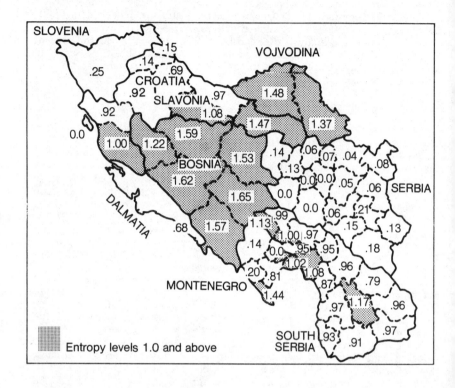

corresponds to its ethnic complexity. Vojvodina's high ethnic variation is not fully mirrored by its level of religious fragmentation (i.e., Catholics may be Hungarians or Croats) but its great complexity relative to other regions does emerge in Figure 2.2.

A corresponding mapping[2] in Figure 2.3 of subcultural heterogeneity based upon ethnic data from the 1971 census reveals that the basic landscape of cultural diversity has not been greatly altered after a half-century, despite the ethno-religious genocide during World War II, and other important demographic changes (migration, deportation, etc.). Although the total population of Yugoslavia increased between 1921 and 1971 by 70 percent and certain minorities (e.g., Albanians) have increased disproportionately while others (Germans, Hungarians) have fallen behind, the overall ratio among the various ethnic groups for the country as a whole, and for each major region, has undergone remarkably little change. For instance, the percentage of the population belonging to each of the six principal "nations" of the country (Serbs, Croats, Slovenes, Montenegrins, Macedonians, and Moslems) has not changed by more than 3.5 percent between 1921 and 1971.

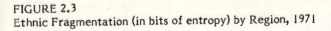

FIGURE 2.3
Ethnic Fragmentation (in bits of entropy) by Region, 1971

While the ethnographic pattern of Yugoslavia remained relatively constant during the country's first half century of existence, the social and economic structure underwent profound changes, especially after World War II. A combination of corruption, political disunity, the world depression, and Yugoslavia's status as an economic satellite of more developed countries (especially Germany) in the interwar era, followed by the debacle of the Second World War and the need for reconstruction, seriously inhibited the country's economic progress before the late 1940s. This is reflected in the data of Table 2.1, which shows that the basic economic composition of the population underwent little transformation throughout the interwar period. By way of contrast, the predominantly agricultural composition of the population was fundamentally altered by the modernization program of the communist regime. As Table 2.1 shows, the proportion of the population working in non-agricultural activities nearly doubled from 1948 to 1971. By the end of the 1970s Yugoslav citizens involved in agricultural activities composed about the same relative size sector of the economy (roughly one-third) as the non-agricultural work force had constituted at the outset of the communist period after World War II. The tempo of urbanization was equally striking: from 17.5 percent of

TABLE 2.1

The Yugoslav Population by Economic Sector

Sector	1921	1931	1948	1953	1961	1971	1980
Agricultural	78.9	76.6	67.2	60.9	50.2	38.2	28.8[a]
Non-Agricultural	21.2	23.4	32.8	39.1	49.8	61.8	71.2
Total	100.0	100.0	100.0	100.0	100.0	100.0	100.0

Sources: Miroslav Pecujlić (1963) Promene u socijalnoj strukturi Jugoslavije. Belgrade: Visoka Škola Političkih Nauka; Yugoslavia (1970) Yugoslavia Thirty Years After Liberation and the Victory over Fascism 1945-1975. Belgrade: Federal Statistical Office, 1976; Dušan Breznik (1982) "The Dynamics of Population in Yugoslavia," Eastern European Economics 20, No. 3-4 (Spring-Summer).

[a]The data for 1980 is an estimate by the Demographic Research Center of the Institute of Social Sciences in Belgrade.

the population in 1931 living in cities of more than five thousand people to 36.7 percent in 1971 (Musil, 1980:141). In the period from 1948 to 1971 alone, 5.5 million inhabitants or 27 percent of the total Yugoslav population left their villages for urban areas (Friganović, 1980:4).

While rapid socio-economic development was a primary aim of the communist leadership, they also sought to overcome the chronic disparities between the more economically advanced areas in the northwestern region of the country and the very underdeveloped southeastern areas. In the view of the new "partisan" elite which took power in 1945, the goal of achieving a more regionally balanced economic structure was inextricably linked to a solution of the country's deep ethnic and sectional conflicts. As Boris Kidrić, the architect of the communist's early postwar economic policy, observed in 1948:

> ... it is clear that we would not be able to speak of a full definitive solution of the national question if inequality existed in the economic respect among the republics, or if, on the other hand, our Yugolav economy were not to develop in the sense and in the direction of a united socialist economic whole. ... A part of the surplus labor of the advanced republics with a higher productivity of labor must necessarily be used in our socialist construction of the less advanced republics. ... Comrades not able to understand this would find themselves on the road to nationalism. ... (Kidrić, 1948:40, 44)

Despite a serious and sustained policy of assistance to the less economically developed areas of the country, the effort to eliminate regional disparities has failed badly. As Table 2.2 indicates, although the per capita annual

TABLE 2.2
Per Capita National Income (at 1966 prices, in thousands of new dinars)

	Per capita national income in absolute and relative terms						
	1947		1955		1964		1973
1. Yugoslavia	1682	100	2306	100	4276	100	6456	100
2. Developed regions	1874	111	2643	115	5087	119	7874	122
Slovenia	2571	153	3958	171	7575	177	12337	191
Croatia	1758	105	2776	120	5048	118	7769	120
Vojvodina	2045	122	2641	115	5189	121	7784	121
Serbia proper	1668	99	2090	91	4258	100	6525	101
3. Less developed regions	1241	74	1592	69	2704	63	3887	60
Bosnia and Hercegovina	1380	82	1770	77	2786	65	4120	64
Montenegro	1332	79	1620	71	2895	68	4383	68
Macedonia	1157	69	1598	69	3284	77	4696	73
Kosovo	839	50	936	41	1528	36	1966	31
Difference, 2-3	633		1051		2383		3987	
Ratio, 3:2	66%		60%		53%		49%	
Ratio, 3:1	74%		69%		63%		60%	

Source: M. Bazler-Madzar, "Regional Development," in B. Horvat, ed., The Yugoslav Economic System. White Plains, N.Y.: International Arts and Science Press, 1976.

income of the country as a whole has nearly quadrupled, the gap between the developed regions and the underdeveloped regions has actually increased. Even after fundamental political changes were introduced in the early 1970s to curtail, among other things, vocal resistance to the transfer of funds from the richer to the poorer areas, regional differences continued to widen. For example, in 1947 the national income of the most developed region (Slovenia) was three times greater than that of the least developed area (Kosovo), but by 1973 the disparity between the two regions had increased to a factor of six. The impact of such wide and growing regional economic disparities on socialist Yugoslavia's persistently delicate ethnic relations has had serious political consequences (especially in the 1960s), an issue which, although frequently referred to in the existing literature, will receive more systematic empirical analysis in the course of this study.

Yugoslavia's appeal as a case-study exemplifying the problems of political cohesion goes beyond the country's extreme cultural fragmentation or the extent to which her uneven economic development has become ethnically contentious. Equally important is the extensive political experimentation with regime-types and strategies designed to cope with these patterns of diversity and deprivation. Despite the country's short history, each of the major regime-types identified in Figure 2.1 has been undertaken. Yugoslavia's modern political evolution begins with the creation of the state in 1918 under a liberal democratic (centrist) regime based upon a unitary system of governmental organization, and including a constitutional monarchy and a multi-party system. This was replaced in 1929 by a right-wing authoritarian regime, again developed along unitary lines but characterized by a royal dictatorship with a restricted party system and a weakened parliament. Following an extremely violent civil war and anti-fascist resistance struggle while the country was dismembered and occupied by foreign authoritarian states (1942-1944), a communist one-party regime organized along federal lines was installed. The communist regime, which has lasted the longest of any Yugoslav political framework, itself can be divided into a number of phases, which to some extent resemble distinct regime-types: (a) administrative socialism from 1945 to 1949, a very centralized period modelled on Soviet theory, but with peculiar Yugoslav features; (b) initial "Titoism" or "national communism" from 1950 to 1962, also called a "transitional period" or "new system" and marked by the introduction of workers' self-management and substantial decentralization of the state and economy; (c) a liberalizing period from 1963 to 1971, in which political and economic reforms broadening the parameters for the expression of cultural diversity were introduced, and (d) the current phase of enhanced party control, greater emphasis on unity, and stricter measures against dissidence which began in 1971 against a background of anxiety over the dangers of excessive pluralism as well as elite concern about the difficulties expected to accompany the post-Tito succession.

The assortment of regime-strategies adopted for the encouragement of political cohesiveness in Yugoslavia is as variegated as the mixture of regime-types described above. In fact, as the dates given in parenthesis in Figure 2.1 indicate, Yugoslav elites have utilized some variant of all three principal management strategies -- syncretic amalgamation, pluralistic accommodation, and group domination -- and, due to the frequent replacement or reorganization of successive regimes, have also adapted most of the actual regime-strategies offered in the typology. The periods of right-wing authoritarian and left-wing communist rule, which comprise the larger part of the country's history, have witnessed the greatest flexibility and innovation in the development of strategies for managing cultural diversity. During the former period, a strategy of authoritarian exclusion in the 1930s yielded briefly to a consociational experiment before being swamped by the ultra-nationalistic purification attempts of wartime extremist groups intent on creating a more ethnically homogeneous future. In the postwar communist period, the first three phases described above correspond to the institution of the three strategies appropriate to this regime-type, beginning with revolutionary fusion, followed by evolutionary merger and ultimately succeeded in the late 1960s by the highly interesting experiment in pluralist socialism. Only the short liberal-democratic phase of the 1920s failed to exhaust the repertoire of available strategies by completely ignoring both melting-pot assimilation and cultural pluralism. The extent to which these different regime types and regime-strategies have met with success in establishing or fostering political cohesion against a background of extreme ethnic heterogeneity and uneven socio-economic change is, of course, the major concern of this study and one to which we shall now turn.

NOTES

1. As indicated above (Chapter 1, footnote 4), the entropy measure is used here to represent the degree of fragmentation of each census district along religious lines. The greater the coefficient in Figure 2.2, the more religiously fragmented the district.

2. The territorial units used in Figure 2.3 are regions which are defined along historical and cultural lines, following the scheme developed by the Federal Statistical Institute of Yugoslavia. This regionalization is discussed more fully in Appendix C. Incidentally, 1971 census data was used here instead of 1981 data in order to present the ethnic picture for the period corresponding to elections most extensively analyzed in this book.

3
Diversity and Divergence: Yugoslavia in the Interwar Years

In this chapter the nature, extent, and evolution of political incorporation in the newly-created Yugoslav state will be explored through the analysis of voting behavior in five national elections held in the interwar years. These elections include the Constituent Assembly election of 1920 and the general elections of 1923, 1925, and 1927 held during the liberal-democratic phase, and the election of 1935 held during the period of right-wing authoritarianism.

The liberal-democratic period is particularly important for our purposes because it represents, particularly in its early years, the only occasion when political expression in Yugoslavia was allowed a relatively free reign. Accordingly, an analysis of these elections should allow us to make a reasonably accurate assessment of the natural propensities of the system before efforts at electoral manipulation began to affect the patterns of voting behavior. This assessment will then be used as a standard of evaluation against which various regime-strategies, such as the 1935 experiment in restricted electoral choice, can be measured. It will also provide a point of comparison with the postwar Communist experiments in electoral participation, with and without candidate choice, which will be discussed in subsequent chapters.

LIBERAL-DEMOCRACY IN YUGOSLAVIA: 1918-1929

The creation of a unified South Slavic or "Yugoslav" state in 1918 resulted from an agreement among various politicans and intellectuals from the region's principal ethnic groups. The idea of establishing such a state was not a new one, and controversy concerning the issue accounted for much of the volatile flavor of Balkan politics before 1918. The major pre-conditions for the formation of the new state were the defeat and disintegration of the Austro-Hungarian monarchy in the First World War, and the earlier defeat of Ottoman Turkey in the Balkan Wars (1912-1913). Both empires had controlled sizeable portions of the Balkan region and had exercized a significant influence on regional political sub-cultures in the area. Serbia's position as a victorious member of the Allies in World War I, along with its previous experience as an independent state (1878-1918) and the Serbs' numerical preponderance relative to the other South Slavic peoples, made it the dominant unit in the new political system.

The new regime's strategy toward cultural diversity was a classic example of the charter-group hegemony model discussed in Chapter 2.

Formally, the three largest Slavic groups in the country, which together comprised roughly 72 percent of the population, shared power in a kind of ruling coalition originally conceived to operate along quasi-federal lines, and which was symbolized in the official designation of the new state as the "Kingdom of Serbs, Croats, and Slovenes." Other groups were either officially classified into one or another of the charter-groups or expected to remain as powerless and permanent minorities. For example, two smaller Slavic groups, the Macedonians and the Montenegrins (4.8 percent and 2.3 percent of the population respectively), which had played an historically significant and sometimes even independent role in the Balkan area, were simply classified as Serbian by nationality. Moreover, the nearly 20 percent of the population that was composed of non-Slavic national minorities, such as Hungarians, Romanians, Albanians, and Moslems, although in some cases allowed schooling in their native languages, were relegated to a subordinate political position (as junior partners of the Serbs in some areas).

In practice, political power in the so-called "Triune Kingdom" was monopolized by the Serbs who, against the vocal opposition of their theoretically equal charter-group allies, quickly organized the political system along highly centralized and unitary lines. The domination of the Serbs over the state's major political and economic institutions, and particularly the top ranks of the state bureaucracy and the army, became the major hallmark and source of contention in the interwar state. Essentially, charter-group hegemony meant Serbian hegemony, as increasingly all of the other major and minor ethnic groups were either eclipsed or alienated by the royal dynasty and governing elite in Belgrade (i.e. by most of the same actors and the same site of control as in pre-1918 Serbia).

Despite these hegemonic arrangements, and formal nonrecognition of certain cultural groups, the first Yugoslav regime made relatively little active effort to alter or contain the expression of traditional ethnic and sectional loyalties. The strategy adopted was one of benign domination and gradualism rather than an attempt at rapid and coercive transformation in basic group identities. Thus, the liberal and majoritarian electoral system allowed members of each cultural group to organize and vote for the political party of their choice. Sovereignty formally resided in a 315 seat unicameral National Assembly elected by universal, direct, and secret suffrage of all males over 21 years of age, with (roughly) proportional representation of parties based on the d'Hondt system (Beard and Radin, 1929). That the Serbian parties controlled the Assembly was mainly due to the numerical plurality enjoyed by the Serbs in the population, the failure of the other ethnic groups and the parties they supported to unite against the Serbian party organizations, and in the case of the major Croatian party, a self-imposed isolation from the legislature for long periods of time.

The regime's strategy thus created a situation in which the country was politically dominated by one cultural group, while it was also politically divided along cultural lines. Moreover, if the first regime's generally liberal and non-energetic strategy toward the country's cultural diversity did little to change the landscape of extreme ethnic differentiation, its policies in other areas provided an equally weak basis for political cohesion. Thus, in such important areas as the legal system and the transportation system, the reality of Serbian political hegemony did not preclude the continuation of what one observer called a "marvellous chaos," including the existence of six distinct "legal areas" for civil and criminal law, and four unintegrated railway networks (Beard and Radin, 1929:275).

The freedom afforded by the new state in the area of party formation was fully exploited by the country's ethnic groups. Two of the most important party organizations, The Radical Party and The Democratic Party, were "self-consciously Serbian" in terms of their social bases and programs (Rothschild, 1974:211).[1] The major party of the ethnic Croats was the Croatian Peasant Party which opposed Serbian political hegemony and the unitary and monarchical organization of the state. Similarly, The Slovene People's Party, or Populists, enjoyed a dominant position among Slovenes. The interests of the Moslems in the country were advanced by two parties, the Yugoslav Moslem Organization in Bosnia and the weaker Dzemjet party composed of Turkish and Albanian Moslems living in Macedonia. A number of smaller parties articulated the special concerns of the German, Hungarian, and Romanian ethnic minorities.

The Communists were the only party which had substantial multi-ethnic appeal. In the constitutional assembly election of 1920, they received 12.4 percent of the total vote and had the third largest share of parliamentary representation (see Chapter 4). Quickly banned in 1921 and driven underground, the Communists did not play a significant role in electoral politics again until after the Second World War. The outlawing of the Communist Party constituted the major exception to the autonomy afforded the political system to develop according to its own natural tendencies in the first years of the country's existence.

The Analysis

Our concern in analyzing the electoral behavior of the 1920s and 1930s is with the natural tendencies of the system rather than with the goals and actions of particular individuals, groups, or parties within it. For this reason, the analysis that follows does not focus on the context, events, or outcomes of each election but on what those elections can indicate about the state of political incorporation in that era and its implications for regime survival. While there are many quantitative analyses of electoral data that have election-specific orientations, only Coleman's (1975) entropy theory, outlined in Chapter 1, purports to deal with the latter concern in a manner that is sufficiently general and predictive for our aims.

In essence, the entropy hypothesis posits an equivalence between the entropy levels that exist in a wide range of structured situations or "event-sets" in a society. As applied to the electoral arena, there are two relevant event-sets: the two-choice event-set of voting or abstaining, and for those who do vote, the event-set constituted by the choice among the "k" parties or candidates. According to the hypothesis, turnout entropy or H(T) should be equivalent to party-choice entropy or H(P) in each of the electoral units of a political system, once differences in their ranges are taken into account. The entropy measure itself ranges from a minimum of zero to a maximum which is equal to the logarithm (to the base two) of the number of choices or alternatives in question. For turnout entropy there are just two choices, voting or abstaining. Its maximum is therefore one, since $\log_2 2 = 1$. Party-choice entropy, on the other hand, can range much higher since any number of parties is theoretically possible; its maximum value is expressed as $\log_2 k$, where k is the number of parties. In formulating the hypothesis, the differences in the ranges of H(P) and H(T) are standardized by dividing each by its maximum or upper limit. Thus the hypothesis is

$$\frac{H(P)}{\log_2 k} = \frac{H(T)}{1}$$

or $\quad H(P) \quad = \quad \log_2 k \, H(T) \qquad$ (Coleman, 1975:41).

Central to the understanding of the entropy hypothesis is the realization that it expresses a relationship, not just between entropy measurements, but between voter turnout and electoral competitiveness. Consider party-choice entropy first. Its minimum value of zero is reached when one party alone receives 100 percent of the votes in an electoral district, and its maximum occurs when each of the k parties gets exactly the same proportion of the vote. It ranges between these extremes according to the extent to which the vote is distributed evenly among the competing parties. It therefore functions as a good measure of the closeness or competitiveness of an election.[2] As for turnout entropy, it is calculated from the proportion of eligible voters which actually did vote and the proportion which did not. Since the one arithmetically determines the other, turnout entropy is in fact solely determined by the voter turnout. Thus, the entropy hypothesis relates voter turnout to electoral competitiveness, standardizing for the number of parties or candidates.

Although the hypothesized relationship is straightforward, the joint behavior it predicts of the two variables is quite surprising. High levels of electoral competitiveness, as measured by H(P), should be associated with high H(T) values, but H(T) achieves its maximum value when the two events in the set, voting and not voting, occur with equal probability; that is, at 50 percent turnout. Therefore the hypothesis predicts that as competitiveness increases, turnout levels should approach, not 100 percent, but 50 percent. Since turnout levels are generally well above 50 percent in the elections we are about to consider, the more competitive electoral districts should therefore exhibit lower turnout rates than the less competitive districts. This expectation runs counter to the more usual assumption that competitiveness stimulates turnout, which has been supported by a considerable amount of evidence (Dawson and Robinson, 1963; Milbraith, 1965; Campbell et al., 1966; Riker and Ordeshook, 1968; Barzel and Silberman, 1973; Silberberg and Durden, 1975; Kim, Petrocik, and Enokson, 1975; but note Ferejohn and Fiorina, 1975; and Sanders, 1980).

The contrast between these two expectations strikes at the very core of the nature of the entropy theory. The prediction that turnout rates will approach 50 percent as electoral competitiveness increases makes little sense if electoral behavior is interpreted in terms of individual voters seeking to express their own political preferences. On the other hand, if voters act under the impetus to express electorally the prevailing levels of social uncertainty or entropy in their communities the analysis of such behavior may be less a means of understanding voters than a means of understanding the state of the political system within which they are acting. This is, of course, precisely what we hope to do.

In Coleman's theory, the state of the system is measured by its entropy level. A system in equilibrium will have a basic equivalence in the entropy levels registered in different event-sets. But what about the relationship among the various communities, districts, regions, or other territorial units that make up the political system? To the extent that they are distinct social entities, one would not necessarily anticipate an equivalence in entropy levels among them, any more than one would expect neighboring countries to exhibit equivalent entropies. If they form the elements of an integrated, cohesive political system, however, there is a certain plausibility to the argument that the hypothesis of entropy equivalence ought to extend to the relationship among them as well.

From this perspective, one would expect that in a completely cohesive and integrated system elections should elicit equivalent entropies throughout the electoral districts of the system, even if different parties win in different districts. Such a situation, however, is unlikely to be obtained in the real world. For one thing, urban and rural districts can be expected to differ in entropy level. "City life is characterized as offering greater diversity, greater occupational variety, heterogeneous social groups, and so forth," Coleman (1975:83) notes. This greater complexity and diversity entails an environment of greater uncertainty; there are simply more choices and thus greater entropy levels in virtually every domain. Coleman (1975:82-91), using data from Japan and India, tested the hypothesis that processes of urbanization and industrialization are associated with higher entropies, and found that the evidence bore him out. Although one should therefore expect a certain degree of heterogeneity across a political system, Coleman (1975:108-9) argues that an integrated system should at least tend towards greater homogeneity in entropy levels over time.[3] The mechanism behind this tendency would be the diffusion of change throughout the system based upon a degree of social interaction or communication among the subsystems. Countries divided into distinct and isolated regions, by way of contrast, tend to go their own ways over time, and in the extreme, civil war or secession becomes a possibility.

The distinguishing characteristic of a system that has the tendency towards homogeneity over time is a "harmonic" distribution of entropy levels across the geographic extent of the system (Coleman, 1975:132). In such a system, the highest and lowest entropy levels should occur in districts located along the borders of the country, where outside influences are most likely to impinge, while between these extremes one should find smooth or continuous increases or decreases in entropy levels as the influence of the extremes makes its way throughout the country. According to Coleman (1975:142-3), "It is easy to think of non-harmonic distributions having occurred many times over in the past several centuries as nation-states in Europe and elsewhere developed from pre-existing aggregations of smaller, semi-isolated, political or social systems." Those systems that survived were presumably able to break down the isolation of the newly-acquired territories over a period of time; the questions we shall explore in the case of the new state of Yugoslavia are, how great was the distinctness and isolation of its "pre-existing aggregations" and did the system in fact move toward greater homogeneity or cohesion over time?

In order to answer these questions, we must first establish the basic validity of the entropy hypothesis, which consists in determining the correctness of the prediction that turnout rates should approach 50 percent non-linearly as electoral competitiveness is heightened. Coleman (1975:51-73) tested the entropy hypothesis on electoral data from the United States, Japan and India in a number of ways, some of them fairly technical. The findings when these tests were applied to the Yugoslav elections of 1920, 1923, 1925, and 1927 are presented in full in Appendix B. For the purposes at hand, however, the evaluation of the hypothesis can be achieved with just two reasonably straightforward tests. The first test is based upon a graphic display in which district party-choice entropy values for a given election are plotted against the corresponding turnout percentages. With the data displayed in this manner, the hypothesis predicts that the array of data-points should take the curvilinear form illustrated in Figure 3.1. In the figure, each semi-circular line or "orbit" represents the relationship between H(P) and turnout for electoral districts with a particular number of competing parties. The lowest semi-circle, for example, gives the relationship that should exist among all districts with "k" parties; the next semi-circle describes the corresponding relationship for districts with k+1 parties; and so forth. There can, of course, be any number of orbits, although only three are pictured in the figure. Each orbit has the same form as the others, but is separated from them according to the value of the $\log_2 k$ coefficient in the entropy equation. Note that all orbits reach their maximum H(P) levels at 50 percent turnout, reflecting the idea that the highest levels of competitiveness will occur when turnout rates are at that level rather than at a higher one, as the standard hypothesis that competitiveness stimulates turnout would suggest.

The test consists of fitting second-degree polynomials of the form $f(t) = a_0 + a_1 t + a_2 t^2$ to the data arranged in the manner of Figure 3.1 in order to determine (1) whether they take on the predicted parabolic, concave downward shape; (2) whether they reach their maxima at or near the 50 percent turnout level; and (3) whether they are symmetrical about these maxima (Coleman, 1975:44-49). Ideally, there should be one polynomial fitted for each orbit in the data. Since Yugoslavia was divided into just fifty-six electoral districts in the elections of the 1920s and there were as many as ten orbits per district, there are too few cases to follow this line of inquiry. A general impression of the nature of the relationship can be gained, however, by fitting a single polynomial to the data for each election. The result when this was performed on the 1923 election data is illustrated in Figure 3.2. Because all districts had turnout rates above 50 percent in this election, the basic expectation is that higher H(P) levels will be associated with lower turnout rates. The distribution of data points in the figure clearly conform to this expectation and the fitted polynomial calculated from these data (and shown in the figure) takes on the predicted parabolic, concave downwards form.[4] The high degree of spread in the data points about the polynomial curve reflects the fact that there is a rather wide range in the numbers of competing parties in these districts.

In Table B.2 of Appendix B, the results of the polynomial-fit test for all four elections are given. The basic finding is that a polynomial of the predicted shape was generated in three of the elections, 1920, 1923, and 1927. The substantial spread of the data-points around the polynomial that is apparent in Figure 3.2 was also in evidence for the other elections, and in consequence the multiple correlations associated with the polynomial fits were all low. One way to compensate somewhat for the large number of orbits would be to divide the data into two roughly equal groups: constituencies with six or more parties and constituencies with five or less parties. When the polynomial-fit test was performed separately on the two groups for each election, it was generally found that the group of districts representing the upper orbits of the data array fit the hypothesis much better than did the other group. Indeed, not only did the upper orbits of the 1920, 1923 and 1927 election data conform to the expected parabolic shape, but the 1925 data, although not parabolic, revealed a negative linear relationship, indicating that even in this election H(P) increased with declining turnout rates.

Coleman (1975:61-66) places great store on the upper contour of the data array. His argument is that the upper contour is more likely to reveal

FIGURE 3.1
Graphic Representation of Entropy Hypothesis

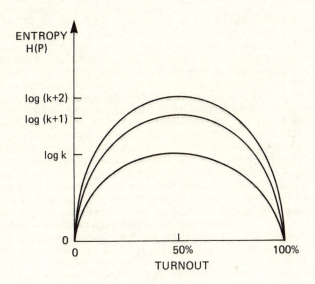

Source: Coleman, <u>The</u> <u>Measurement</u> <u>and</u> <u>Analysis</u> <u>of</u> <u>Political</u> <u>Systems</u>, 1975:43.

the entropy relationship accurately because data-points located in that region will have achieved their maximum entropy values; data-points at lower levels, on the other hand, may represent constituencies that are undergoing entropy change that cause them (temporarily) to be located between orbits. In political systems with a wide range of orbits, the data-points will be especially unlikely to conform to their predicted orbits, and the overall shape of the distribution, especially as defined by the upper contour, is the better indicator of the validity of the hypothesis.

The second test that we shall employ here does allow us to assess the magnitude of this orbit-by-orbit error. The entropy hypothesis, as originally stated, took the form of an identity between H(P) and H(T), once each is divided by its maximum possible value. The maximum value is always equal to the logarithm of the number of alternatives or choices. Accordingly, we can produce a new version of the party-choice entropy variable by dividing the H(P) value for each district by the logarithm of the number of

FIGURE 3.2
Single Polynomial-Fit to 1923 Election Data

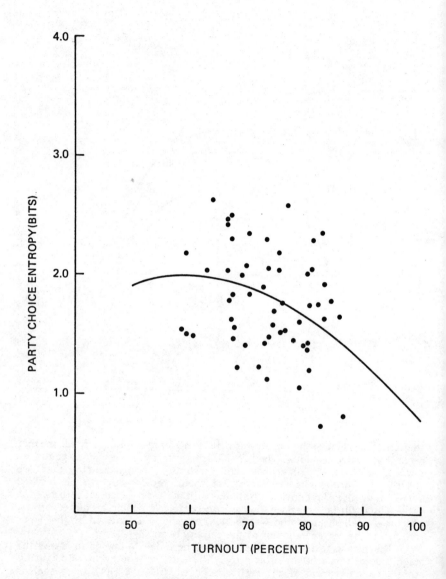

competing parties in the district. We shall term this new variable the "degree of electoral competitiveness," since it ranges between zero and one according to the extent to which the votes are evenly spread among all the competing parties, regardless of how many there are. By the entropy hypothesis, it should be identically equal to H(T), which also ranges between zero and one. Conversely, the degree to which these two variables are not identical will be an indicator of the overall degree to which the data-points lie off their appropriate orbital curves.

In Table 3.1, the results of a regression analysis of electoral competitiveness on turnout entropy for the elections of the 1920s are presented. According to the hypothesis, the intercept produced by the regression should be zero and the slope (partial beta coefficient) should equal one. We should also expect to find a high degree of correlation between the two variables. The findings reported in Table 3.1 indicate that the first two elections, in 1920 and 1923, go a considerable way towards meeting these expectations. The correlations between electoral competitiveness and H(T) are substantial and in the predicted positive direction, supporting the "counter-intuitive" interpretation of the relationship between these variables. The regression slopes, it is true, are both somewhat less than one and the intercepts are not quite zero, but the amount of error is not inconsistent with that reported by Coleman (1975:57) for other political systems. The 1925 and 1927 elections, however, deviate much more substantially from the hypothesis: the variables are only slightly related in 1927 and even less related in 1925, and as a result the slopes and intercepts are remote from their predicted values.

It is possible to interpret the latter finding as a disconfirmation of the entropy hypothesis, at least as it applies to these data. An alternative explanation would be that the hypothesis is valid for all four elections but that its high degree of error in 1925 and 1927 is the result of the influence of some factor or factors that caused certain districts to deviate systematically from their expected entropies in those elections. In what follows, we shall attempt to show that the latter alternative is the more valid one, and that one intruding factor was the attempt made by the regime to influence voting behavior in the face of an increasing degree of non-incorporation in the political system in the latter years of this period.

For the purpose of establishing this point, we shall assume for the moment that the entropy theory is correct and that the extent of political incorporation in Yugoslavia can be discovered by an examination of the spatial distribution of entropy levels across the country. One such distribution is presented in Figure 3.3, which maps H(P) values by constituency for the 1923 election. It is evident from the figure that the pattern closely mirrors the pattern of ethnic heterogeneity presented in Figures 2.2 and 2.3, with Bosnia and Vojvodina, in particular, showing H(P) levels much higher than in other regions. This follows, of course, from the predominantly ethnic basis of the party system. What is more important for our purposes are the sharp lines of disjuncture between high and low entropy areas, with little in the way of transitional districts to act as buffers (note the border of Serbia with Bosnia and Vojvodina, in particular).[5] Clearly, this high entropy ridge which slices the country through the middle violates the condition of a harmonic distribution of entropy levels that should exemplify a cohesive and stable political system. In fact, it is similar in nature to the pattern that Coleman (1975:142) showed for the United States in 1860, which was interpreted as predictive of an imminent attempt at secession in order to produce smaller, more homogeneous political systems.

36

TABLE 3.1
Regression Test of the Entropy Hypothesis, 1920 to 1927 National Elections

Dependent Variable	Election	Independent Variable: Turnout Entropy (H(T))		Correlation
		Intercept (a_0)	Slope (a_1)	
Electoral Competitiveness ($H(P)/\log_2 k$)	1920	0.18	.70	.41
	1923	0.26	.60	.48
	1925	0.68	.03	.03
	1927	0.62	.15	.12

FIGURE 3.3
Party-Choice Entropy by Electoral District, 1923 Election

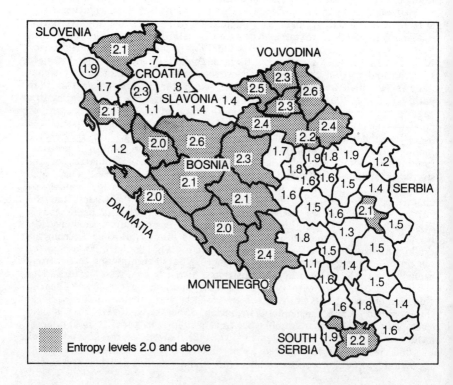

A non-harmonic distribution of entropy values is to be expected in a new political system composed of separate entities. But one would also expect that a process of incorporation or integration in the system would gradually lead to a relaxation in the sharp discontinuities in entropy levels. In the case of the new Yugoslav polity, however, it turns out that the opposite is closer to the truth. This can best be demonstrated by categorizing the fifty-six electoral districts into larger units and comparing their mean entropies over the four elections. For purposes of comparability across regimes as well as ethnic and historical validity, the units we have employed are the six republics and two autonomous regions (provinces) into which the country was divided in 1945 when it became a federal state.

The statistical method most appropriate for this purpose is an analysis of variance. In Table 3.2, we present an analysis of variance of party-choice entropy in each election by republic (for simplicity's sake, we shall refer to both republics and autonomous provinces as 'republics'). The coefficients listed are eta's; they generally range between zero and one according to the degree to which variations in the dependent variable can be accounted for by sorting it into the categories of the independent variable or "factor" (which in this case is the republic in which the electoral district is located). The findings in Table 3.2 show that over the four elections there is a consistent trend towards larger eta coefficients, indicating that the republics were becoming increasingly homogeneous internally and therefore more sharply differentiated each from the other in entropy values.[6] The increasing differentiation by republic is illustrated by the multiple classification analysis, also given in Table 3.2, which lists the mean $H(P)$ deviations of the republics from the country-wide mean $H(P)$ level for each election. Examination of the pattern of deviations reveals that the republics to the south and east of the central ridge -- Serbia, Kosovo, and Macedonia -- were falling further below the national average over the four elections. Although Montenegro, with just one electoral district, actually moved closer to the national average in 1927, Bosnia in the central ridge stays well above that average and Vojvodina actually increases its exceptionally high entropy levels. Finally, Croatia, which contains both low and high entropy districts, remains on average moderately deviant (although changing from below average to above average), and Slovenia slips to slightly below the national mean and hence becomes more sharply differentiated from the central ridge of high entropy formed by Bosnia and Vojvodina. Without question, the Yugoslav polity in this era was demonstrating an increasing resemblance to a collection of distinct subsystems rather than a single, cohesive political system. It was, in effect, divergent rather than convergent over time.

Could this tendency be related in any way to the failure of the regression test of the entropy hypothesis on the 1925 and 1927 data? This is a possibility, for certain processes of change do affect the hypothesis significantly. In particular, we have noted the expectation that districts which are changing orbits (i.e. changing numbers of competing parties) from one election to the next may not be able to achieve their new equilibrium $H(P)$ and $H(T)$ values all at once. Eventually, they should find new $H(P)$ and $H(T)$ values that conform to the hypothesis, but in the meantime it is possible for them to find intermediate entropy values that place them well off the hypothesis. Large numbers of such changes could affect the overall test of the hypothesis quite substantially.

Our data show that there was, indeed, much changing of party numbers in the 1923-25 and 1925-27 intervals; the mean change in party numbers per

TABLE 3.2
Party-Choice Entropy by Republic, 1920 to 1927 Elections

A. ANALYSIS OF VARIANCE

Dependent Variable	Election	Factor Republic[a]	Explained Variance
Party-Choice Entropy (H(P))	1920	.61	.37
	1923	.68	.46
	1925	.73	.53
	1927	.86	.74

B. MULTIPLE CLASSIFICATION ANALYSIS

Depend. Variable	Elec-tion	Grand Mean	Std. Dev.	Slo.	Cro.	Bos.	Voj.	Ser.	Kos.	Mon.	Mac.
Party-Choice Entropy (H(P))	1920	1.94	.44	.31	.02	.50	.07	-.01	-.53	.60	-.18
	1923	1.79	.44	.11	-.23	.39	.62	-.14	-.38	.30	-.08
	1925	1.67	.38	.26	-.25	.15	.58	-.08	-.31	.57	-.18
	1927	1.74	.51	-.07	.34	.42	.76	-.24	-.46	.15	-.65

(Deviations from Grand Mean by Republic)

[a]Coefficients are correlation ratio's (eta's).

district is 0.95 and 1.31 respectively. In order to assess the possibility that this accounts for the deviations of the data from the hypothesis, residual H(P) values were calculated for the 1925 and 1927 data by subtracting from each district's H(P) value, the H(P) value that would have been predicted from its turnout level and number of parties according to the entropy equation. These two residual H(P) variables were then correlated with variables representing the net change in the number of parties in the district over the same period. The results were significant and virtually identical correlation coefficients of -.246 and -.247 for the 1923-25 and 1925-27 periods. Evidently, the more deviant H(P) values tended to occur in districts that were experiencing orbital change, with districts that were increasing orbits tending to undershoot their expected H(P) levels and vice versa. Since changes in the choice spectrum do seem to be a contaminating factor, it is worthwhile to look at changes in electoral competitiveness and turnout entropy controlling for changes in party numbers. The partial correlation of the change in H(P) from 1923 to 1925 with the change in H(T) over the same period controlling for the changes in the number of competing parties is .248. The corresponding change partial correlation for the 1925-27 period is a similar .277. Thus, the process of change from 1923 to 1925 to 1927 was generally in the direction predicted by the entropy hypothesis, but with the result that, cross-sectionally, the data increasingly deviate from the hypothesis. This would appear to be consistent with Coleman's (1975:67) suggestion that the entropy hypothesis cannot completely describe systems where there is a wide variation across districts in the numbers of competing parties, as when rapid systemic change is occurring.

Exactly how much of the error in the 1925 and 1927 elections can be attributed to widespread change in party numbers and H(P) levels is unclear. For one thing, determining how many parties there are in a district is fairly arbitrary. For a party to affect electoral behavior, the voters have to perceive it as a component in the choice spectrum offered them. We employed Coleman's (1975:149) cutoff point of 1 percent of the popular vote as indicating that a party existed as a valid choice, but it is possible that this criterion counts parties that may not even be perceived by the mass of voters, much less taken into account. Accordingly, the correlations cited above should be treated as indicative of a tendency whose true strength is anyone's guess.

There is another, and potentially more important, factor to bear in mind. Examination of the residuals from the entropy relationship for the 1925 and 1927 elections reveals that the errors consisted principally of certain districts having negative residuals caused by turnout rates too low for their H(P) levels, and that these districts are concentrated to a very high degree in the ethnically more homogeneous northwest and southwest regions of the country. Figure 3.4, which maps the 1925 residuals, shows this pattern very clearly. It is true that these areas experienced larger-than-average changes in their numbers of competing parties, which may account for some of the deviation from the hypothesis. But even in those districts that did not change orbits (by the rather arbitrary counting rule we have adopted), the tendency remains the same. This geographically-based pattern of deviation from the hypothesis, which became more pronounced over the course of these elections, would seem to be intimately related to the process of increasing centrifugality in entropy levels over time.

Historical works in this period may provide clues to account for the phenomenon. In the 1925 election, the pro-government parties apparently set out to enhance support for the regime by "encouraging" voting for the government bloc of parties rather than for the opposition parties. Methods used to this end included opposition party intimidation, press control, invalidation of certain party lists, pressure applied to electoral commissions, destruction of ballot boxes, and police presence at polling stations (Ćulinović, 1961:447-57). This pressure seems to have been applied quite generally throughout the country (Beard and Radin, 1929:89-90), but its effect might have varied depending on the social make-up of the district. For instance, there is evidence that in ethnically homogeneous regions like Slovenia where the position of an ethnically dominant party was

40

FIGURE 3.4
Party-Choice Entropy Residuals by Electoral District, 1925 Election

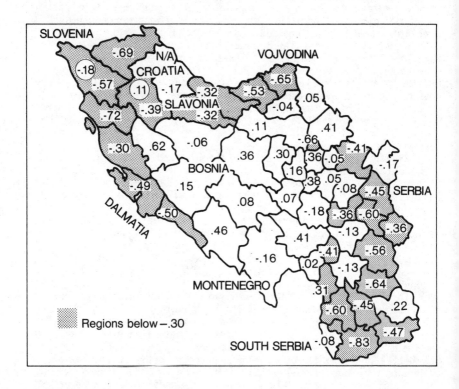

assured, non-support for the regime commonly found expression in abnormally high levels of abstention (Rakočević, 1937:59-60). In the ethnically more heterogeneous districts, on the other hand, it is possible to speculate that the ethnically-based party competition was so intense and so central that the expression of protest through exceptionally low turnout levels or reduced party competitiveness was not as attractive an option. In these areas, voters responded in ways suggested by the entropy hypothesis, regardless of the pressures put on them by the authorities.

This explanation is, of course, highly speculative, but it is consistent with the findings of the polynomial-fit tests. Those findings showed that over the four elections, districts with more than five competing parties conformed more closely to the entropy hypothesis than did districts with less than six parties. Given the ethnic basis of the party system, it is precisely the districts with large numbers of parties that are likely to have been more ethnically heterogeneous. This does not "prove" that the particular interpretation we put on the tendency for the ethnically heterogeneous districts to fit the hypothesis better is correct, but it does underscore the fact that the changes that caused the entropy hypothesis to not work as well in 1925 and 1927 are systematic, patterned, and very probably related to the increasing degree of non-incorporation in the Yugoslav political system in these years.

If these explanations for the pattern of deviation from the entropy hypothesis are generally acceptable, two fundamental points stand out in our analysis of the elections of the liberal-democratic era. First, we have found basic confirmation that the entropy hypothesis is an appropriate tool for analyzing Yugoslav electoral behavior, and therefore that such behavior is a collective reflection of the state of the system rather than merely an expression of individual political preferences. Second, we see evidence of a non-incorporated political system whose centrifugal propensities were becoming increasingly pronounced as the decade wore on, and in which abstention was becoming a major manifestation of protest against the system, particularly in the more ethnically homogeneous regions.

It had long been apparent that the authorities were actively concerned with the problem of regime stability and survival under conditions of extreme fragmentation and mutual hostility between rival ethnic groups. Their interventions into the electoral process did not meet with success and, indeed, may have been counterproductive. As Beard and Radin (1929:89-90) point out, "if ... there is some reality to the [government] 'terror' about which complaints are made, it remains a fact that the Bosnian Moslems, the Croatian Peasant Party, the German Party and the Slovene Populist Party managed to sweep their districts with mechanical regularity losing very few seats to the government, if any, as a result of influence from the centre." Meanwhile, events at the center were reinforcing the feeling that a more sweeping intervention in the political system was desirable. By 1929, the extreme fragmentation and polarization of the party system, which had resulted in twenty-four governments in eleven years, culminated in a major crisis. The virtual paralysis of the National Assembly, along with the murder of the principal Croatian party leader by a Serb nationalist, induced the King to take actions which altered the regime significantly. In the next section, we shall consider the nature and effects of those changes on the fundamental problem of weak and declining political incorporation that our data analysis has revealed.

THE EXPERIMENT WITH RIGHT-WING AUTHORITARIAN CONTROL, 1929 TO 1939

The changes that the monarch inaugurated in 1929 were indeed drastic. Rejecting proposals for the federalization of the country, the King abrogated the Constitution of 1921, suspended the National Assembly, banned the existing parties, and severely curtailed civil liberties. In a quest for a legitimating formula that would cross-cut traditional cleavages and create a supra-ethnic consciousness, a number of other changes were made: the trinational designation of the country was dropped and replaced by the name "Yugoslavia"; the historical regions of the state were reorganized into new administrative units and renamed in a manner designed to undermine customary patterns of identity and behavior; and Serbian army units -- the core of the state's military structure -- were obliged to turn in their cherished regimental colors and receive new "Yugoslav" insignia.

The propaganda accompanying the new regime-strategy implied that Yugoslavia consisted of a single nation, and that the national question would be solved by the creation of a new "integral-Yugoslav national unitarianism." Superficially, this rather vague formulation had certain similarities with the strategy of syncretic amalgamation discussed in Chapter 2. In fact, however, the new "Yugoslav" (i.e. South Slav) notion of patriotism was another variant of group domination which we have termed a strategy of authoritarian exclusion. Thus, while the regime symbolically encouraged a modest degree of cultural amalgamation and greater political unification among the state's three major ethnic groups (Serbs, Croats, and Slovenes) the new strategy toward cultural diversity continued to ignore -- both in theory and practice -- the political aspirations of the numerous other nationality groups in the country.

The initial wave of domestic and foreign optimism which first greeted the new arrangements proved to be short-lived as the royal dictatorship gradually assumed a more authoritarian, centralized, and Serbian character. Serbian control over the military and state bureaucracy remained intact while the legal extermination of traditional ethnic symbols only further alienated the non-Serbian groups who previously had enjoyed the use of their "tribal" nomenclature and cultural customs. Group domination continued but under an authoritarian dictatorship controlled by Serbian bureaucrats, police, and military officers, rather than by Serbian party politicians.

While the new strategy made only cosmetic changes with respect to basic ethnic relations, the new regime was determined to avoid the relatively free expression of societal diversity which had characterized the earlier period. To that end, the new Constitution of 1931, designed to rationalize the authoritarian regime, established a much weaker parliamentary structure with real power left in the hands of the monarch. Overtly religious, regional, or ethnic parties were prohibited, and parliamentary candidates were required to prove that they were running on the lists of genuinely "Yugoslav" parties. A new law stipulated that the party obtaining a plurality of popular votes would receive two-thirds of the seats in the Assembly.

A blatantly manipulated and open ballot election -- really a rigged plebiscite -- was held in November 1931. Although uncontested by the now illegal parties (who clandestinely encouraged their supporters to boycott the event), the regime claimed a great "victory" in receiving the support of an alleged 65.3 percent of registered voters who cast ballots.[7] Even using the regime's very suspect statistics, this would mean that over a third of the entire population abstained, and that some regional levels of abstention were even more unfavorable (65.5 percent in Dalmatia, 45.5 percent in Croatia, and 47.9 percent in Slovenia). The new parliament, labelled the "police assembly" by the opposition, was dominated by Serbs, even though they constituted only a minority of the population. Politically overcentralized, ethnically biased, corrupt and very unpopular (even among the Serbs), the King's exercise in nation-building was both ill-devised and ill-fated.

In 1934, the King, increasingly aware of the regime's many shortcomings, dismissed the General who had been serving as Prime Minister since 1929, and moved to "civilianize" the political process by organizing a new mass government party, the Yugoslav Radical Democratic Party (co-opting the names of three former Serbian-based parties). A new, but hardly less authoritarian, electoral law was also adopted whereby the party list winning a plurality in the next election would receive only three-fifths of the seats in parliament (rather than the earlier two-thirds). The former parties, however, remained illegal and violations of human and political rights continued to give the regime a cast that was decidedly authoritarian, if slightly more benign than some other right-wing dictatorships in Europe at the time.[8] Blocked from any legal outlet, ethnic, and regional demands increasingly took an extreme ultra-nationalist and violent character. In October 1934, on the eve of contemplated liberal reforms, the King was assassinated by a joint squad of Macedonian and Croatian separatists. A moment of inter-ethnic solidarity and outrage at the assassination's foreign (Hungarian and Italian) sponsorship soon evaporated as central control passed to a regency headed by the late King's cousin, Prince Paul, and the same Serbian clique that had supported the authoritarian regime.

In May 1935, seeking a semblance of popular legitimation, the new regency and the government called an election. For the occasion, an Opposition Bloc was permitted to compete with the government party, which was renamed the Yugoslav National Party. The Opposition Bloc artificially combined most of the major ethnic and regional parties that had competed during the 1920s (including the Croatian Peasant Party, Serbian Democrats, Serbian Independent Democrats, Serbian Agrarians, and the endorsement, but not the participation, of the Yugoslav Moslem Organization). Two other groups were also permitted to run slates: a dissident faction of the government party and a fascist "corporatist bloc" centered in Serbia.

The outcome of this four-slate electoral contest, which included the by now normal amount of police intimidation and statistical falsification, was another massive government victory. The regime claimed 60.6 percent of the vote, with the Opposition Bloc allegedly receiving 37.4 percent and the other two groups sharing 2 percent of the vote. Given the regime's character, the results seemed rather predictable, if still scandalous. The question that concerns us is: did the attempt to structure electoral participation into forms more compatible with the objectives of political incorporation and stability constitute an effective regime-strategy?

The Analysis

The first step in answering this question is to determine whether the entropy hypothesis functions as an adequate means of accounting for electoral behavior in this highly contrived electoral context. The results of the hypothesis testing, presented and discussed in detail in Appendix B, indicate that it does. By the time of the 1935 election, the original fifty-six electoral districts had been subdivided into 353 constituencies, of which 325 were competitive. Since the numbers of orbits had been constrained to just three (the number of competing parties ranges from two to four per district), the polynomial-fit test could be performed separately for each orbit. The findings indicate that a parabola of the hypothesized concave-downwards form was generated at each level (Table B.3).

One interesting feature of the polynomial-fit test is that the amount of explained variance for each parabola is quite small, indicating that there is a considerable amount of scatter about the fitted parabolic curves. The regression test, presented in Table 3.3, yields a similar conclusion. The regression of electoral competitiveness ($H(P)/\log_2 k$) on turnout entropy, although in the expected positive direction, produces a correlation of just .15, and also indicates slope and intercept coefficients well off their predicted values. Surprisingly, however, when the regression was performed on $H(P)$ without standardizing for the number of parties, the regression fit improved noticeably. The slope, for example, increased from .31 to .57 -- still well below 1.0 but much closer to the slope estimates derived for the 1920 and 1923 elections.

TABLE 3.3
Regression Test of the Entropy Hypothesis, 1935 Election

Dependent Variable	Independent Variable: Turnout Entropy $(H(T))$		Correlation
	Intercept (a_0)	Slope (a_1)	
Electoral Competitiveness $(H(P)/\log_2 k)$	.37	.31	.15
Party-Choice Entropy $(H(P))$	.32	.57	.23

We cannot examine the possibility that the deviations from the hypothesis which have appeared are the result of processes of change taking place, because the elections nearest in time to this election are either too rigged to be meaningful (1931) or are unavailable (1938). The nature of the deviations can allow us, however, to make some guesses about the error. The fact that the regression test works better when the number of choices is not controlled suggests that the number of choices is not a particularly meaningful factor. When this point is considered in conjunction with the fact that the third and fourth parties together amassed just 2 percent of the vote, it is safe to assume that the 1935 election was perceived and responded to by the electorate primarily as a two-choice event-set. On this assumption, a third test of the hypothesis, the estimation of the $\log_2 k$ coefficient in the entropy equation, produces a result (0.96) remarkably close to the value (1.00) predicted by the hypothesis (see Appendix B). Clearly, despite the highly manipulated character of the 1935 election, the data findings indicate that the electorate's response followed the lines of the entropy hypothesis.

This conclusion implies that the regime's attempts to engineer electoral behavior so as to disguise the non-cohesive state of the political system may have failed, even if the Government Bloc did win a commanding majority. Examination of the geographic distribution of $H(P)$ values and of the patterning in the $H(P)$ residuals (errors) reveals considerable evidence to support this view. In order to achieve comparability with the 1920s data, and to enhance interpretability of the mapping of $H(P)$ values, we first performed an analysis of variance of $H(P)$ by a new variable, "region," which classifies the 353 constituencies of 1935 into the fifty-six districts employed in the earlier period. The result was quite strong (eta = .66), indicating that there is considerable within-region similarity in $H(P)$ levels. This is our justification for presenting a spatial distribution of mean 1935 $H(P)$ values for the fifty-six regions in Figure 3.5. The figure reveals that much the same pattern of sharp discontinuities in $H(P)$ levels separate off the centre of the country from the northwest

FIGURE 3.5
Party-Choice Entropy by Region, 1935 Election

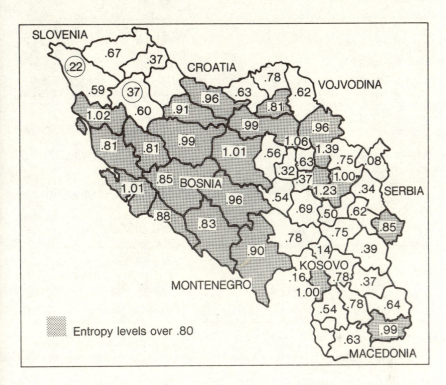

(Slovenia, part of Croatia) and the southeast (Serbia, Kosovo, and Macedonia). There are some slight changes, such as a significant reduction in entropy levels of northern Vojvodina and a relative rise in H(P) levels in parts of Croatia, reflecting the fact that Vojvodina was incorporated into the Government Bloc and Croatia, a centre of opposition, experienced intense competition in its more ethnically-mixed areas. In general, however, the continuity in patterns is very high, given the extent of constitutional manipulation and government interference that took place.

An examination of the residuals (shown in Figure B.3) reinforces the above conclusion. The northwest and southeast regions of the country are the principal areas whose districts showed negative H(P) residuals, resulting from the fact that turnout rates were much lower than the low levels of competitiveness would lead one to predict. Evidently, the same ethnically more homogeneous regions that withheld participation in 1925 and 1927 did so again in 1935. By way of contrast, Croatia and Bosnia, regions of maximum contestation between government and opposition slates, show positive residuals: H(P) values, artifically restricted to very low orbits, rise above their predicted orbital positions. These ethnically diverse, high-entropy regions conformed closely to the hypothesis for the 1920s; the effect of limiting their party-choice entropy levels seems to have been to generate more error than had been the case in the earlier elections.

The implication to be drawn from these findings is that the experiment in right-wing authoritarian control, with popular electoral expression permitted only in a highly restricted format, did not have the intended effect of decreasing the centrifugal tendencies in the country. An analysis of variance of H(P) by republic, presented in Table 3.4, reveals this fact most clearly. Although there is a very large reduction in the mean H(P) level across the country in 1935, the constituency-by-constituency variation in that variable, indicated by its standard deviation, is nearly as great as it had been in the earlier elections (compare with Table 3.2). Moreover, the analysis indicates that the republics still constitute units which have a reasonable degree of internal homogeneity in H(P) levels and are differentiated from one another.[9] Finally, the pattern of high entropy and low entropy republics is basically the same as it was in the 1920s, with, as mentioned earlier, the sole exception of Vojvodina.

The experiment with a highly manipulated election was, then, not a particularly successful one from the regime's standpoint. If anything, the government's manufactured statistical victory in the 1935 election seemed to hasten the erosion of support for the regime. In protest at the transparent electoral chicanery, the Opposition Bloc, led by the Croatian Peasant Party, decided to boycott participation in the legislature, and several key members of the cabinet even resigned in protest against the government's insensitivity to ethnic and regional interests. Efforts to rationalize the authoritarian political system and hegemonic regime-strategy continued over the next few years (e.g. the restructuring of the officially-sponsored government party on a more mass and multi-ethnic basis), but the Serbian-dominated central government was unwilling to meet the minimum opposition demands for inter-ethnic accommodation, i.e. the abandonment of dictatorial methods and the federalization of the country. Spurned by the opposition, the Belgrade government became increasingly illiberal in character, even flirting with various fascist-style practices (uniformed para-military fomations, ritualistic salutes, and a leadership cult) which foreshadowed the more brutal regime-strategy soon to be implemented throughout most of Europe under Axis direction. The response of the Croatian and Serbian opposition party organizations to such authoritarian developments was to work together more closely in order to channel the widespread popular alienation with both the government and regime. Electorally, this rising dissatisfaction found expression in the 1938 election, in which the Opposition Bloc actually increased its share of the popular vote from 37.4 percent to 44.9 percent, despite systematic police repression and the utilization of a non-secret ballot. The position of the Croatian leadership on regime change (democratization) and constitutional reform (federalization) was now buttressed by a substantial popular mandate that could no longer be safely ignored.

The last period of interwar Yugoslavia was a classic case of positive measures being taken too late to matter. With war in Europe imminent, and pressure on Yugoslavia from all sides, the regime's top leaders became desperate to find a basis for inter-ethnic and regional cohesion. Prince Paul and the new government began intensive confidential negotiations with the Croatian leadership to find a solution to the country's difficulties. In August 1939, just a week before the start of World War II, a constitutional agreement (Sporazum) was reached which essentially federalized the relationship between Croatia and the rest of the state. A completely new

TABLE 3.4
Party-Choice Entropy by Republic, 1935 Election

A. ANALYSIS OF VARIANCE

Dependent Variable	Election	Factor Republic	Explained Variance
Party-Choice Entropy (H(P))	1935	.32[a]	.10

B. MULTIPLE CLASSIFICATION ANALYSIS

Depend. Variable	Election	Grand Mean	Std. Dev.	Deviations from Grand Mean by Republic							
				Slo.	Cro.	Bos.	Voj.	Ser.	Kos.	Mon.	Mac.
Party-Entropy (H(P))	1935	.75	.35	-.13	.02	.17	.07	-.06	-.35	.10	-.15

[a]Correlation ratio (eta).

and quite sizeable province, to be known as "Croatia," was established out of existing regions. The province included approximately 30 percent of the population and territory of the entire state and roughly 76 percent of its inhabitants were ethnic Croats. The new province was given its own legislative assembly and an executive officer who was to be appointed by the monarch (or regent) but responsible to the provincial legislators. The province was given broad budgetary and administrative authority, as well as control over economic and social affairs. The central government in Belgrade continued to exercise power over the rest of the country and retained exclusive jurisdiction over foreign relations, foreign trade, defense, security, transportation, and communications. To consummate the agreement, several top leaders of the Croatian Peasant Party joined a new coalition cabinet in Belgrade, thereby relinquishing the policy of obstruction and abstention which had characterized most of their relationship with the hegemonic Serbian political elite and dynasty in Belgrade throughout the preceding twenty years. The Parliament was dissolved pending a new election which unfortunately was never held as external events overwhelmed the country.

In making the 1939 agreement, the Croatian Peasant Party leadership had abandoned the other ethnic and sectional parties in the Opposition Bloc (a move especially resented by the Serbs in Croatia) in order to get the most favorable results for Croatia. On the other hand, for the first time since the creation of the state, the Serbian leaders gave up the dogma of national unity or "Yugoslav unitarianism," which in practice had meant Serbian hegemony, and recognized the principle of "Croatian national individuality." Essentially the agreement represented the acceptance of a new consociational approach to ethnic conflict. In the (usually secret) bilateral negotiations at the elite level which had resulted in an agreement to govern jointly, each sub-elite was authorized to control matters in their separate ethnic-territorial communities. Based on the last election, Croatian leaders could justifiably claim to have, as consociational theory requires, a popular mandate to act as ethnic spokesmen, an enviable position which could not be asserted by Prince Paul (the principal regent) and the Serbian government leaders. As in the case of the two previous regime-strategies, however, the consociational-type model of 1939-1941 took no account of the several other smaller Slavic and non-Slavic nationalities in the country. The elite-managed and ethnically-limited character of the new agreement was quickly attacked by the underground Communist party leaders who, as we discuss in Chapter 4, were in the process of formulating an entirely new solution and regime-strategy of their own.

The agreement was, nevertheless, a very positive development for the mangement of ethnic hostility, and suggestions were soon advanced to create similar quasi-federal units out of Slovenia and the "Serb-lands." In addition to initiating a process that might have led to the federalization of the Yugoslav state, the settlement reached between the Serbian and Croatian spokesmen also aimed at the general liberalization of the political system. Thus, the agreement included the termination of the authoritarian electoral law of 1931 which had prevented a free range of party organization and voter preferences. A constitutional court in Zagreb with jurisdiction over possible disputes between the central government in Belgrade and the Croatian government was also to be established.

Given enough time, attention, and further modification, the new institutional arrangements had a reasonable chance of success. Yugoslavia, as one knowledgeable observer put it at the time, was now poised for "the substitution of a democratic for a camouflaged authoritarian regime. . . . In this situation, everything depends upon securing immunity from war" (Seton-Watson, 1976:358, 364). Unfortunately, no such immunity was forthcoming. During the next year and a half, Prince Paul and the government were preoccupied with a vain effort to maintain Yugoslav neutrality. When pressure by Hitler finally forced them to join the Axis in March 1941, the regime was quickly overthrown by a coup arranged by pro-Allied military officers. Using the event as a pretext, the Fascist powers invaded, rapidly defeated, and then dismembered the Yugoslav state. The war was soon to expose the depth of regional and ethnic fragmentation in the country which the innovative but short-lived quasi-federal arrangements of 1939 could not possibly reverse after two decades of squabbling parliamentary government and inept authoritarianism. Future experimentation with the institutional management of cultural diversity was not to include the politicians and parties that had dominated interwar Yugoslavia.

NOTES

1. Programatically, the Democrats took a more "Yugoslav" position than the Radicals, and at the outset enjoyed a small amount of support among the Croatian and Slovenian middle class. As time went on, however, its ethnic basis became increasingly Serbian (Gligorijević, 1969:176).

2. A measure of competitiveness which can take into account any number of competing parties is clearly more valuable than the commonly-used percentage difference between the two largest parties. Whether an entropy-based measure or Rae's (1967:47-64) index of fractionalization is to be preferred has elicited some debate, however. If one accepts Elkins' (1974:682-700) point that the critical feature of the concept of competitiveness is uncertainty, then entropy has the advantage. Its use is not unprecedented in political science: some time ago Wildgren (1971) introduced an index of hyperfractionalization which is simply the antilogarithm of entropy.

3. Coleman's use of the term "integration" follows the discussion in Chapter 1. It is closely related in meaning to cohesiveness, except that it implies a particular mechanism, social interaction, as the cause. This makes sense in terms of Coleman's theory, but as we have no evidence concerning social interaction processes, we shall interpret the findings that follow in terms of cohesiveness rather than integration.

4. The maximum or turning-point of the fitted polynomial for this and the other elections are substantially higher than the predicted 50 percent turnout level. The reason for this is closely connected with the explanation of the error given later on in the discussion, and is elaborated in some detail in Appendix B.

5. Interestingly, the very marked disjuncture in electoral behavior along the border between Croatia and Bosnia closely parallels the frontier of the Croatian military border created by the Hapsburgs to resist the expanding Ottoman Empire (Rothenburg, 1966).

6. This would not be the case if the overall variance in H(P) levels across the country were diminishing. As the standard deviations in Table 3.2 indicate, however, 1925 registered a slight decline but 1927 saw a much larger increase in H(P) variance.

7. The level of turnout claimed by the regime was attacked as fallacious by the former parties and bears a rather strange similarity to the lowest level of turnout under the former electoral system, 64.9 percent in the election for the constitutional assembly in 1920. It seems plausible that the authoritarian regime did not want to appear any less legitimate than its liberal predecessor.

8. Commenting at the time on the new regime's capacity for institutional engineering, Britain's most eminent specialist on interwar Eastern Europe noted in a private memorandum that the "King and Prime Minister are, by reason of their education and mentality, complete amateurs in the theory of constitutional and representative government and political science. The task of drafting a new constitution is obviously beyond them

and they seem to prefer the assistance of other amateurs rather than the advice of the (admittedly few) experts whom the country possesses ... there is a tendency to treat Absolutism not as a regrettable and temporary necessity, but as desirable, and as an end in itself" (Seton-Watson, 1976:193).

9. The finding that the correlation ratio for 1935 is considerably below those for the elections of the 1920s (Table 3.2) is largely a function of the six-fold increase in the number of electoral districts and the correspondingly greater variability across constituencies in H(P) levels.

4
The Communists and Cultural Diversity

After two decades of ethnic divisiveness and increasing centrifugal pressures, the young Yugoslav state had little chance to withstand the onslaught of the invasion and war which engulfed the country in April 1941. The combination of internal and external forces which had triggered the rapid collapse of the interwar state also produced one of Europe's bloodiest cases of communal violence, and led to a radical restructuring of the country's political system.

The major political beneficiary of the war was the Communist Party of Yugoslavia which came to power at the end of 1944, and has been in control of the country since that time. In this chapter we will examine the communists' changing strategy toward cultural diversity both before and immediately after the party attained political control. By looking at the various ideas and programs with which the communists have addressed the national question, as well as the socio-political demography of communist support, we will be in a better position to empirically assess and explain the evolving state of political incorporation of the Yugoslav mosaic during the post-World War II period.

COMMUNIST VIEWS ON THE NATIONAL QUESTION: FROM FACTIONALISM TO A REVOLUTIONARY STRATEGY, 1919-1941

The changing attitudes of the Yugoslav communists towards the multi-ethnic features of their environment before World War II can be divided into three stages. The first period from 1921 to 1923 was characterized by continuous and very intense polemical struggles between the right and left factions of the newly-founded Communist Party of Yugoslavia (KPJ) about how to deal with the nationality issue (Vlajčić, 1970). The right faction led by Sima Marković, a Serb, maintained that the national question could be solved through institutional reforms that would give each of the three major ethnic groups (Serbs, Croats, and Slovenes) in the new kingdom broader "autonomy" vis-à-vis the central government than under the Constitution of 1921. This essentially meant working within the framework of the existing state's tri-national ethnic formula and, if not explicitly accepting the existence of Serbian hegemony, at least downplaying the national issue in the party's strategy to attract popular support. The right faction opposed the idea of federalizing the state or of recognizing the political and cultural aspirations of non-charter-group nationalities and minorities, fearing that such a development would strengthen ethnically-based centrifugal forces and weaken class solidarity.

In a more democratic state, according to the right-wing leader, "federalism would not have any special justification from the point of view of the proletariat" (Avakumovic, 1964:68). Concentrating entirely on a "pure class struggle" which aimed at the establishment of a Soviet Socialistic Yugoslavia along republican and centralized lines within the framework of a broader Balkan revolution, the right faction foreclosed the party's tactical use of appeals such as the devolution of power to minority groups or the ethnic dissolution of the state.

In contrast, the left faction in the party, which supported the views of the Communist International based in the USSR, saw ethnic rivalry and dissatisfaction in the new state as an opportunity to be exploited. For the left faction, a strategy advocating the reorganization of the state along federal lines (favored by most other non-Serbian oriented political parties, and some Serbs as well), combined with a Leninist tactical appeal for the "self-determination" of peoples, seemed more likely to hasten the creation of a revolutionary situation. Moreover the left-wing in the party drew attention not only to the grievances of large groups such as the Croats and Slovenes, but also to the potential for mobilizing the dissatisfaction of politically unrecognized groups such as the Macedonians and Montenegrins, as well as minorities (e.g. the Hungarians, Slovaks, and Romanians in the Vojvodina) who wished to assert their autonomy from Serbian control. Although party pronouncements fluctuated back and forth on the national question, depending on the ascendency of one or another group in the party leadership, the position of the right faction exercised the most weight in this period. Members of the right faction were concentrated primarily in Serbia and tended to look at the ethnic problems of the state from a centralist and therefore basically pan-Serbian perspective, rather than from a more pluralistic or multi-national point of view. The latter outlook was more prevalent among both Croatian and Serbian communists working in the the Croatian party organization, who appeared to have a sharp sensitivity to the country's multi-ethnic character (a situation with certain similarities to the division of communist views after 1945).

The success of communist appeals to the geographically "peripheral" and politically dissatisfied ethnic groups in the early 1920s gave some credence to the more ethnically sensitive and less centralist strategy of the left faction in the party. Thus, in the municipal elections held during 1920, the communists scored significant electoral victories in Croatia and Macedonia as well as in Serbia. In April of the same year, the party helped to organize a strike of transport workers across the country, with particular success in Slovenia and Vojvodina. The high point of Communist success as a legal opposition movement in interwar Yugoslavia, and an indicator of the party's potential for multi-national and cross-regional mobilization, was the November 1920 election for the Constituent Assembly. The KPJ emerged as the third strongest party in the country with 12.4 percent of the popular vote and 58 seats in the legislature. Even more important with regard to the formulation of a "national strategy," the Communists were the only political party, apart from the Democrats, (the second most influential Serbian-oriented party) to gain seats in every province of Yugoslavia. Nevertheless, as Figure 4.1 indicates, their appeal was not uniform across the entire country. The communists' greatest electoral success was concentrated in Macedonia and Montenegro, areas of considerable discontent, which at the time were officially considered as parts of Serbia. The Communists also achieved impressive support in other areas of the country experiencing nationality unrest, including parts of

FIGURE 4.1
Communists' Share of Popular Vote by Electoral District, 1920 Election

Kosovo, Vojvodina and present-day Croatia (Dalmatia and Slavonia) as well
as the southern area of Serbia proper and the principal urban areas
(Belgrade, Zagreb, and Ljubljana). Although the communist electoral
achievement cannot be attributed solely to ethnic or territorial factors (e.g.
efficient organization, an emergent urban proletariat, and economic
distress were also at work), on the whole they did much better in areas that
were becoming increasingly alienated from the strategy of Serbian
charter-group hegemony practiced by the central government in Belgrade.
Paradoxically, the communists were able to attract a large number of
voters offended by the regime's strategy toward cultural diversity even
though the party's own right-wing position on the national question tended
to neglect the importance of ethnic and regional dissatisfaction as a basis
for revolutionary change.

Despite the communist leadership's general neglect of the national
question, and their commitment to the existing state boundaries (if not to
the regime), the growing attraction of the party as a rallying point for
discontented elements of the population soon drew a sharp response from
the state authorities. In 1920 and 1921, the regime first drastically curbed,
and then completely outlawed the Communist Party. As leaders of an

illegal and politically isolated movement, the energies of the Yugoslav communists were increasingly devoted to factional squabbling on a variety of theoretical and tactical issues, including the national question. Although communist activity had little bearing on the immediate political life of the country, it did have an important impact on the evolution of the party's strategy and its future role in Yugoslavia. During 1922 and 1923, the party leaders from the right and left factions engaged in a vigorous debate on the national question. The right-wing was attacked for seriously underestimating the revolutionary potential of nationalism and anti-centralist feeling in the country, and for having inadequately prepared the party for coping with its illegal situation. The impact of the left-wing charges was accentuated by the growing success of the legal "bourgeois" parties in mobilizing voters on the basis of ethnic and regional appeals (very apparent to the communists from the 1923 election results), and also by the increasing support given to the left faction by the Comintern. Criticizing the Yugoslav communists in 1923, the Executive Committee of the Comintern (ECCI) argued for the importance of adopting a Leninist conception of "national self-determination," and even advocated separatism for aggrieved ethnic groups who wished to form their own independent states. The communists were pressed to form united-front alliances with nationalist parties (such as the Croatian Peasant Party) in order to overthrow capitalism. Such blatant exploitation of ethnic divisions and especially the encouragement of tactical alliances with anti-communist nationalists was strongly resisted by the right-wing members of the party, who maintained "that so much significance cannot be attributed to the national question as to thrust back socio-economic and class interests in a secondary place" (Gruber, 1974:103). In practice, the deep factional differences on the national question and other theoretical issues had little immediate effect on the political fortunes of the KPJ except to further weaken the unity and effectiveness of the illegal communist organization, and allow for the greater intrusion of the increasingly Soviet-dominated Comintern into Yugoslav party affairs.

The second period, from 1924 to 1934, began with a basic re-formulation of communist strategy on the national question which, while not eliminating factional dissension over this and other issues, established the dominant "line" in the party over the next decade. As early as the third regional party conference in December 1923, the left faction was able to push through a resolution supporting the principle of self-determination by the various nationalities in Yugoslavia up to, but not necessarily including, outright secession from the existing state. The resolution also advocated a constitutional revision which would insure equal rights for the Macedonian people and the country's ethnic minorities (a proposal which still ignored the existence of a Montenegrin nation or the creation of autonomous regional units for Vojvodina and Bosnia). This new left-wing view received strong encouragement from the Fifth World Congress of the Comintern in June 1924, which called for "separating Croatia, Slovenia, and Macedonia from Yugoslavia, and creating independent republics of them ..." (Gruber, 1974:134). The Comintern thus demanded that secession be supported as a general principle, and again urged the KPJ to undertake alliances with the bourgeois nationalist parties. In November 1924, the left-led KPJ adopted a platform agreeing with the Comintern position, and offered to fight with other nationalist parties for the right of the different South Slav peoples (including Montenegrins) to form independent states. When the leader of the still vital right faction stubbornly refused to swallow this new multi-national approach to revolutionary change, he was sharply rebuked by

Stalin himself. The Soviet leader attacked the view that a solution to the conflicts among the nationalities of Yugoslavia should be reduced to a "constitutional question," and argued that the right-wing in the KPJ had underestimated the revolutionary potential "in the movement of the Croats for national emancipation." Arguing for a more "Leninist" and therefore more tactically agile exploitation of the national question, Stalin observed that

> the right to secede must be provided for those nationalities that may wish to secede, and the right to autonomy must be provided for those nationalities that may prefer to remain within the framework of the Yugoslav state.

Of course he also went on to point out that

> the right to secede must not be understood as an obligation, as a duty to secede. A nation may take advantage of this right and secede, but it may also forego the right. ... We must not confuse a right with an obligation. (Gruber, 1974:143)

In April 1925, the Comintern passed a resolution which urged the KPJ to

> spread its propaganda and agitation to the utmost to convince the toiling masses of the oppressed nature of Yugoslavia that the destruction of the pan-Serb bourgeoisie is the only way towards the solution of the national question. Fear of inflaming national passions ought not to keep the Party from appealing with all its might to the masses on this most important question. (Avakumovic, 1964:80-81)

By the time of the Third Party Congress in Vienna in 1926, even the right-wing leadership admitted to having committed errors on the national question (and were quickly rewarded by the Comintern by being allowed to reassert their control of the party apparatus). Communists were now urged to fight for the right of self-determination up to secession "to win the confidence of the broad masses of the oppressed nations and thus broaden its revolutionary front" (Avakumovic, 1968:81). Tito (who in 1926 was the secretary of the metal and leather workers union in Croatia) later observed that it was only after Stalin's intervention "that the KPJ as a whole finally took a correct stand of principle in connection with the national question" (Tito, 1948:26).

At the Fourth Party Congress in 1928, the Yugoslav communists supported the formation of independent states for Croatia and Macedonia, the unification of Kosovo with Albania, and the right of the Hungarian national minority in Vojvodina to secede. The fact that these demands were almost identical with the views of the various domestic and foreign ultra-nationalistic political forces in the 1930s was regarded by the communists as highly beneficial to their revolutionary secessionist tactics (ironically, such nationalist demands are very similar to certain dissident programs advanced since 1945 in communist Yugoslavia, but which are naturally viewed as "counter-revolutionary").

The disagreement on the national question in the mid-1920s was not the last time that the policies of Stalin and an international communist organization would collide with the views of the Yugoslav communist leadership. For the moment, however, it ended effective controversy concerning what position the KPJ should adopt toward the national question. Although factionalism remained rampant in the party, the right-wing was forced to accept the left's "nationalist-separatist" line and to cooperate with Comintern-Soviet manoeuvering in the Balkan region. Since this stage of communist thinking about ethnic relations coincided to some extent with the harshest period of the authoritarian royal dictatorship (1929-1934), the new tactics of the illegal KPJ had little practical effect on political development.

Perhaps the most important change in the Yugoslav party during this period, and one which would later influence their popular appeal, was the gradual entry of more non-Serbs into the communist leadership. By the late 1920s, the center of communist activity had shifted to Croatia, where the party found it possible to exploit the anti-Serb and anti-centralist opposition to the existing state. In fact, during 1927, the party headquarters in Belgrade accused the Zagreb branches of displaying nationalistic tendencies. If the Yugoslav communists were not in agreement on their strategy to the national question, they were at least becoming more sophisticated in turning the country's ethnic diversity and conflicts to their own advantage.

From 1935 to 1941, during the last stage in the evolution of communist strategy on the national question prior to World War II, the party ended its tactical support for the dismemberment of the Yugoslav state, while at the same time intensifying its commitment to the self-determination of dissatisfied ethnic groups. Faced with the aggressive ostpolitik of an emergent Nazi Germany, the Soviet Union and Comintern decided that the dissolution of states such as Yugoslavia would be counter-productive. Thus, the new Popular Front policy adopted by the Comintern during 1934 and 1935 encouraged parties like the KPJ to continue their struggle for regime transformation, but within the frame-work of existing state boundaries. The earlier emphasis on nationalist-separatist secessionism, it was argued, would only create a host of small nation-states which would easily fall prey to fascist aggression rather than serve the Soviet Union's urgent need for a buffer zone against Germany.

The Yugoslav communists quickly adapted to the "new tactical orientation" of the Communist International. At the Fourth Territorial Party Congress in December 1934, the old policy of immediate secession for the larger national regions and the self-determination of minorities was downplayed. Stress was now placed on the establishment of revolutionary worker and peasant governments in the various regions of a still unified country. A major innovation adopted at the 1934 Congress was the proposal to create separate "national" party organizations in Slovenia, Croatia, and Macedonia -- a decision which was implemented in the first two regions in 1937. Thus, while the communists no longer wished to dismantle the Yugoslav state along ethnic and regional lines, they were still determined to give the party a multi-national image and appeal. Communist party leaders continued to criticize vigorously the existing regime, but the attacks on the integrity of the Yugoslav state by separatist movements within or outside the country were sharply condemned. Increasingly throughout 1935 and 1936, the concept of self-determination in party pronouncements was equated with the creation of a communist federation based upon "equality and brotherhood" among peoples. As Tito, now the new Soviet-appointed organizational secretary of KPJ, stated in a 1937 article distinguishing the party's policy toward the Croats from the strategy of the ruling regime:

> Communists are resolute opponents of any forcible assimilation
> (fusion, merger) of individual peoples. Because of this, they
> condemn and refute all attempts by Belgrade rulers to wipe
> Croats from the face of the earth, to transform Croats into
> Serbs or Yugoslavs, to make of Croats a tribe within a
> three-name [Serb-Croat-Slovene] nation. Communists consider
> the Croats, Serbs, and Slovenes are three separate, brotherly
> peoples. (Tito, 1978:4)

Starting the interwar period in support of a centralized and tripartite
charter-group formula, and then shifting for a decade to an equally extreme
secessionist position, the communists, by the late 1930s, had developed a
new program which urged the unification of the South Slav peoples, but only
on the basis of national equality and federalism. The communists' new
policy had immense tactical advantages. It allowed the party to endorse
the classical marxian struggle for a social revolution which would establish
bonds of class consciousness among the country's culturally-diverse
proletarians, while still being able to exploit the revolutionary potential of
ethnic and sectional grievances. The new approach also enabled the KPJ to
appeal to both the larger ethnic groups and the smaller minorities, as well
as to groups having a territorial identity, since the general notion of a
future federal system implied that every group would be accommodated in
one way or another (an ambiguity which party leaders encouraged).
Moreover, the shift in tactics also allowed the party to continue criticizing
the regime, while still condemning its more extreme separatist opponents
who were in competition with the communists to take power.

By the Fifth Party Congress in October 1940, less than six months
before Yugoslavia was drawn into World War II, the communists had finally
devised a revolutionary, coherent, and flexible "tactical orientation" on the
national question that was a considerable improvement upon earlier
approaches. Although twenty years of factional polemics and tactical shifts
had contributed to a good deal of dissension and confusion in the party
ranks, the communists had also acquired considerable theoretical prowess
and practical sensitivity in dealing with nationality issues, experience that
was to serve them well during the events of the next five years and would
ultimately help them to acquire control of the country. What the
communists actually believed, as Marxists devoted to a trans-ethnic notion
of proletarian internationalism, and what policies they would endeavor to
implement once they came to power, were however, entirely different
matters.

WARTIME: ETHNIC STRATEGIES IN CONFLICT

The Axis-led invasion of Yugoslavia in April 1941, rapidly followed by
the collapse of the last interwar regime and the dismemberment of the
country, added an entirely new dimension to the national question.
Determined to exploit the existence of deep cultural and territorial
cleavages which had hastened their conquest of Yugoslavia (e.g. most of the
non-Serbs in the Yugoslav Royal Army had shown little enthusiasm to
defend the regime), the invading powers generally supported the pro-fascist
elements within each region and, wherever possible, played each local
ethnic community and pro-Axis group off against the other.

This divide-and-rule policy (which ultimately also tended to divide the
pro-Axis forces along ethnic lines) began with the dismemberment of the

Yugoslav state. Croatia (as constituted under the consociational regime-strategy of 1939-1941) was enlarged to include most of Bosnia and proclaimed as an independent state under the control of the ultra-nationalistic Ustashe organization which modelled its "racial" policy and party structure along Fascist principles. Serbia became a German Protectorate under a puppet regime headed by a conservative military officer and manned by a combination of Serbian fascists and collaborators. Most of Slovenia, which had so jealously endeavored to protect its special interests in the tri-national interwar state, was integrated directly into the Third Reich. Other areas of the country were partitioned among Germany's allies. Hungary was given a large part of Vojvodina where the presence of large Hungarian and pro-fascist German minorities enhanced Budapest's control of the region (in the election of 1935, the Germans of Yugoslavia had voted almost en bloc for the pro-Axis ruling party). The Italians received most of the Dalmatian coast and Montenegro, while the Bulgarians were given the major part of Macedonia and a portion of Serbia.

In the Independent State of Croatia (NDH), the pro-Axis regime adopted a strategy of ultra-nationalistic purification toward non-Croats (i.e. non-Catholics and non-Moslems). Carried to its most brutal extreme by the Ustashe organization, this policy involved the deportation or liquidation of the Jews, Gypsies and those Serbs (approximately one-third of the NDH population) who would not renounce their Orthodox faith. In a banquet speech made on 6 June 1941, the Minister of Education and Religion in the new state outlined the strategy: "We shall kill some of the Serbs, we shall expel others, and the remainder will be forced to embrace the Roman Catholic faith. These last will in due course be absorbed by the Croat part of the population." When asked what the government's policy would be toward the non-Croat racial and religious minorities, the Minister replied, "for them we have three million bullets" (Maclean, 1957:84-85).

In the execution of this ambitious program, it is estimated that between 500,000 and one million Serbs were murdered from 1941 to 1945. Although it is sometimes overlooked that the historical roots of Ustashe racial strategy "lay in the hegemonistic violence done to the Croatian nation in Monarchic Yugoslavia" (Tudjman, 1981:164), it is indisputable that the ethnic slaughter committed under the NDH regime, which lasted for only five years, far surpassed the extent and brutality of ethnic persecution during the interwar period. Fascist authorities also collaborated in programs of ethnic violence in other regions such as Hungarian-occupied Vojvodina and Bulgarian-controlled Macedonia, but without the "strategic" ideological thrust, systematic character, and magnitude of the effort in Croatia. Despite their own dedication to ethnic genocide in Yugoslavia (mainly against the Jews) and elsewhere in Europe, the Nazi authorities actually had mixed feelings about their fascist allies' violent campaigns of racial purification which tended to alienate more and more of the population from Axis control.[1]

Two major resistance movements to the Axis occupation and the fascist satellite regimes emerged in 1941: (1) the Chetniks, Serbian remnants of the Royal Army, operating in territories having a Serbian population in the central and southwestern part of the country, and responsible to the government-in-exile in London; and (2) the Communist-led Partisans, a broad mass movement that was multi-ethnic in terms of its leadership and program, and which maintained an organizational network throughout the entire country. The shape of the wartime struggle which gradually emerged on the territory of the truncated

Yugoslav state was extremely complicated and included the following major features: first, a resistance war against the Axis forces and their internal fascist allies waged primarily by the Partisans, and to a much lesser extent by the Serbian Chetniks; secondly, an ethno-political civil war between the Croatian Ustashe, on the one side, and the predominantly Serbo-Montenegrin membership of the Chetniks and the communist-led Partisans (whose ranks gradually became more multi-ethnic) on the other; finally, a socio-political civil war between the Communists and the royalist Chetniks (the latter sometimes acting in collaboration with the Ustashe and Axis forces) for postwar control of the country. The enormous loss of human life from this multi-sided struggle -- almost one-tenth of Yugoslavia's population -- and its searing impact on the surviving population decisively influenced the context of political development and the national question following the war.

The Chetniks, who supported a return to the prewar unitary state and social structure, were predominantly Serbs from within "Old Serbia" (i.e. Serbia Proper). In reaction to the slaughter of Serbs in the Independent State of Croatia, the Chetniks carried out reprisals against Catholic and Moslem Croats, particularly in multi-ethnic Bosnia, which became a major base of operations and killing ground for all the principal actors in the wartime struggle. The Chetniks viewed their own ethnic violence not only as a way to ensure continued Serbian hegemony in the postwar period, but also as justifiable retribution for both the Ustashe murders, and the alleged Croatian betrayal of the interwar Yugoslav state.

The strategy of nationalistic purification adopted by the Chetniks did not have the backing of a locally constituted regime (the Serbian puppet state was a less independent and radical authoritarian variant than the NDH), but in areas which the Chetnik guerrilla fighters occupied or roamed, the effect was just as devastating and brutal as the Ustashe atrocities in Croatia. A Chetnik manual (Tomasevich, 1975) of December 1942 clearly indicated the movement was prepared to use ethnic terror against the Croats during and after the war. According to the manual, "the problem of revenge" against the Croats was not simply to involve disorderly and unsystematic acts of punishment, but collective retribution carried out by organized state authorities, including special courts and troops. "One should not fear," the manual points out, "that the retribution executed in this manner would not be complete as far as the number of executed is concerned. If there are not more, then there are at least as many, Frankovici [nationalist Croats] ... as there were Serbs who were killed" (Tomasevich, 1975:261). In a telegram to the Royal Yugoslav government in London in 1942, the main Chetnik commander, Draža Mihailović, explained "we are exterminating the Ustashe wherever we find them. We shall destroy everything that is of the Ustashe mercilessly because of the 600,000 Serbians massacred by them" (Zalar, 1961:83). At a secret meeting held between Mihailović and Tito to discuss joint resistance, Tito later reported that the Chetnik leader (thinking the communist chief was a Russian rather than a Croat) told him that the "Croats, Moslems, and all others must be severely punished, and after certain retribution completely subordinated to the Serbs. When I [Tito] opposed this, he said his attitude was completely correct because all Croats are guilty of Ustashe crimes and the treason which had delivered Yugoslavia to the Germans" (Mužić, 1969:252). Estimates of the number of Croats murdered by the Chetniks range as high as 500,000, although as in the case of Croatian-managed atrocities, the highest figures appear to be inflated in the heat of postwar polemics by

60

survivors on both sides.

Concentrating on terror or counter-terror against their ethnic (Croatian) and political (Partisan) enemies, the Chetniks became increasingly lethargic in their resistance efforts against the Axis. The Chetniks also feared that a more vigorous resistance would invite Nazi reprisals against the civilian population and, together with the Ustashe's activities, would significantly reduce the size of the Serbian population in the postwar state. Faced with this situation, the Western Allies gradually shifted (in 1942 and 1943) their support to the Chetniks' principal political foe, the Communist-led Partisans. This development strengthened the Partisan movement, and significantly, if not decisively, influenced the internal struggle for power.

The KPJ began the war as a small, mainly urban movement composed largely of young members of the intelligentsia and some workers. Although they had not played a very significant role in Yugoslav politics after being banned in 1921, the Communists had acquired considerable experience in underground organizational activity and in propaganda techniques. While the party leadership had dissipated much of its energy in factional and ideological struggles, it had also attracted a sizeable and committed following among the country's radical youth, especially in Serbia (Avakumovic, 1964:186).

The communists' tactical program on the national question, worked out during the extensive prewar polemical debates, became an integral part of the Partisan political and military strategy which took shape after the occupation of the country. As Tito (1978:8) explained to his forces in 1942:

> the present liberation struggle and the national question are inseparable. . . . The word 'national liberation struggle' would be only an empty phrase, even a fraud, if in addition to its all-Yugoslav meaning, it did not have a meaning for each people separately, i.e. if in addition to the liberation of Yugoslavia, it did not at the same time mean the liberation of the Croats, Slovenes, Serbs, Macedonians, Albanians, Moslems, etc. . . .

Despite their propaganda efforts and attractive multi-ethnic program, support for the communist-led national liberation movement developed very unevenly throughout the country. In fact, the actual ethnic and geographical composition of the Partisans was affected more by the exigencies and circumstances of the war than by the communists' program. As Figure 4.2 indicates, the initial areas of Partisan military activity were in Western Serbia, Montenegro and Bosnia, as well as in limited sections of Croatia. Although the multi-ethnic communist leadership made a determined effort to organize units among all the national groups in the country, the Partisan forces were overwhelmingly Serbian in ethnic composition during the first part of the war.[2] Unlike the Chetnik movement which consisted primarily of Serbs from Serbia proper, the Partisans were especially successful in attracting support among Serbs living in other regions of the country, most of whom were seeking refuge from the genocidal policies of the Ustashe and other fascist occupying forces.

If one compares the regions of Partisan strength in 1941 (shown in Figure 4.2), with the areas of communist electoral success twenty years earlier in the election of 1920 (Figure 4.1), the marked shift in the party's basis of support becomes more apparent. Whereas the party previously had been strong in urban centers, and in certain ethnically discontented border

FIGURE 4.2
Area of Military Operations of Tito's Partisans, 1941

(Derived from Djonlagić, et al., Yugoslavia in the Second World War, 1967)

areas (e.g. Macedonia, Dalmatia, Vojvodina), the circumstances of wartime struggle led to a concentration of communist activity in hinterland and rural areas and in Montenegro where the communists had always had a strong appeal. Ethnic discontent still played an important role in communist recruitment, but it was now derived from peasant nationalism directed against the country's occupiers and the ultra-nationalistic ethnic terror of the Ustashe and Chetniks. In the initial phase of the war this discontent was predominantly Serbian, unlike the situation in 1920 when electoral protest was directed against centralized Serbian hegemony.

When the military situation at the end of 1941 forced the Partisans to withdraw from most parts of Serbia, they retreated to the rugged interior of Bosnia (illustrated in Figure 4.3) which then became their core area of operations during the war. Bosnia, which was experiencing an intense and bloody conflict among its mixed Serbian, Croatian, and Moslem population, became an important laboratory for Partisan nationality policy. In Bosnia, the Partisans could appeal as protectors to the Serbs against the Ustashe and Moslems, and to the Croats and Moslems as protectors against the Chetniks, promising all ethnic groups a better deal within a multi-national communist framework. The communists were least successful in their appeal to the Moslems, who did not join the movement until the end of the war, and even then not in very large numbers (see below).

62

FIGURE 4.3
Liberated Territory of Yugoslavia at the End of 1942

(Derived from Djonlagić, et al., Yugoslavia in the Second World War, 1967)

FIGURE 4.4
Liberated Territory in the Autumn of 1943

(Derived from Djonlagić, et al., Yugoslavia in the Second World War, 1967)

It was only in the second half of the war, when the Partisans were able to expand the geographical range of their operation (Figure 4.4) and the outcome of the struggle was clearer to the population, that the communists were really able to broaden their support among the non-Serbian nationalities and minorities. Separate combat units were gradually set up for groups such as the Albanians, Hungarians, Moslems, and other much smaller nationalities that were still only weakly committed to the Partisans. The real strength of the Partisan movement remained, however, heavily Serbian in ethnic composition and geographically rather concentrated until very near the end of the war. Thus, a large influx of ethnic Croats into the Partisans only occurred after the capitulation of Italy in September 1943, and the Croatian capital of Zagreb was not captured by Partisans until a week after Hitler's death. Macedonia, where the Communists polled more votes than any other party in the election of 1920, did not have an organized Partisan division operating on its territory until August 1944. Slovenia as an integral part of the Third Reich was also very difficult for the communists to penetrate on a broad scale, although some scattered Partisan units did operate there throughout the war.

New and previously unreported empirical data on the veterans of the Partisan struggle presented in Table 4.1 offers greater insights into the fascinating pattern of ethnic representation in the different regions of the country. Based on a 1977 survey of surviving Partisan veterans and families of deceased veterans from the entire wartime period, the data reveal the Serbs' overall numerical majority in the movement as well as their over-representation when compared to their relative position in the total population. Such over-representation is most striking for the Montenegrins who are the Serbs' closest ethnic bretheren. Persons who identify themselves as "Yugoslavs", a generalized supra-national designation frowned upon in the 1970s but currently in vogue again (see Appendix A) are also over-represented, which is probably due to the strong commitment by many communists during (and after) the war to the goal of transcending ethnic divisions. Apart from the Slovenes and Croats, who are well represented among the total veteran population, all the other ethnic groups are quite significantly under-represented, with the Albanians being the least committed to the Partisan cause.

The regional picture gives even more striking evidence of the Serbian role in the Partisan movement. In all of the important regions troubled by ethnic heterogeneity and conflict -- Vojvodina, Bosnia, Croatia, and Kosovo -- the Serbs are heavily over-represented. If Montenegrins are considered together with Serbs, as they are by most of the population in these regions, the pattern becomes even more lop-sided. Thus, while Albanians compose 75 percent of Kosovo's population, they make up only 51 percent of the veterans in that region (they are also very under-represented among the partisans of Macedonia and Montenegro). In Vojvodina the equivalent figures for Hungarians are 22 percent and 7 percent. Moslem under-representation in Bosnia and Montenegro also attest to the communist failure to attract this group during the war.

Although support for the Partisan movement was very unevenly distributed, by the end of the war it was the only organized political force in the country whose membership genuinely cross-cut the major lines of ethnic, religious, and sectional divisions. Tito and his fellow revolutionaries had convinced at least some members of all the ethnic groups that the realization of their national aspirations was linked to a social revolution led by the communist party. To some extent this was due to the Partisan's

TABLE 4.1
The Ethnic and Regional Composition of Partisan Veterans as of December 31, 1977a

Ethnic Group	Yugoslavia Total Pop.	Vets.	Serbia "proper" Total Pop.	Vets.	Vojvodina Total Pop.	Vets.	Kosovo Total Pop.	Vets.	Croatia Total Pop.	Vets.	Bosnia Total Pop.	Vets.	Montenegro Total Pop.	Vets.	Macedonia Total Pop.	Vets.	Slovenia Total Pop.	Vets.
Serbs	39.7	53.0	89.5	90.4	55.8	74.8	18.4	34.7	14.2	29.2	37.3	64.1	7.5	1.7	2.8	3.0	1.2	1.6
Montenegrins	2.5	5.5	1.1	3.0	1.9	3.9	2.5	11.0	0.2	0.4	0.3	0.6	67.2	88.5	0.2	0.5	0.1	0.3
Macedonians	5.8	2.7	1.1	0.3	0.8	0.5	0.1	0.1	0.1	0.1	—	—	0.1	—	69.3	82.4	0.1	—
Slovenes	8.2	9.2	0.2	0.2	0.2	0.2	—	—	0.7	0.9	0.1	0.1	0.1	—	0.1	—	94.0	94.8
Croats	22.1	18.6	0.7	1.1	7.1	4.3	0.7	0.7	79.4	63.3	20.6	8.8	1.7	0.8	0.2	0.2	2.5	2.1
Moslems	8.4	3.5	2.4	0.5	0.2	0.1	2.1	1.7	0.4	0.2	39.6	23.0	13.3	4.5	0.1	0.9	0.2	—
Yugoslavs	1.3	2.5	1.4	2.4	2.4	3.7	0.1	0.6	1.9	2.9	1.2	2.9	2.1	2.2	0.2	0.3	0.4	0.4
Albanians	6.4	1.7	1.2	0.2	0.2	—	73.7	50.8	0.1	—	0.1	0.1	6.7	2.0	17.0	8.7	0.1	—
Hungarians	2.3	1.1	0.1	0.1	21.7	7.1	—	—	0.8	0.4	—	—	0.1	0.1	—	0.1	0.5	0.2
Others	3.3	2.2	2.3	1.8	9.7	5.4	2.4	0.4	2.2	2.4	0.8	0.4	1.2	0.2	10.1	3.9	0.9	0.6
TOTAL(%)	100	100	100	100	100	100	100	100	100	100	100	100	100	100	100	100	100	100

Source: Computed on the basis of data in Yugoslavia (1980) "Borci, Vojni invalidi i porodice palih boraća," Statistički Bilten, Savenzi Zavod za Statistiku, 1174 (April).

aIn the table, all persons entitled to benefits under federal regulations for veterans of World War II are added together, i.e., whether they are living veterans or families of veterans killed in the war. Noteworthy regional ethnic comparisons are underlined.

position on the national question expressed by the slogan "brotherhood and unity" among the peoples of Yugoslavia, as well as the more tangible promise of a federal system to be established after the war.

The establishment of this federal system actually took place during the war in a series of meetings held in liberated areas and attended by both central and regional partisan leaders. At the second such session held in Bosnia in November 1943 (and thereafter considered the official birthdate of the new regime), it was announced that "Yugoslavia is developing and will develop according to the federative principle which would guarantee full equality and rights to all the nationalities and minorities" (Nikolić and Atlagić, 1967:203). In a jab at the prewar regime's rather belated effort to resolve the nationality conflict in the country by means of a consociational strategy, Edward Kardelj, who was to become the major architect of the communists' postwar institutional framework, observed that the

> new Yugoslavia is not being created as a result of a compromise between the Serbian nation and other nations that were oppressed in old Yugoslavia, or better to say as a compromise between the ruling Serbian and Croatian reactionary cliques, but rather as a result of a conviction of the nations of Yugoslavia that a federal Yugoslavia is the best and strongest form of maximum guarantee of the free development of each of them. (Yugoslavia . . ., 1980:7)

The national question and the Partisan struggle may have been "inseparably linked," as the communists suggested, but the reasons for their victory in the wartime struggle are more complex than simply a correct application of a "tactical orientation" in response to the country's cultural diversity. There is no doubt that the genocidal ethnic policies of the occupation and pro-fascist forces created recruits for the Partisan movement. Tito, perhaps thinking of the inter-nationality dissension which appeared within his own ranks, and also the virulent nationalism found within the groups which failed to respond to the communist's, program, later observed that ethnic hatred was basically a "negative factor":

> The national question was one of the powerful levers in the liberation struggle. The Communist Party of Yugoslavia, thanks to its correct line on the national question which it persistently carried out both up to the war, and also during the war, waged a persistent struggle against chauvinism and national intolerance, . . . succeeded in overcoming that negative factor, succeeded in averting further reciprocal extermination and sparks of national hatred. . . . That wasn't an easy job. Here one had to operate very delicately, very deliberately, one needed a great deal of patience, self-restraint, and persistence by each fighter while it was being accomplished. . . . Consequently it would be absurd to affirm that national inequality in Yugoslavia and national hatred which was influenced by the old regime and the occupiers had a positive effect on the Yugoslav liberation struggle. On the contrary, such national hatred was a great evil against which the people were obliged to persistently fight in the course of the war, as against other enemies. (Nikolić, 1967:201)

By the end of 1944, the Communists' tenacity and military success, combined with the Allied decision to support the Partisan movement, placed Tito in a position to control the postwar political system. The KPJ had become transformed from a small, factionalized, underground movement closely responsive to pronouncements from Moscow, into a large centralized, multi-class and multi-ethnic organization with some basis of support in all sections of the country.[3] Despite the party's basic pro-Soviet orientation and wartime radio communication with the USSR, the Yugoslav communist victory was largely a self-directed operation carried out by a talented and independent-minded indigenous political leadership composed of individuals from all of the major ethnic groups. While the Partisans did not engage in explicit ethnic-oriented terror along the lines of the ultra-nationalist groups, the communist leadership did condone ruthless "collective retribution" against their own political enemies (Djilas, 1977:338, 446-447), irrespective of national origins. As the communists came face to face with the realities of political management in a highly diverse society, their wartime habits of self-reliance and pragmatism as well as their direct experience with the consequences of violent ethnic conflict, significantly influenced the various strategies and policies which they adopted.

THE PARTISANS IN POWER: 1945-1950

To a certain extent, the approach that the communists adopted toward the national question in the first years after the war represented an extension of their policy over the previous decade. Fulfilling the Partisans' wartime promise, the Constitution of 1946 established a federal system with six republics. Three of the federal units (Serbia, Croatia, and Slovenia) were designated as regions for the three ethnic groups which had enjoyed recognition and a quasi-federal relationship in the interwar regimes. The three other republics (Bosnia-Hercegovina, Macedonia, and Montenegro) and the "autonomous" areas of Serbia (Vojvodina and Kosovo-Metohija) represented the first real recognition by a Yugoslav state of territories or nationalities which had earlier chaffed under one form or another of charter-group hegemony. The model for the new political system was Soviet federalism, or what Edward Kardelj at the time called "the most positive example of the solution of relations between peoples in the history of mankind" (Hondius, 1968:137).

The new arrangements were designed primarily to formally express the existing diversity and alleged equality among the nationalities of the country, rather than to provide a dynamic framework for the real distribution and exercise of political power among the federal units. It would be wrong, however, to regard the theory and practice of Yugoslav strategy on the national question after the war as simply a carbon copy of Soviet federalism and Stalinist practices. It was in this period, for example, that the regime launched an ambitious program to develop the economically less advanced regions of the country by means of assistance from the more developed regions -- a policy ultimately having quite unintended consequences (see below). In an effort to portray their regime as a showcase of ethnic equality, the communists also provided the country's many minority groups with genuine opportunities for the preservation of their linguistic and cultural distinctiveness. The policy promising "equality of peoples" was also expressed in the recruitment and training of new elites from ethnic groups which had previously been denied control of their own regional areas. The new treatment and legal status of the various nationalities, although often mainly symbolic in character, constituted a fundamental departure from the practices of the former regime, and as such had an important psychological impact on the population which helped to legitimate the communist system.

There was, however, another side to the Yugoslav regime's approach to nationality issues in this period. Many members of the communist leadership felt that the national question had essentially been "solved" by the end of the war as a result of the party's multi-national policy and the creation of a federal system, and that it was time to move rapidly ahead toward the creation of a new trans-ethnic (if not pan-ethnic) "Yugoslav socialist patriotism." Advocates of this view shared an expectation that the new regime's program of rapid socio-economic transformation and political centralization would quickly foster a new "socialist consciousness" based upon the population's loyalty to the state and the party. The new focus of identity would parallel and eventually supercede the attraction of traditional cultural identities along with the panopoly of federal institutions and multi-national symbols introduced by the communists. The latter features were regarded as politically necessary and temporarily inviolable, but were also seen as a basically inconvenient tactical accommodation to residual nationality differentiation from the pre-socialist period. This mentality or outlook on the part of those party leaders who looked forward to a more "homogeneous socialism" (Vrhovec, 1970:145) approximated a strategy of syncretic amalgamation based upon increased ideological uniformity, economic interdependence, and popular mobilization, or what we have earlier termed the <u>revolutionary fusion</u> approach to cultural diversity.

A number of factors converged to encourage support for such a fusionist strategy. First, many Yugoslav communists, as Marxists, believed that social factors must be given priority over national factors (a feeling reminiscent of the right-wing factional position in the 1920s) despite the need to temporarily and emblematically recognize the multi-ethnic features of the country. Writing about the immediate postwar period, one Yugoslav sociologist points out:

> Our communist movement, like the communist movement anywhere in the world, did not ignore the nationalities question. But it did not consider it more important than the social question -- the question of how, regardless of the national structure and identification of people, to organize the authority of the people that would carry out socialist goals. What is more, the nationalities question -- and this is not difficult to prove -- was not then treated as a question of equal importance with the class, social question. It was simply considered that the nationalities question would find its authentic solution by solving the class, social question. (Šuvar, 1971:67)

Second, there was the experience of the Soviet Union, which had long been regarded as a sacred model for communists and which was still admired by many of the Yugoslav party leaders and party members. Following Soviet theory and Stalinist practice, it was possible to combine a spurious federal system and facade of nationality rights with a highly centralized and revolutionary commitment to the elimination of traditional cultural values. Although the Yugoslav communists were unwilling to emulate the most coercive and manipulative features of the Stalinist system (a "flaw" which contributed to their growing quarrel with Moscow), the early postwar nationality policy of the regime still revealed traces of its Soviet paternity. Evidence of this inheritance included a broad definition and punitive suppression of "chauvinistic" tendencies, the use of crude political indoctrination and propaganda methods to undermine traditional cultural and religious beliefs (Shoup, 1968:142), and the tendency to either mask, deny, or ignore problems which still existed among the various ethnic groups.

Finally, and closely related to the issue of Soviet influence, another important factor encouraging a fusionist outlook on the national question in this period was the extreme centralization of the state and party apparatus. The great concentration of power at the summit of the political system reduced the elegant constitutional and statutory division of powers between the various units of the federation and party to a largely formal and "decorative" (Djordjević, 1969:9-10) matter. Any real possibility for the open political expression of divergent nationality and sectional interests or grievances was lacking, although the top party leaders sometimes functioned (behind closed doors) as ethnic and regional group spokesmen. A Yugoslav historical analysis of this period indicates the contradictory impact of centralization on the cohesion of the political system:

> Centralistic tendencies, which appeared very early in the phase of reconstruction, led to a decrease in the jurisdiction of republican and local organs and constraints on their initiatives. ... In opposition to such phenomena and their domination there appeared the first signs of other manifestations. These were efforts, on the one side, to defend one's self-governing sphere of work, and on the other side, to express the tendency to sanction the decentralization from the wartime period, the autarkic position in relation to the whole, or to guide the centralistic usurpation over the local organs of authority. (Petranović, 1969:271)

The Yugoslav break with the Soviet Union, although not directly connected with internal nationality policy (except perhaps to the extent that Tito and his colleagues were emboldened by confidence in their own methods and support in that area), changed the entire atmosphere with respect to ethnic relations in the country. Two concerns assumed paramount importance for the Yugoslav leadership as a result of its quarrel with the Soviet Union in 1948. First, it was considered necessary to demonstrate that the policies adopted by Belgrade were not revisionist deviations from communist principles, as Stalin and the Cominform suggested. Second, it was necessary to shore up the internal unity of the Yugoslav party and regime in order to survive the attack made on them. Both requirements encouraged an even more explicitly fusionist strategy toward the national question than had existed prior to the split with Moscow. Speaking to a group of academicians in Slovenia in November 1948, only a few months after the explusion of the KPJ from the Cominform, Tito remarked

> the reason that I don't say anything about the national question is not because it is posed in our country in one form or another. No, the national question has been solved in our country, and

very well at that, to the general satisfaction of all our nationalities. It has been solved in the way Lenin and Stalin have taught us [author's own emphasis]. ... The role of the Communist Party today is to watch vigilantly to see that no national chauvinism emerges and develops within any of our nationalities ... and to educate people in the spirit of internationalism. ... During the Liberation War period, however, we placed relations between the national groups on other, new, and better foundations. We formally separated ourselves in order that we might in true fact be better united [author's own emphasis]. ... (Hondius, 1967:182; Tito, 1963:97-99)

Although in later years copies of this speech by Tito would not include the mention of Stalin's name (e.g. Tito, 1968:97; 1978:13), the Yugoslavs nevertheless found it exceptionally important to stress their ideological continuity concerning the national question. They would continue, for instance, to imply that Stalin and the Comintern played a positive role in defeating the right-wing factional position in the KPJ during the 1920s, while also building up Tito's role in the development of prewar strategy (Yugoslavia, 1980:4-5). On another occasion in 1948, Tito reminded his listeners that it was necessary to construct "one powerful Yugoslav national state" and that "to love your federal unit means to love a monolithic Yugoslavia." "The people," according to Tito, "needed to arm themselves with a consciousness, so that a Croat worries about events which take place on the borders of Macedonia, and a Serb for those things which happen in Istria [on the Dalmatian coast of Croatia]" (Petranović, 1969:39). The fact that such remarks were made at the founding congress of the Communist Party of Serbia (continuing an approach which began in 1937 with the formation of "national" party organizations in Croatia and Slovenia) shows that there was no question of abandoning a recognition and tactical use of the country's nationality differences, but only of shifting the emphasis from a celebration of diversity, which had been so prominent in the wartime propaganda, to a concern with unity and cohesion.

The candor expressed by some Yugoslav leaders about the fusionist outlook which co-existed alongside the framework of federal institutions and ethnic rights during this period contrasted markedly with the more duplicitious approach of their Soviet comrades. Rejecting proposals in 1950 to add a provison to the 1946 Constitution which would give each region the "right" to voluntarily secede from the federation (as in the USSR Constitution), one top Yugoslav party functionary (Hondius, 1968:143) pointed out:

We do not wish to include such a provision in our Constitution for it would be insincere as it is in fact in the Soviet Union. ... It is theoretically possible that some people or people's republic would bring up the matter of its secession. But that would be a thing to be solved in concreto, either as a revolutionary or as a counter-revolutionary case, according to the development of [socialist Yugoslavia]. There is, so far, no reason to surmise that this would happen. ... [4]

On the other hand, Yugoslav leaders were careful not to associate themselves with a policy resembling the assimilation or integration of peoples into some new Yugoslav ethnic identity. Instead, they stressed the need for a stronger popular identification with the regime and its ideology, i.e. Yugoslav socialist patriotism. The danger, as critics were later to point out, was that this emphasis on trans-ethnic patriotism might be carried too far. Although different in content from the prewar regime's formula of "integral Yugoslav national unitarianism," the communist policy might be equally devastating to the preservation and expression of cultural diversity. In 1949 and 1950, however, the fear of fusion and a new "unitarianism" was overshadowed by the regime's effort to survive as an independent state.

Despite the frequent public claims that the national question had been "thoroughly solved," the great stress placed on unity by the Yugoslav regime in the immediate wake of the rift with the Soviet Union revealed the party leadership's anxiety about the state of ethnic relations. As we have shown earlier, the party had achieved very uneven success in its wartime appeal to the country's different nationality groups, and had been conspicuously unsuccessful among groups such as the Albanians, Hungarians, and Bosnian Moslems. Despite a massive increase in party membership immediately after the war, there was still a marked imbalance in the communist's ethnic composition, as well as very serious signs of internationality tensions within the party ranks (Petranović, 1969:38-46, 180-202).

The results of the first postwar election in November 1945 for the new Constituent Assembly indicated that the Yugoslav leaders had good reason to be concerned about the political cohesiveness of the new regime. Although no political parties except the Communist-organized Peoples' Front were allowed to offer a list of candidates, citizens were allowed to vote against the Front by dropping their ballot in the so-called "box without a list." A choice for the "box without a list," popularly referred to as the "black box" or the "widow" (because it bore the name of no political party), was generally regarded as an endorsement for the few non-communist parties still allowed to compete openly in 1945, or at least an act of protest against the regime.

An examination of votes against the Peoples' Front (or what constituted political dissent in the election of 1945) reveals striking sectional differences which were closely related to the still troublesome national question. For example, in the popular vote for the Assembly (Chamber) of Nationalities in the Constituent Assembly, the list of the Peoples' Front obtained the support of 88.7 percent of the citizens who turned out to cast their ballots, while 11.3 percent chose the "box without a list." Three areas registered electoral dissent above the country-wide mean: Vojvodina (19.4 percent), Slovenia (17.8 percent), and Serbia (12.7 percent). Croatia, which had been an area of mixed support for the Partisans during the war, had very close to the mean level of dissent (10.8 percent), while the four other federal units in the country all had very low levels of dissent. The lowest levels of regime non-support were in Montenegro (2.7 percent) and Macedonia (4.1 percent), precisely the areas which had been most supportive of the communists a quarter of a century earlier in the election of 1920 (for another Constituent Assembly), and whose "national" aspirations had been suppressed by the group-domination strategies of the former regimes. The recognition of Montenegrin and Macedonian nationality by the communists (even before the war), and the creation of separate federal units for these two "peoples" in the new state, undoubtedly had a bearing on the outcome of the 1945 election.

There is reason to believe that ethnic factors were also at work in the regions registering the highest levels of political dissent against the regime. In Vojvodina, the previously noted resistance among the Hungarians was manifest in the election, while in Slovenia the dissent was due to the activity of "clerical circles" whose active propaganda succeeded in changing to some degree the results of the election at the expense of the Peoples' Front (Petranović, 1964:205). Serbia Proper, which had been more of a Chetnik than a Partisan stronghold during the war, also exhibited a high level of dissent. A more detailed analysis (Petranović, 1969:204-205) of the 1945 election also indicates the importance of nationality as a factor in political dissent even in regions of the country (e.g. Kosovo, Bosnia, and Croatia) where the overall regional vote against the Peoples' Front was below the mean for the entire country. Although the communists had few doubts, as one of their top spokesmen later remarked (Djilas, 1977:355), about an election "held under our supervision, and on the ruins of the old regime," the marked imbalance in their popular support must have given the party leaders some pause for reflection during this difficult period.

As the Yugoslav leadership grappled with the repercussions of its expulsion from the Soviet bloc, the continued problem of ethnic rivalry and regional differences intensified the need for greater internal cohesion. There was no question that the new regime had been extremely innovative in addressing the national question compared to the prewar leaders of Yugoslavia. At the same time, however, the communists were acutely aware that the bitter memories of wartime strife and ethnic genocide still lingered on, and that Yugoslavia's neighbors -- both capitalist and communist -- were eager to turn such divisions to their own advantage. Unless Tito and his comrades could successfully jettison the legacy of the Stalinist past and find a new formula for political cohesion and survival as an independent communist state, the same problems which had helped to destroy the interwar state might reappear to threaten the new regime. In the next chapter we will examine the strategies developed by the communists to meet that challenge over the next 20 years, and assess their record in developing political incorporation.

NOTES

1. A German report referring to the period September to December 1941, noted that "from the territory ... which had been turned over to Hungary, more than 37,000 Serbs, about 100,000 from Croatia and 20,000 from Bulgarian Macedonia were expelled into the remaining Serbian territory all without any belongings and in the most abject misery. These hordes of refugees had in many cases been witnesses to the murder of their dependents. They had nothing more to lose ... therefore they allied themselves by the thousands to the [insurgent] bands." Commenting on the treatment of the Serbs by the Ustashe, the German General in Zagreb reported that "the sacrifice of the blood of its citizens which the Croatian State had demanded since its inception surpassed by far that of Yugoslavia during its entire existence" (Hehn, 1979:70).

2. An official analysis (Prelević, 1970:127-129) of the Partisan forces points out "the historical conditions in which the First Proletarian Brigade was formed [December 1941] determined that it was composed mainly of the members of two nationalities: Serbians 61.7% and Montenegrins 31.4% [i.e. 1,118 out of 1,199 individuals in six battalions]. In addition to them, the Brigade had 20 Croatian communists, a Slovene detachment (27), 17 Jews and others. Owing to its socio-political and military strategic role

in the National Liberation War, the Brigade later filled itself out with recruits from all the regions of Yugoslavia . . ." By the spring of 1944, Tito reported (1945:180) that the nationality composition of the Partisan movement was 44 percent Serb, 30 percent Croat, 10 percent Slovene, 4 percent Montenegrin, 2.5 percent Muslim and 6 percent other.

3. A 1960 survey (Graovac, 1974:39-40, 59) of 907,949 living veterans of the Partisan forces indicated that following social composition: peasants, 61.1 percent; workers, 30.8 percent; employees and military personnel, 6 percent; and others (artisans, merchants, free profession, etc.) 2.1 percent. Approximately 60 percent were less than 25 years old when they joined in Partisans, 21 percent were women and 49 percent joined the Partisans after 1943, i.e. with victory in sight.

4. Pijade's remarks are particularly interesting in light of more recent (1981-83) nationalist demands for secession (see Chapter 7). All subsequent Yugoslav constitutions (1953, 1963, and 1974) have repeated the original and highly ambiguous formulation that was included in the 1946 document, namely, that secession was a right enjoyed by those nations who united to form the new socialist state, but was not a right enjoyed by the federal units thereby established.

5
Incorporation Under Communism, 1950–1969

The dramatic break with Stalin necessitated the development of a distinctly Yugoslav model of communist development, one which would preserve the Marxian lineage of the new political system, yet distinguish it completely from the "statist socialism" of the Soviet type. A number of rather novel domestic features were introduced to effect this transformation, among the most significant of which were the changes designed to decentralize the system. Such changes included the establishment of the now-famous councils for workers' self-management of the economy, a scaling down in the operational scope and size of the party (renamed the League of Yugoslav Communists or SKJ), and a decentralization of the state bureaucracy and system of economic planning. Equally important, a series of measures were introduced to loosen the state's control of the electoral process (Cohen, 1977a). Provisions were made for increased citizen participation in the nomination and slating of candidates and for the introduction of plural-candidate (i.e. competitive) contests for legislative seats in a very limited number of districts at all levels of government. There was also a noticeable decrease in overt intimidation by the authorities to influence voter participation.

In order to enhance the cohesiveness of the political system during this difficult period of transition away from Soviet Marxism, the Yugoslav leaders decided to further de-emphasize the federative and multi-national features of the political system and society (a policy already begun in some earnest in 1948), and to concentrate on the creation of closer social bonds among citizens based upon the allegedly similar position and common interests of "producers" in all groups and sections of the country. As Edward Kardelj (1978:7-8) put it in his remarks at the inauguration of the new constitutional system in 1953, the Yugoslav socialist community was founded "on the common interests of working people, regardless of their nationality, and is therefore stronger than any other possible community." The strong encouragement of measures to weaken traditional group identities by establishing greater class consciousness and economic linkages throughout the population -- eventually resulting in support for the gradual amalgamation of ethnic cultures -- together with the regime's more "liberal" and cautious experimentation during the period, comprised a strategy which we have termed evolutionary merger.

The new strategy was expressed in a number of different ways. As part of the reorganization of the legislative system, the Chamber of Nationalities was abolished as a separate branch of the Federal Assembly and replaced by a Chamber of Producers. The latter body was designed to express the interests and "leading role" of the working class and included representatives elected from industrial enterprises and agricultural cooperatives. As the national question had supposedly been solved, the Chamber of Nationalities itself became a committee-like component (70 out of 350 deputies) of the popularly-elected Federal Chamber which was to meet only if the vital interests or equality of the nationalities and regions were at issue. In fact, given the prevailing strategy toward the national question, this weakened and encapsulated Chamber of Nationalities held a limited number of short and perfunctory sessions during 1954 and 1955 and then completely ceased to function for the remainder of this period.

A related consequence of the new strategy was the reduction in both the formal and real power of the republican and provincial governmental authorities during the 1950s. Although there was a slight shift in political decision-making power from the party apparatus to the agencies of the state structure, the main beneficiaries of this change were the federal rather than the republic legislative and executive organs. The striking decrease in the size and direct functions of the central (federal) bureaucracy was not accompanied by any growth in the real political power of the republican administrative organs. Political control continued to be structured in a hierarchic manner, a situation accentuated by the persistent influence of both the central party leadership and the central security organs. The reality of Yugoslav federalism during this period consisted more of a devolution of administrative personnel and functional responsibilities for policy implementation, rather than a genuine de-concentration of power on important matters.

The most interesting and notorious component of the regime's ethnic strategy in this period was the attempt to encourage greater cultural integration among Yugoslavia's diverse citizenry. The new strategy undoubtedly was influenced by the unacknowledged fear on the part of the communist leadership throughout the 1950s that the national question had not been as thoroughly solved as publicly suggested, and that any sign of internal disunity would serve the interests of foreign powers. Despite the communists' tactical support for ethnic diversity since the mid-1930s, there was also a latent Marxian impulse to move beyond traditional ethnic and regional loyalties toward the creation of a new "all-Yugoslav" consciousness. Unlike efforts in the preceding period (1945-1950) to quickly develop a new "Yugoslav socialist patriotism" which would co-exist alongside of traditional group identities, the new policy anticipated a gradual transcendence and replacement of various older cultural bonds through the commitment of the whole population to a completely new value system referred to as "socialist Yugoslavism." This rather vague formula anticipated the eventual merger of pre-socialist customs and beliefs into a new cultural amalgam which would be heavily infused with the regime's current ideological creed. The most coherent expression of the new strategy was advanced by Edward Kardelj in 1958. In a new preface to the second edition of his 1938 book on The Development of the Slovenian National Question, which had originally helped to launch the communists' prewar tactical program recognizing ethnic and cultural diversity, Kardelj (1960:52-54) reaffirmed support for that earlier position, but he now added that recognition of "the individuality and equality of the Yugoslav peoples . . . is only one side of the question." It was now necessary, he argued, to move ahead with the "general unification of these peoples":

There is no doubt that the ethnic and cultural affinity of the peoples of Yugoslavia is a very important factor in their merger. ... But at present that isn't the decisive feature of the Yugoslav community of nations. A firm community of the Yugoslav peoples doesn't depend on this or that treatment of ethnic and cultural problems as much as upon the common social, material, and by that also political interests of the peoples of Yugoslavia. In short the essence of present-day Yugoslavia can only be the socialist interests and socialist consciousness ... of the kind which arises on the basis of inexorable socio-economic tendencies. ... It is evident that the result of that process will be the even greater cultural merger of the Yugoslav peoples.

Kardelj and other party leaders went to great pains during this period to contrast the formula of "socialist Yugoslavism" with earlier schemes (by interwar communist factions and the old regime) for ethnic assimilation or the creation of a new "nation." It was impossible to conceal the fact, however, that the "merger" of cultures, even on a supposedly ideological and universal basis, meant the diminished vitality and eventual disappearance of traditional group bonds. Thus, the effort in the mid-1950s to establish greater cultural uniformity in such areas as language reform, historiography, education, and the arts, evoked considerable resistance by those groups and individuals who feared that such a centrally-engineered policy would ultimately favor the culture of one group or section of the country. In the northwestern sections of Yugoslavia, particularly, the strategy of evolutionary cultural merger emanating from top decision-making bodies in Belgrade, was seen as a plot to reimpose Serbian group hegemony by means of a new formula. When a leading Serbian literary figure suggested that inter-regional cooperation would be enhanced only "when there were no more republics," a Slovene writer compared the new sponsorship of Yugoslavism to the prewar "unitarian integralists" and "centralists who do not know what republics are and what people are" (Shoup, 1968:197).

Despite the controversy over regime-strategy regarding the national question, the effort by the Yugoslav communist leadership to legitimate their unique model of non-totalitarian and anti-Soviet communism appeared to have met with considerable success. By the mid-1950s Tito's regime, bolstered by assistance from the West and encouraged by Stalin's death, had survived the boycott and ostracism of the Soviet bloc and had begun to achieve impressive levels of economic growth. In the federal elections of 1953, 1958, and 1963, the level of dissent as measured by ballot invalidation had steadily dropped, while the rate of voter turnout gradually increased. The relative economic and socio-political progress of Yugoslavia compared to the other communist states, together with the regime's campaign to mobilize support and the continued presence of an authoritarian security apparatus to constrain both prominent dissenters and local trouble-makers, seemed to be having the desired effect on electoral behavior.

Other developments, however, were also taking place during the 1950s that were soon to result in both a fundamental shift in political development and a change in the regime's approach toward ethnic diversity. Two inter-related factors were most important: (1) growing regional economic nationalism, and (2) increasing intra-party factionalism regarding the issue of political liberalization. The first factor can be traced to the regime's failure to reduce the gap between the advanced and less developed sections of the country. By the beginning of the 1960s, despite a vigorous policy of modernizing the economically-backward sections of the country, the economic disparity between the more advanced and less advanced regions was actually greater than in 1945. Added to this, the functional decentralization of tasks and economic planning during the 1950s, together with the system of enterprise self-management, had tended to encourage the growth of divergent interests and perspectives among elites on the republican, provincial, and local levels of the system. These trends stimulated inter-regional competition and "particularism" which, given the close correspondence between ethnic and developmental cleavages in the country, often assumed a nationalistic character resembling the prewar pattern.

The second factor -- intra-party factionalism regarding political liberalization -- turned largely on the question of how to deal with the impact of economic nationalism. Briefly, the more liberal members of the party leadership, concentrated in the relatively developed northwestern sections of the country and deriving support from the emergent post-revolutionary professional and managerial elites (found throughout the country), favored greater decentralization of political decision-making and the creation of a more "polycentric" federal system. These liberals, while committed to economic development, opposed the idea of grandiose and economically inefficient show projects and politically-motivated investments in the underdeveloped areas, as well as central party and government interference in other spheres of policy such as education and culture. The more conservative wing of the party, led by Aleksander Ranković, the head of the security apparatus, favored a continuation of both strong central controls to insure the political unity of the country and the prevailing modes of resource allocation which were designed to redistribute the wealth from the more economically advanced regions to the less fortunate areas. The conservatives had a stronger political base among Serbian party members of the partisan generation and, not surprisingly, among elites in the less developed areas. It was no coincidence that the more conservative members of the party leadership, who felt that the "equality" of regions could best be achieved through centralized methods, also equated the open expression of regional and ethnic grievances as a threat to the state's "monolithic" unity (even though the grievances were often generated by their own hard-line policies), and tended to be more supportive of an evolutionary merger strategy designed to create a single integrated "Yugoslav socialist consciousness." Since classical Marxist-Leninist theory advocated the elimination of pre-socialist cultural beliefs, the conservatives could also count on the support of the more ideologically dogmatic party members in this particular area.

One of the first signs of the growing ascendency of the liberal faction in the party leadership was the unpublicized abandonment of evolutionary merger as a regime-strategy. Although the elements of a new strategy were not immediately apparent -- perhaps reflecting the quandary and conflict within the party leadership about how to proceed on this issue -- it was clear by the beginning of the 1960s that efforts to reduce the existing regional and ethnic plurality of the Yugoslav landscape had lost official support. The formula of "socialist Yugoslavism," which had been included in the widely disseminated 1958 Party Program, simply dropped from view, as did support for the merger of cultures. Party leaders (and particularly Tito, who seemed to have suffered a defeat on this matter) still spoke about the dangers of regional economic nationalism and about the "integration" of the population on the basis of common socialist values, but only after acknowledging that the long-term preservation and further development of distinct ethnic cultures was not in question. "Our federation," Kardelj remarked in 1962, "is not a frame for making some new Yugoslav nation, or the frame for the kind of national integration which various advocates of hegemonism or denationalizing terror have been daydreaming of" (Hondius, 1968:242). While direct and sometimes vocal resistance to the idea of cultural integration was undoubtedly a factor in the change of policy, it appears that a complex pattern of political conflicts and personal animosities (e.g. between Kardelj and Ranković) played an important if still not completely understood role in this matter (Shoup, 1968:225-226).

A number of steps taken by the regime in the early 1960s provided evidence that a fundamental change in strategy was taking place. Under a new constitution drafted in 1962 and adopted in 1963, the republics received more decision-making authority, and greater attention was given to public procedures for the resolution of conflicts among different sections and groups in the country (e.g. a new Constitutional Court). The new constitution also included provisions for republican-provincial representation in the federal government and administration on a parity basis, and specified that greater "attention be given to the proportional representation of personnel from all the major nationality groups" (Secretariat of the Federal Assembly Information Service, 1969). These measures opened the way for the institutionalization of ethnic and sectional competition in the central decision-making process, a trend which was to cause increasing frustration and opposition on the part of more conservative party leaders in the years ahead. During the debate on the draft constitution, it was also hinted that the self-designation of citizens as "Yugoslavs" was no longer considered to be acceptable (although it was technically permitted in the final version), a view that was soon to become official policy. Persons were encouraged to declare themselves on the basis of traditional ethnic categories, and, in an unprecedented departure from earlier policy, the classification "Moslem" was recognized as an ethnic rather than religious designation.

The economic reform package of 1965, which emphasized further decentralization, individual enterprise autonomy, and the role of market-type forces, gave indirect support to the regional elites and interest groups who had been longtime allies in the liberal coalition. It was in this period that Yugoslav politicians and academics openly acknowledged the existence of serious conflicts in their society, including those deriving from residual cultural cleavages and emerging economic difficulties (Cohen, 1978). Collectively, these developments may be termed a new strategy of pluralist socialism, which among other things, legitimized the recognition and political expression of divergent ethnic and regional interests.

The most important impetus for the new strategy of pluralist socialism was the removal of Aleksander Ranković and the purge of the secret police in mid-1966. Ranković had not only opposed the liberal measures described above, but had also managed the systematic and covert repression of ethnic minorities such as the Albanians in Kosovo, a policy which was to have far-reaching consequences for the regime's future stability (see Chapter 7). The dismissal of Rankovic and his cronies opened the way for the further political articulation of the country's ethnic and regional plurality.

Between 1967 and 1969, a series of constitutional amendments transformed the previously inert and decorative Chamber of Nationalities within the Federal Chamber of the Federal Assembly into an independent legislative branch with primary responsibility for the consideration of all federal legislation. "We consider," wrote the President of the strengthened Chamber of Nationalities (Borba, 1967:2), "the existence of several peoples and nationalities in Yugoslavia as being an advantage for our socialist community rather than a necessary evil which has to be disposed of as soon as possible by some kind of supra-national structure on the basis of Yugoslav unitarism." The method of selecting members of legislative assemblies was also liberalized to provide more opportunity for the nomination of candidates by the public and to give voters a degree of choice among candidates on the final ballot. In 1967, a choice among candidates appeared in several contests for seats to the Federal Assembly, and the numbers of such plural-candidate races on the republic-provincial and local levels were greatly expanded over their 1965 levels. In 1969, the availability of candidate choice at all levels was augmented even further, with consequences that will be fully explored in this and the next chapter.

By the second half of the 1960s, the regime had fully embarked on a new approach toward ethnic and regional diversity as part of a broader change in the direction of political development. It was now conceded that the national question was far from being solved, and would likely persist for some time to come. By allowing problems among the nationalities and regions to be expressed openly through various formal channels, the party leadership hoped to dissipate the tensions accumulated from the neglect of such issues in the past, and also to give all the sections and groups in the country a stake in the successful formulation of central policies. In that spirit, the party re-organization of 1967 strengthened the republic-level centers of the League of Communists at the expense of the central apparatus in Belgrade, and created more opportunities for the intrusion of regional and ethnic viewpoints in intra-party debates. Increasingly, the party organization was described as a kind of broker to help channel and resolve divergent groups interests. As a 1969 party pronouncement (Komunist, 1969:49) put it:

> The League of Communists is a very significant factor of ideological integration and political cohesion in our multi-national socialist community. Such a role cannot be created as any kind of supra-national organization which transforms the republican organizations into transmission belts. In place of their central connection, the League of Communists of Yugoslavia [the federal apparatus] establishes a creative ideological-political synthesis of views, attitudes, activities and initiatives of the League of Communists of the socialist republics.

This strategy was, of course, a rather risky gamble for a political leadership which was also completely opposed to the institutionalization of interest group pluralism through a multi-party system, and that was operating in an environment still seriously divided along ethnic and sectional lines. The centrifugal political developments and vitriolic ethnic conflict which had helped to destroy the old regime remained a vivid memory for Tito and the top communist elite still ruling Yugoslavia in the 1960s. The question at issue was, would the new forces, experiences and values generated by the communist-sponsored regime-strategies, as well as the regime's program of modernization, act to dampen or to exacerbate the serious lack of cohesiveness which the war years had so vividly evoked?

THE PATTERNS OF DISSENT

It is the premise of this study that electoral results collected over the period of the 1950s and 1960s provide a broad, systematic, and unique source of information on the critical issue of cohesion raised above. This premise rests upon the notion that the extent of political incorporation in the system can be assessed through the analysis of levels of ballot invalidation and electoral turnout. It can, of course, be argued that these phenomena, although clearly manifestations of discontent or dissent in most cases, should be seen as pertaining solely to the individual citizen and not as indicative of the state of the political system itself. In Chapter 3 we were able to demonstrate that electoral data gathered from millions of individual voting (and non-voting) acts can be interpreted to reveal the state of incorporation of the political system. It is now necessary to establish that the postwar elections, in which there was no possibility of party choice, can be employed to the same end.

The argument that the above-mentioned indicators of dissent can be interpreted at a level higher than that of the individual, essentially depends on the degree of _patterning_ that such indicators manifest. A purely individual or idiosyncratic interpretation of ballot invalidation or abstention would be consistent with a finding that there is a fairly random distribution of such behaviors across the electoral districts, regions, and republics of the country. Conversely, to the degree that dissent is concentrated geographically, especially if such concentrations can be tied to particular ethnic groups, it becomes reasonable to assume a less-than-complete state of political incorporation of those areas and ethnic groups in the system. This, in turn, may be regarded as symptomatic of a lack of political cohesion in the country as a whole.

We do not wish to minimize the fact that the manner in which the degree of political incorporation is assessed has changed significantly from Chapter 3. Before the communist takeover, ballot invalidation was not a significant factor, and our attention was concentrated on the party fragmentation of the vote; after 1944, the competitive party system had disappeared and we are left with invalidation as the sole voting alternative to the expression of support for the regime.[1] Moreover, in the Communist era, there were sharp limits in the extent to which even invalidation or abstention was tolerated by the regime. The absolute levels of invalidation or abstention, therefore, may not necessarily mean a great deal in themselves.

Despite the enormous changes that occurred after the war in the institutional context of elections and the difficulties in interpreting postwar voting behavior, there are also important lines of continuity with our investigation of electoral behavior in the interwar era that should be emphasized. Voters in the communist period, although certainly under some restrictions, were still permitted enough leeway through the invalidation and abstention options to register tendencies and patterns which challenged the regime and its efforts to engineer cohesion. The degree of overall political cohesion can still be assessed by the extent of convergence and divergence in the patterns of voting behavior that do emerge across the electoral units of the country. Finally, divergence in the patterns can still be interpreted as challenging the durability of the regime, provided, of course, that the divergence follows ethnic or other lines that would fit such an interpretation.

The most obvious way that a patterning in voting behavior in federal elections might appear would be at the level of the republics that comprise the Yugoslav state. In Chapter 3, we discovered that party-choice entropy levels in the 1920s and 1930s did tend to group by postwar republican boundaries; that is to say, constituency entropy levels within individual republics were highly homogeneous in comparison with the variability of entropy levels across the whole country. Could this also be the case for the postwar invalidation levels?

This possibility was tested by performing an analysis of variance of constituency invalidation levels by republic for each postwar election where data were available in the appropriate form. The usable data included all the elections between 1950 and 1969, but excluded the 1945 election for which invalidation levels were not reported by constituency, and the elections of 1974, 1978, and 1982 which were held under a very complex indirect format that precluded the existence of federal constituencies. The elections of 1965 and 1967 are treated as a single election because one-half of the seats of the Federal Chamber were slated for election in each of those years.

The results of these analyses are reported in Table 5.1. In this table, "republic" is defined exactly as it was in the interwar electoral analyses, with the autonomous regions of Kosovo and Vojvodina -- which report their electoral results separately -- treated as separate republics. The findings presented in Table 5.1 clearly demonstrate that there was a sizeable grouping effect of invalidation by republic: between 17 percent and 64 percent of the variance in invalidation levels are accounted for by that factor, depending on the election in question.[2]

Since the republics do exhibit a substantial degree of internal homogeneity in their levels of ballot invalidation, they may be treated as distinct entities whose voting behaviors over time can be recorded separately. This is done in Figure 5.1, which contains graphs of the mean invalidation levels of each republic over the entire range of postwar elections, including the 1945, 1974, and 1978 elections for which invalidation rates by republic were published. The inclusion of these latter elections in the figure is based on the assumption that the grouping effect noted in the elections of 1950 to 1969 is valid for these other elections as well.

The overview of ballot invalidation trends provided by Figure 5.1 reveals two rather striking tendencies in the data. First, the mean levels of invalidation, while clearly forming a pronounced trend over time, do not move consistently in any single direction. As one might suspect, this lack of monotonicity corresponds to shifts in regime-strategies. Thus, the trend in the 1950s, a period of consolidation, was downward from the high invalidation levels of the 1945 and 1950 elections (particularly for certain republics) to a minimum of 2.8 percent mean invalidation in 1963; the subsequent elections of the 1960s revealed a rapid rise in invalidation levels encouraged by the greater freedoms and opportunities provided by this more liberal phase in official policy; the maximum reached in 1969 (6.9 percent nation-wide), which exceeded every election but that of 1945, was followed by a revamping of the electoral system, a clamping-down on participation and dissent, and a resultant return of invalidation rates in the 1970s to the more "acceptable" levels of the 1958-63 era.

An equally striking characteristic of the trend-lines in Figure 5.1 is

TABLE 5.1
Analysis of Variance of Constituency Invalidation Levels by Republic, Federal Elections of 1950 to 1969

Dependent Variable	Election	Number of Constituencies	Factor Republic[a]	Explained Variance
Invalidation	1950	405	.56	.31
Level per	1953	282	.61	.37
Constituency	1958	300	.61	.37
	1963	120	.80	.64
	1965/67[b]	118	.49	.24
	1969	120	.41	.17

[a]Coefficients are correlation ratio's (eta's). See fn. 2 for details.
[b]This election took place in two stages: half the Federal Chamber was elected in 1965, the other half in 1967.

the extent to which they converge over time. The 1945 election, the results of which provoked no small amount of alarm within the ruling party elite because of the lack of cohesion they revealed, is shown in the figure to have been quite atypical. In subsequent elections, the trend-lines converge substantially, and stay converged even with the rapid increases in levels of invalidation during the 1960s. Thus, although the trend in levels of invalidation is not monotonic, the extent of convergence in the trend-lines is monotonic for the most part, and these gains in terms of uniformity across republics were not affected by the fluctuation in dissent levels that occurred.

Figure 5.1 provides a very interesting picture of the over-time and cross-republic patterning of ballot invalidation. The implications that emerge from that pattern -- that republic invalidation levels tended to converge over time and tended to respond quite sharply to variations in regime-strategy -- are worthy of closer analysis. Grouping the data on invalidation levels by republic is not, however, the most instructive manner of exploring such matters. While within-republic similarities in invalidation are quite evident, the levels of explained variance (eta^2) in Table 5.1 indicate that, with the one exception of the 1963 election, within-republic differences in invalidation levels constitute the greater source of variation in that variable. If we are to trace and analyze the over-time trends in invalidation with precision, and relate them to patterns of economic development and ethnicity, it will be necessary to employ a finer unit of analysis than these eight rather large and heterogeneous entities.

FIGURE 5.1
Ballot Invalidation Levels by Republic, Federal Elections of 1946-1978

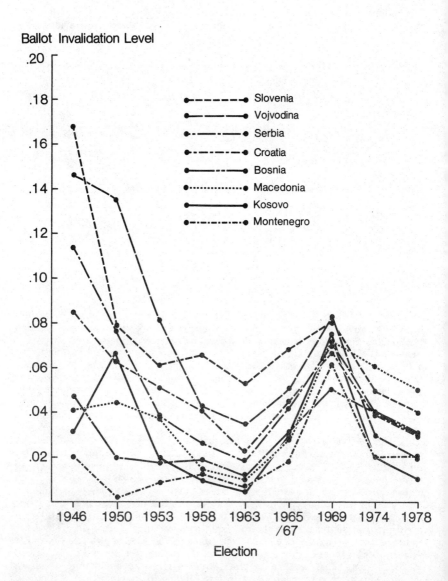

The most advantageous levels of analysis would be, of course, the individual constituencies. Unfortunately, such constituencies can only be matched up across elections for the 1960s, for as the listing of the number of constituencies per election in Table 5.1 implies, their sizes, shapes, and numbers were altered with every election up to and including that of 1963. In the analyses that follow, we shall use a constituency-to-constituency matchup over the three elections of the 1960s where appropriate, but in order to tie in the elections of the 1950s, we shall rely more heavily upon a unit of analysis of our own design. This unit, which we designate by the term "region," was constructed to correspond in general terms to the geo-historical divisions employed by the Yugoslav Federal Statistical Institute (Yugoslavia, 1963) during the 1960s for the collection of socio-economic and ethnographic census data.

The precise manner of the construction of the original classification is discussed in detail in Appendix C. For the present purposes, however, the appropriateness of categorizing the country into fifty-five regions for the study of time trends in the postwar elections can be assessed by the extent to which it patterns electoral behavior. It is important not only that constituency invalidation levels group by region for each election in the 1950-1969 period, but that the grouping effect be substantially stronger than that achieved by republic; otherwise the introduction of this factor would be of no advantage. In Table 5.2, the results of the analyses of variance of constituency invalidation levels by region are presented. A comparison of the magnitudes of explained variance in that table with the explained variances produced by republic in Table 5.1 indicates that region is consistently the much more powerful factor. Indeed, unlike republic, region is able to account for half or more of the variance in invalidation levels in every one of the six elections. The degree of within-region homogeneity in invalidation levels, revealed by the findings of Table 5.2, provides a strong measure of justification for using the regional invalidation means for the fifty-five regions as a unit of analysis in itself for over-time comparisons. Since the regional categorization respects republican boundaries, the region variable includes and adds to the grouping effect of republic.[3]

The first utilization of the regional classification for over-time comparisons is contained in Table 5.3, which presents an analysis of the election-to-election continuities in regional invalidation levels by means of correlation coefficients. The upper part of the table gives an intercorrelation matrix of invalidation levels for all available elections. The intercorrelations reveal a substantial degree of similarity in the pattern of high and low invalidation areas across all elections, and an especially large degree of continuity between consecutive elections (note the correlation coefficients on the diagonal of the matrix). Only the 1969 election differentiates itself from all the other elections, but as we shall see, it was an unusual election in a number of respects. The connections between absolute levels of invalidation and the amount and direction of change in those levels is indicated in the lower half of Table 5.3. The negative correlations across the entire period indicate that no matter whether invalidation was increasing or decreasing, the further the region was from the mean invalidation level of the country at one election, the more it tended to move towards that mean in the next election. This substantiates the trend toward convergence suggested by the republican trend lines in Figure 5.1. In general terms, the pattern is quite simple: in the 1950s it was the regions of higher invalidation that reduced their invalidation levels

TABLE 5.2

Analysis of Variance of Constituency Invalidation Levels by Region, Federal Elections of 1950 to 1969

Dependent Variable	Election	Factor Region (eta)	Explained Variance (eta^2)
Constituency	1950	.78	.61
Invalidation	1953	.75	.57
Rates	1958	.72	.52
	1963	.94	.89
	1965/67	.76	.58
	1969	.71	.50

more, whereas in the 1960s, the regions of somewhat lower invalidation tended to increase their rates of invalidation more, thereby producing a radical improvement across the political system in the homogeneity or similarity of ballot invalidation levels.[4]

In discussing Figure 5.1, we noted that while the republican rates of invalidation tended to converge, they did not tend to diminish; instead the decline of the period up to 1963 was followed by a rapid expansion in invalidation levels until 1969, whereupon they once again receded. The explanation we alluded to consisted in associating these movements with the changes in regime-strategies that occurred across this period. This explanation is, of course, totally inferential, but the electoral data do afford a more direct means by which the effect of the change in regime-strategy from evolutionary merger to pluralist socialism can be established and measured. Although the beginnings of the liberalization process can be traced to 1962, the critical stage in the changeover to pluralist socialism was reached in 1966, with the dismissal of the chief hardliner in the party hierarchy, Aleksander Ranković, and the purging of the secret police which he headed. These developments occurred precisely in the midst of the election of the 1965/67 assembly; the 1965 half-election had already occurred, the 1967 half-election followed shortly thereafter. Now, if this regime-strategy change did strike a popular chord, there should be some evidence of it in the differences in voting behavior between these two half-elections. The very weak coefficient of -.20 between the invalidation levels of 1963 and the change in invalidation between 1963 and 1965/67 (Table 5.3) suggests just such a discontinuity. Let us explore this suggestion more thoroughly.

TABLE 5.3
Inter-Election Correlations Among Regional Invalidation Levels, Federal
Elections of 1950 to 1969

		Invalidation Level of:				
		1953	1958	1963	1965/67	1969
Invalidation	1950	.67	.40	.43	.28	.39
Level of:	1953		.67	.67	.48	.40
	1958			.87	.60	.31
	1963				.62	.38
	1965/67					.29

		Invalidation Level of:				
		1950	1953	1958	1963	1965/67
Change in	1950 to 1953	-.24				
Invalidation	1953 to 1958		-.59			
From:	1958 to 1963			-.56		
	1963 to 1965/67				-.20	
	1965/67 to 1969					-.66

We are fortunate in having at our disposal a complete
constituency-to-constituency match-up for the 1963, 1965/67, and 1969
elections, since standard constituencies were used during this period. This
permits a comparative examination of the process of expansion in
constituency invalidation levels according to whether elections were held in
1965 or in 1967. Table 5.4 presents a breakdown in the change in
constituency invalidation levels by year of election. The data in the table
show a striking time-based pattern to the expansion of invalidation between
1963 and 1965/67: the mean increase of 2.0 percent is decomposable into
mean increases of 3.4 percent in those districts that had their election in
1967 and of just 0.5 percent for those districts that went to the polls in
1965. In other words, almost all the increase in invalidation took place in
districts that voted after the critical events of 1966. The process of

TABLE 5.4

Change in Ballot Invalidation by Year of 1965/67 Election

Dependent Variable	Mean	Year of Election		Correlation (eta)
		1965	1967	
Change in Invalidation Level, 1963 - 1965/67	2.0%	0.5%	3.4%	.71
Change in Invalidation Level, 1965/67 - 1969	2.7%	3.8%	1.5%	.43

expansion in constituency invalidation levels between 1965/67 and 1969 reversed the process: the districts that had elections in 1965, and therefore had not sizeably expanded their invalidation, engaged in an enormous "catch-up" process, registering mean gains in invalidation of 3.8 percent (vs. 1.5 percent for those districts that had elections in 1967). The extent of the catch-up process is indicated by a large negative correlation coefficient of -.54 between change in invalidation between 1963 and 1965/67 and change in invalidation between 1965/67 and 1969. The end result, incidentally, was a virtual levelling out of invalidation levels in 1969: those districts which had gone to the polls last in 1965 registered a mean 1969 invalidation level of 6.8 percent, while those districts which had last voted in 1967 had a mean 1969 invalidation level of 6.9 percent.

The massive rise in invalidation levels which took place after the reforms and purges of 1966 does not in itself indicate or suggest its causes. What we have discovered, essentially, is that after 1965 the electorate seized upon the opportunity presented to it for the more open expression of dissent. On the other hand, we have also ascertained from the intercorrelation matrix in Table 5.3 that the end result, the 1969 pattern of regional invalidation, did not bear a particularly strong resemblance to the pattern of any of the previous elections. Moreover, the analyses of variance of invalidation by republic and by region make it clear that the republican pattern had largely broken down in 1969, and also that the regional pattern was not particularly pronounced. The final section of this chapter is devoted to a search for the causes or correlates of the evolving pattern of regional invalidation levels, with particular attention to the expansion of invalidation during the experiment in pluralist socialism in the late 1960s. Before turning to that search, however, it would be useful to consolidate our understanding of the patterns of political expression in this era by examining the other widespread means by which dissent or dissatisfaction might have been indicated, namely, levels of voter turnout.

Our discussion of turnout levels will be quite succinct, for virtually everything we have discovered about the patterning of invalidation turns out to be true of voter turnout as well. Analyses of variance on turnout levels for the elections of 1950 to 1969 reveal that turnout groups by republic and by region, although not as strongly as was the case for invalidation. The weaker spatial patterns associated with turnout may be a result of the fact that turnout is more amenable to the mobilizing pressures of the party, whereas invalidation, although discouraged, is less difficult to actually influence. Whatever the case, there is nevertheless a fairly high degree of continuity over time in the patterning of turnout by region, with the same general tendency for the turnout intercorrelations to be highest for adjacent elections. Moreover, a pattern of negative correlations between regional turnout levels from one election to the next also appears in the data in a fashion that closely mirrors the corresponding relationships for invalidation levels. This finding indicates a tendency for turnout levels to become more similar across the regions of the country, and is a further reflection of the convergence of electoral behavior that seems to characterize the Communist experience in Yugoslavia. Finally, the two-step process of invalidation expansion in the 1960s was matched by a two-step decline in turnout, with the key factor being whether the district went to the polls in 1965 or 1967.

All of the similarities revealed in the results produced by the statistical analysis of invalidation and turnout suggest the possibility that these two indicators of dissent may be related to each other. The pattern we would anticipate is one in which districts with high invalidation would have low turnout, and vice versa. Simple correlations between the levels of constituency invalidation and turnout provide evidence for this in some elections: the correlations are $-.39$ (1953); $-.13$ (1958); $.02$ (1963); $-.30$ (1965/67); $.15$ (1969). (The 1950 election is excluded because turnout figures are not available.) It is possible, however, that the relationship between invalidation and turnout are interfered with by a third variable, that of region. Region affects the two variables differently because the regional grouping effect on invalidation is much stronger than that on turnout. Accordingly, the connection between invalidation and turnout might be more fruitfully assessed if region were controlled. This is effected in Table 5.5, which presents an analysis of variance of constituency invalidation levels with region as a factor and turnout levels as a covariate. In this table, the beta coefficients associated with region have changed little from Table 5.2; nevertheless, in four of the five elections a negative unstandardized regression coefficient connecting turnout to invalidation does emerge. The 1969 election once again appears as a special case.

Both the degree of patterning for turnout and its negative association with invalidation are further evidence that voting behavior in the Communist era can be used to make inferences about the state of political incorporation in the system. Invalidation is, of course, the better indicator since it is less amenable to distortion by the electoral practices of the authorities; the fact that the connection between them is fairly weak need not, therefore, raise too much concern. Significantly, the trend in both variables over time points to the same fundamental conclusion: the political system was experiencing a process of convergence over this period with the result that, in the 1960s, national stimuli such as the purging of the secret police and related actions could produce a common response across all regions of the country.

It is perhaps worth mentioning at this point that our analysis can be given an entropy theory interpretation. If we treat turnout as a two-event set, as we did before, and the choice to invalidate the ballot as another two-event set, entropy theory (presumably) would predict an equivalence between them. It will not be a one-to-one equivalence, because abstention is generally much higher than invalidation for obvious reasons.

TABLE 5.5

Analysis of Variance of Invalidation Levels By Region and Turnout Levels, Federal Elections of 1953 to 1969[a]

Dependent Variable	Election	Factor Region	Covariate Turnout	Explained Variance
Constituency	1953	.72	-.28	.64
Invalidation	1958	.72	-.08	.54
Rates	1963	.96	-.11	.89
	1965/67	.76	-.32	.72
	1969	.70	.02	.50

[a]Turnout figures not available for 1950 Election.

Nevertheless, the negative association between turnout and invalidation in four of the five elections analyzed in Table 5.5 is consistent with the basic entropy hypothesis, for those negative relationships would translate into positive relationships between turnout entropy and invalidation entropy. It is not necessary to press this interpretation of the findings because either way one looks at the two variables -- as entropy measures or as indicators of dissent -- the conclusion remains the same: dissent (entropy) fell and rose with the regime-strategy changes, but in either case it came to increasingly resemble a country-wide, rather than a regional phenomenon.

THE DEMOGRAPHIC BASES OF DISSENT

The patterns of electoral invalidation and abstention are strongly suggestive of a general enhancement of political incorporation in Yugoslavia during the first twenty-five years of Communist rule. In order to establish this interpretation, however, it is necessary that the ethnic or other bases for these patterns be explored. Our expectation is that improved levels of political incorporation will be manifested in a general decline in the importance of ethnicity as a basis for differential invalidation rates. Regional variations in invalidation persisted even in 1969, however, and in light of this fact we shall entertain the possibility that the rapid economic growth of the country during this period has entailed the emergence of economic factors as significant bases for political behavior. Findings of this sort would be indicative not only of improved political cohesiveness but also of a significant degree of modernization of Yugoslav society.

The importance of exploring these possibilities with quantitative data cannot be exaggerated, especially in view of the fact that these fundamental questions have not been treated in a systematic fashion in the literature on Yugoslavia.[5] The methodological problems that such questions raise are, however, very considerable. Basically, they fall into two categories: there is the problem of matching up data from a wide variety of geographic units (communes, districts, regions, constituencies, etc.); and there is the problem of making inferences that may turn out to be ecologically fallacious.

The procedures and tests that were employed to cope with these problems are discussed in full in Appendixes C and D. There is some value, nonetheless, in pausing at this point to indicate the general nature of the problems and the ways in which they were handled. The dimensions of the first issue can be appreciated quite readily by considering the data that we have assembled. From the 1953 and 1971 censuses (Yugoslavia, 1959, 1972), the ethnic composition by communes (1953)[6], the percent of the work force employed in agriculture by commune (1953 and 1971), and the mean personal income by commune (1971) were taken. Income data were not published by commune before 1963, but income data reported for some 107 districts in 1955 (Ivanović, 1964:56-57) has been used as a substitute. Not only do these latter districts not equate with communes, but communes in 1953 and 1971 do not correspond with one another (there are 301 communes in 1953 and 504 in 1971). Moreover, none of these units match up with the electoral constituencies, which themselves vary in size and number across the series of elections under study. Since this plethora of different units of analysis could not all be linked directly to one another, the only alternative was to find a different unit of analysis to which all could be transposed. The unit of analysis we adopted is the one that stood us in such good stead in the preceding section, that is the fifty-five regions which we defined along ethnic and historical lines. (Indeed, it was largely in order to effect such a linking up of demographic and electoral data that the regions were derived).

Converting data reported for communes into regional means proved to be a straightforward task; the communes represent such fine subdivisions of the country that in most cases they fit into the fifty-five regions quite readily. The 107 districts into which the 1955 income data was reported presented a much greater problem, however, because no indication at all was given as to how these districts were defined. The variable is quite essential to our analysis because it allows us not only to measure income levels in the period before 1971, but also to assess the relative rapidity of economic development over the period by calculating the change in income levels per region between 1955 and 1971. The attribution of these 107 districts to regions was ultimately effected purely on grounds of nomenclature. Moreover, in contrast to the data taken from censuses, whenever two or more districts were combined into a single region there was no information on the district populations by which the relative contributions of district means to the regional mean could be weighted. In the end, we made the assumption that the districts were of approximately equal size and weighted them accordingly.

The possibility of inaccuracy in this procedure is, of course, considerable. One means of verifying the validity of the income (1955) variable would be to relate it to the income (1971) variable, which was regionalized without problem. Despite the considerable economic growth between 1955 and 1971, and its somewhat uneven character (Table 2.2), one would expect a substantial degree of correlation between the two income measurements. In fact, the correlation of .69 between the measurements over the fifty-five regions is quite considerable. More significantly, the relationship of the two income measures to invalidation levels per region is remarkably similar over all elections. This data, reported in Table C.1 of Appendix C, shows that only slight differences exist between the two variables in their degree of association with the principal dependent variable in this chapter. It seems reasonably safe to assume that income (1955) is a satisfactory indicator of mean regional income levels for that year. Accordingly, both income (1955) and income (1971) were standardized and a third variable, change in income (1955-71) was produced by subtracting the former from the latter.

The facility with which data reported at the level of communes can be transposed to regions provides no assurance that results calculated on the basis of regions will bear a close resemblance to what would have been produced if it had not been necessary to introduce this higher unit of analysis. It is a common finding in aggregate data analyses, for instance, that grouping data into higher units of analysis tends to inflate the degree of association or correlation among variables (Blalock, 1972:107), or even to produce sizeable correlations among variables at the higher level where no correlations existed at the initial level of analysis. By taking the fifty-five regions as the common unit of analysis, it is possible that correlations might be generated that would not have appeared at the constituency or commune level.

Fortunately, the possibility that our interpretations might be erroneous because of the presence of this correlation-inflating effect, technically known as the ecological fallacy, can be assessed. Careful study of the divisions of the country into 301 communes and 282 electoral districts in 1953 revealed that it is possible, without too much distortion, to match communes directly to constituencies for that election and census year. A comparison of the correlations produced at that level with those produced at the level of regions for 1953 should provide a very good indication of the degree of inflation or other distortion in the coefficients that is generated by the regional grouping.[7]

With respect to the correlations between invalidation levels and the proportional sizes of various ethnic groups, the comparison showed that very little inflation or distortion took place as a result of the grouping of constituency and commune data into regions (Table D.1). This is not to say that corresponding correlations are identical at the two levels of analysis: in most cases, the coefficients calculated at the regional level are clearly larger in magnitude than the corresponding constituency-level coefficients. But what is significant for our purposes is that in no case did a small constituency-level correlation coefficient become a large one because of the grouping of the data into regions. No matter which of the two levels of analysis is considered, the correlations of invalidation with the percentages of Hungarians, "Yugoslavs" (i.e. principally Moslems in this period), Albanians, Slovenes, and Montenegrins, in that order, stand out. This is not the case, however, for the agricultural employment variable. The modest (negative) correlations between this variable and invalidation that appeared at the regional level is not matched by a similar finding at the constituency level. Since we have no grounds for believing that the region-level correlation is not simply an artefact of the regional grouping procedure, this variable will not be included in the analyses that follow.

To have shown that region-level findings reflect, in most cases, constituency-level findings is an important step in the analysis, but to be able to move to the level of the voter is equally crucial. Throughout this study, we have eschewed the individual level of analysis in favor of making inferences about the state of the system and its territorial components. In order to proceed in the intended direction of causal analysis, however, it is necessary to break this rule to some extent. Unfortunately, there is a risk involved. Consider the positive correlations noted above between the percentage of Hungarians in a given constituency or region and its level of invalidation. It is natural to interpret the finding as indicating that Hungarians invalidated their ballots to a disproportionately high extent. This may be and probably is the case, but the correlations do not in themselves prove this interpretation for it is also possible that they resulted from a tendency of non-Hungarians in highly Hungarian areas to invalidate their ballots. Alternatively, the correlations could have emerged simply because the Hungarian population is concentrated in Vojvodina, a relatively developed part of the country, and the more developed regions of Yugoslavia generally tend to exhibit higher invalidation rates. The first interpretation seems rather implausible given that there is considerable other evidence pointing to the Hungarians as high invalidators (Petranović, 1964:205), but what of the alternate interpretation?

One way to answer this question is to look within individual republics. For example, if Hungarians as an ethnic group were invalidating more, we would expect to find that within Vojvodina itself the more Hungarian the constituency the higher the invalidation rate. Conversely, if levels of economic development or some other republic-wide factor were at the root of the relationship, this would not be the case. When this test was performed, we found that for each of the principal ethnic correlates of invalidation, the relationship does hold within the relevant republics, adding weight to a straightforward ethnic interpretation of the correlations (Table D.2).

This test does not rule out the possibility of a misleading interpretation being made; it simply makes it less likely. Moreover, the test is only possible where there is a matching-up of constituency-level electoral data with census data; that is to say, for the 1953 election. To some extent this latter limitation has been dealt with through the application in Appendix D of a generalized version of the test to the region-level data for all election years from 1950 to 1969. Even if that test were not limited by the small number of cases available at that level of analysis, however, the initial objection would remain. Public opinion surveys provide the only sure way of linking demographic factors to individual voting behavior, but it is unlikely that survey questions on such sensitive matters as ballot invalidation would yield accurate results, and in any case they are not available. We shall therefore proceed with the analysis of the aggregate data, remaining aware of the dangers of making fallacious inferences about the behavior of particular categories of voters, and in general making inferences only when they are plausible, the evidence is strong, and the risk worth taking.

The range of demographic variables that have been gathered in order to aid us in the search for causes is quite large. First of all, there are the proportions per region of the nine largest ethnic groups and the ethnic fragmentation (entropy) per region. Next, there are the two measures of mean personal income per region, for 1955 and 1971, and the amount of change between them. Although, theoretically, a multiplicity of indicators could be used to assess the levels and rapidity of economic development, it is our position that these three variables are the best all-round indicators of this concept.[8] Finally, there are two variables that can be employed to represent the effect of political developments in the 1960s: the year of election for the split election of 1965/67, and the number of candidates competing in the elections of 1965/1967 and 1969. The former reflects, as we have seen, the degree of response to the reforms of 1966, while the latter will allow us to assess the effect of the offering of electoral choice on the pattern of invalidation. These two variables, in other words, are both indicators of the experiment in pluralist socialism. Since neither variable is defined at the regional level, the exact variables we shall employ are the proportion of constituencies in the region which had their 1965/67 elections in 1967 and the mean number of candidates per constituency in the region. Fortunately, the precise effects of both of these variables can be established at the constituency level to verify that no distortion in findings has taken place as a result of transforming them into regional means for the purposes of this analysis.

In order to assess the relative effects of these various independent variables on regional invalidation levels of the 1950-69 period, we shall rely upon multiple regression analysis. Initially, our approach involves the regression of invalidation on all the independent variables for each election. The normal criterion for inclusion or exclusion of an independent variable in the final version of a regression equation -- the statistical significance of its partial regression coefficient -- is inappropriate for these data because they do not constitute, in practice or in principle, samples of a larger universe of cases. We have therefore adopted the somewhat arbitrary expedient of excluding any variables that yielded a standardized partial regression coefficient or beta weight of less than .10 with invalidation.[9] This cut-off point indicates a contribution to the explanation of variance in the dependent variable of the order of 1 percent, other things being equal. Given the fact that we are dealing with aggregated data which can be expected to show quite strong statistical relationships, the criterion can be characterized as generous. This accords with our intention to include all variables that could possibly be considered as having an effect on the dependent variable.

In Table 5.6, the final version of the regression equations are given in standardized form; that is to say, each coefficient (beta weight) indicates the relative effect of the independent variable on invalidation, controlling for the influences of other independent variables and standardizing for variations in the ranges (standard deviations) of those variables. The Table, it will be remembered, contains three types of independent variables: ethnic, economic (income and change in income), and political (year of election and mean number of candidates). Among the ethnic variables, there appears to be a high degree of continuity across the elections. In particular, the presence of Hungarians and Slovenians is generally associated with higher invalidation rates, while the presence of Albanians, Moslems (Yugoslavs) and Montenegrins is associated with invalidation levels that are lower than average. It is interesting to note that these five ethnic groups are the same groups that were found to be most strongly associated with invalidation rates at the constituency level in 1953. All of these correlations were re-calculated within the appropriate republics (Table D.2) in order to demonstrate that they did not simply reflect differences among the republics in invalidation levels. The present results show us that these correlations hold up even when regional levels of income are controlled. It seems clear that a definite ethnic effect is at the root of these relationships.

This conclusion is consistent with the evidence cited in Chapter 4 concerning the dissident behavior in the 1950 election of Slovenes and Hungarians, and the regime-supportive behavior of Montenegrins, whose activity in Tito's partisan movement was rewarded by the creation of a Montenegrin republic. The association of low levels of invalidation with the presence of Albanians and Moslems should not, however, be interpreted as indicative of high levels of regime support. Instead, the operative principle

TABLE 5.6
Multiple Regression of Invalidation Levels per Region (1950–1969) on Demographic Variables

Dependent Variable	Independent Variables[a]											Change in Income	Year (% 1967)	Mean No. of Cands.	Multiple Correlation (R)
	% Serbs	% Hung.	% Alb.	% Turks	% Mos.	% Croat.	% Slov.	% Mace.	% Mont.	H(E)	Income				
1950	.23	.70	--	--	-.25	--	.14	--	-.13	-.15	--	--	--	--	.79
1953	--	.50	-.26	--	-.40	--	.18	--	-.18	.16	.17	--	--	--	.83
1958	.31	.28	-.15	--	-.18	.34	.91	--	--	.12	--	--	--	--	.84
1963	--	.26	-.18	-.20	-.22	--	.69	--	-.11	.13	--	-.12	--	--	.87
1965/67	--	.16	-.19	-.10	-.13	--	.28	--	-.16	--	.29	--	.46	--	.83
1969	--	.14	--	--	-.46	-.15	--	--	-.10	--	--	-.11	--	-.27	.58

[a]Coefficients are standardized partial regression coefficients (beta weights). Variables with coefficients less than .10 were deleted from the equations.

seems to have been that protest was expressed in high invalidation rates among certain dissatisfied ethnic groups such as the Slovenes and Hungarians who had been active in prewar politics and whose political culture may be characterized as "participant" in Almond and Verba's (1965) sense, while a more backward or "parochial" political culture in which dissatisfaction was not channelled through the electoral system characterized the Moslems and Albanians.

Aggregate data cannot take us beyond this point, but it is much less important for our purposes that each ethnic group's particular voting behavior be accounted for correctly, than that the phenomenon in question be recognized as ethnic in its essence. This is so because the hypothesis that the postwar era was one of rising incorporation depends not on which ethnic group did what, but rather on how much ethnicity influenced electoral behavior in total. There is little doubt that Hungarians registered high levels of invalidation in the early years and that the Slovenians took over as the leading dissenters in the 1958 and 1963 elections; this much was strongly suggested in the trend lines of Figure 5.1 and is affirmed in Table 5.6. What is crucial is the relative importance of all these ethnic effects in comparison with effects that are more correctly considered economic or political.

This comparison can be effected more readily if Table 5.7 is considered in conjunction with Table 5.6. The data reported in Table 5.7 are the results of a transformation of the variables in Table 5.6 into the three broad categories: ethnic, economic, and political.[10] The coefficients are still beta weights, but they indicate the relative importance of each of the three categories of variables, rather than that of the individual variables themselves, in determining regional invalidation patterns. We note in Table 5.6, for instance, that the higher levels of invalidation recorded in 1953 for the northern parts of the country are associated to some extent with higher levels of income as well as with particular ethnic groups. On the other hand, the contribution of the income variable, while undeniably present, is shown in Table 5.7 to be rather small in comparison with the total influence of the ethnic variables. The pattern of ethnic predominance in determining regional invalidation levels is even more apparent in the 1950 and 1958 elections. In the 1950 election, the main source of high invalidation is the Hungarian population; in the latter election the major invalidators are the Slovenes; in both cases, economic (income) variables register no effect at all.

This situation changes very considerably, however, after 1964. In the 1965/67 elections, the increased levels of invalidation are strongly associated with two non-ethnic variables: mean income and especially the year of election. The association of higher income with invalidation might be interpreted as the re-emergence of the income effect that was evident in the 1953 election, and therefore as a phenomenon to be expected whenever regime pressures on political behavior are relaxed. But a general interpretation of this election as being a "return-to-normal" one is not fully justified. Although the by-now standard pattern of ethnic relationships is evident for this election, it is highly significant that invalidation rates in 1965/67 are virtually as closely associated with the year of election, that is to say with a nation-wide change in political climate, as they are with behaviors specific to ethnic groups. The relative decline in importance of ethnic effects in 1965/67, as recorded in Table 5.7, is indeed very large.

If one would expect that the 1969 election would reveal a further decline in ethnicity in favor of economic and political effects, the findings which are reported in Tables 5.6 and 5.7 will certainly come as a surprise.

TABLE 5.7
Relative Effects of Ethnic, Economic and Political Factors on Regional
Invalidation Levels, Elections of 1950 to 1969

Dependent Variable	Election	Independent Variables[a]			Multiple Correlation (R)
		Ethnic Factors	Economic Factors	Political Factors	
Regional	1950	.79	--	--	.79
Invalidation	1953	.77	.17	--	.83
Rates	1958	.84	--	--	.84
	1963	.85	(-).12	--	.87
	1965/67	.49	.29	.46	.83
	1969	.52	(-).11	(-).27	.58

[a]Coefficients are beta weights.

It remains the case that the contribution of ethnic variables to the
explanation of invalidation is weak, with only the Moslems exhibiting low
levels of invalidation. But even more striking is the decline of effects from
the political and economic variables.[11] The absence of a strong political
effect is related to the fact that its main indicator has changed: by 1969
the two-step expansion in invalidation is complete and the proportion of
1965/67 elections conducted in 1967 is no longer relevant to invalidation
levels. Its place has been taken by the mean number of candidates per
constituency, a variable which proves to have a substantial but
nevertheless much weaker effect on the dependent variable. The conclusion
that economic factors were of little importance in the 1969 election also
needs to be qualified. The 1965/67 election witnessed the emergence of a
positive relationship between income and invalidation; for that relationship
to disappear in the 1969 election, there must have been a process of
catching-up on the part of lower income areas from 1965/67 to 1969. In
other words, the very absence of an income effect in the 1969 electoral
data suggests the presence of an income effect on the change in invalidation
levels between the 1965/67 and 1969 elections. This suggestion can best be
evaluated by examining the determinants of change in invalidation levels
between the two elections.

In Table 5.8, the results of a regression analysis of the changes in
invalidation levels from 1963 to 1965/67 and from 1965/67 to 1969 are
displayed. A comparison of the two regression equations makes it clear that
there was a two-step effect associated with income as well as with the year
of the 1965/67 election. Regions that had conducted higher proportions of

elections in 1967 and/or had higher mean income levels moved ahead in invalidation in the first period; those regions with more 1965 elections and/or lower mean income quite clearly experienced larger increases in invalidation in the second period. Indeed, the catching-up phenomenon even extends to certain ethnic groups (Turks, Albanians) that manifested traditionally low levels of invalidation. One consequence of these processes was a very considerable levelling-off in invalidation across the entire country in 1969. Because of this, few of the regularities noted in earlier elections seem to work: in 1969 Hungarians and Slovenians did not invalidate at exceptionally high levels relative to other groups; Albanians and Montenegrins were not especially low invalidators; and income no longer made any significant difference at all. Only the Moslems persisted in their normal pattern of electoral behavior. As a result, the set of independent variables as a whole explains much less variance for the 1969 election than for any of the other elections.

If the net result of the above analysis is a reduction in our ability to explain invalidation in 1969, the process by which this reduction occurred is itself highly explicable: across the country, between the elections of 1965/67 and 1969, there was an extraordinary expansion in invalidation by poorer, less developed regions and by ethnic groups which, for one reason or another, had previously been unwilling to indicate dissent. Moreover, if ethnic variables still hold the preponderance of influence on the invalidation levels of the later 1960s, it is clear from Table 5.8 that the processes of change in those years are much more closely associated with economic and political factors, even when the ethnic dimension of the catch-up phenomenon is taken into account.

We previously noted a number of ways in which the electoral results of the 1969 election deviate from the pattern of earlier years: invalidation levels in 1969 group weakly by republic; they are not related to turnout; and their degree of association with invalidation in previous elections is rather slight. What we have now shown is that the 1969 election violates the essentially ethnic patterning of invalidation in earlier elections as well. It is clear that a new demographic picture of political behavior emerged in 1969, namely, one in which more backward southern regions were just as willing to express dissent as the developed regions of the north; in which traditionally "quiescent" ethnic groups registered similar levels of dissent as the traditional dissenting groups; and in which all regions responded very quickly to more liberal political initiatives with rapid increases in protest voting (and, incidentally, with significant declines in electoral turnout as well).

These findings make it difficult to interpret the events of the 1960s in a simplistic fashion, for what we have found, in effect, are contradictory signposts. On the one hand, voting across the entire country demonstrated a substantial uniformity rather than ethnic divergence. Our basic hypothesis is thus affirmed by the data at hand. But what did uniformity entail in terms of the regime's durability? Was the convergence in electoral behavior an indication that the regime's survival was assured at last, or did it perhaps reflect a trans-ethnic consensus on the undesirability of the regime?

It is very evident that the political elite adopted the more pessimistic interpretation of the election. As we shall see, the leadership chose to take steps which disallowed any opportunity for electoral behavior of the sort exhibited in 1969 to find expression in the future. From their point of view, this may have been justified. Perhaps they had expected that the provision

TABLE 5.8
Regression Analysis of Regional Invalidation Levels, 1963 to 1965/67 and 1965/67 to 1969

Dependent Variable	Independent Variables										Multiple Corre-lation
	% Alb.	% Turks	% Yug.	% Slov.	% Mace.	% Mont.	Income	Change in Income	Year (% 1967)	Change in No. of Cands.	
Change in Invalidation Levels, 1963 to 1965/67	-.12	-.15		-.23		-.11	.25	.10	.68		.77
			-.29					.31	.68		.77
Change in Invalidation Levels, 1965/67 to 1969	.25	.48	-.23	-.14	-.38		-.27		-.58	-.18	.82
			.45				-.27			-.57	.82

of candidate choice within the framework of a single-party regime would have resulted in a reduction in dissent. Instead, invalidation rose substantially in this period.

This does not mean, however, that the offering of candidate choice to the electorate had no effect at all. For example, the 1969 regression produced a substantial negative coefficient from the mean number of candidates variable: apparently, the greater the number of candidates the lower the invalidation. This effect was not strong enough by itself to counteract the effects of the other influences which were causing invalidation levels to increase, but might not a more extensive use of the candidate-choice stratagem (only a minority of districts had more than one candidate in 1969) eventually have served to check and perhaps roll back the growth in invalidation across the system?

Let us consider the effect of multi-candidacies more closely. Despite the emphasis placed on the effect of choice in 1969, there were multiple candidate races in four of the six federal elections in the 1950-1969 period. In Table 5.9, we present an analysis of covariance of constituency invalidation levels for each of these elections by region and number of candidates, with turnout as a covariate. Two aspects of these analyses stand out. First, the size of the coefficient associated with the number of candidates per constituency increases over time. This most certainly is a function of the greater number of constituencies permitted multi-candidacies in later years (in particular, the extent to which multi-candidate races were permitted in 1969 far exceeds that of the other elections). Second, the direction of influence of the number of candidates variable is reversed in 1969. This is shown in the multiple classification analysis in the lower half of Table 5.9, where the mean deviations from the grand mean invalidation level are given according to the number of candidates per constituency for each election. In the elections of 1953, 1958, and 1965/67, the general tendency is for constituencies with more than one candidate to have higher than average invalidation rates (indicated by positive deviations). It is only in the 1969 election, when candidate choice becomes more than an idiosyncratic curiosity, that the offering of choice had a dampening effect on invalidation. Indeed, since the forty-three districts which sponsored two candidates in 1969 had an average invalidation rate that was 0.8 percent lower than the overall or grand mean of 6.9 percent (while the seventy-one districts with just one candidate averaged 0.5 percent above the grand mean), one can speculate that the presentation of two candidates in every district would have resulted in an overall invalidation rate of nearly 1 percent less than actually occurred. At this level, invalidation in 1969 would only have been slightly higher than in 1967 (6.1 percent vs. 5.3 percent).

The findings of Table 5.9 give us some reason to believe that a large-scale experiment in candidate choice within the context of a more liberal political climate may ultimately have achieved the regime's dual electoral goals, namely, greater cohesiveness and lower dissent. This possibility remains in the realm of speculation, however, for the 1969 election represents the end rather than the beginning of this unique era of pluralist socialism. It is very difficult, therefore, to render an overall verdict concerning the efficacy of this strategy on the basis of the evidence of federal elections. Fortunately there is another avenue that can be pursued. In 1969, candidate choice was offered on a much more extensive basis in the elections to republic assemblies. In the next chapter, we shall extend our analysis of the electoral impact of candidate choice in the late

TABLE 5.9
Invalidation per Constituency by Region, Number of Candidates and Turnout, Federal Elections of 1953, 1958, 1965/67, and 1969[a]

A. ANALYSIS OF VARIANCE

Dependent Variable	Election	Factors		Covariate	Multiple Corre- lation
		Region	No. of Candidates	Turnout	
Constituency Invalidation Rate	1953	.73	.05	-.28	.83
	1958	.71	.07	-.08	.54
	1965/67	.85	.17	-.32	.74
	1969	.71	.28	-.02	.74

B. MULTIPLE CLASSIFICATION ANALYSIS

Dependent Variable	Election	Grand Mean	Deviations from Grand Mean by No. of Candidates			
			1	2	3	4
Constituency Invalidation Rate	1953	4.3%	-0.0% (267)[b]	0.5% (13)	-1.3% (2)	--
	1958	3.2%	-0.0% (294)	1.1% (6)	--	--
	1965/67	4.2%	-0.1% (103)	0.9% (11)	1.0% (3)	-2.1% (1)
	1969	6.9%	0.5% (71)	-0.8% (43)	-0.2% (5)	-0.8% (1)

[a]There were no multi-candidate races in 1950 or 1963.
[b]Number of constituencies given in brackets.

1960s by examining the republic-level elections of this period in order to achieve a more precise indication of the effect of the experiment in pluralist socialism on political incorporation in Yugoslavia.

100

NOTES

1. According to Yugoslav electoral laws, invalid ballots are those on which more than one candidate's name is selected by a voter, a ballot on which a new name is indicated, a ballot which is not filled out, or a ballot filled out in a manner that makes it impossible to determine which candidate the elector chose. It is impossible to systematically distinguish those invalid votes which can be considered an expression of political dissent from those ballots spoiled due to negligence or misunderstanding of correct electoral procedure. Yugoslav voting analysts regard the number of invalid votes due to ignorance, indifference, or negligence to be very low, however, and feel that ballot invalidation generally functions as "an indicator of the political mood because their number can be an expression of concealed protest at the ballot or at the political situation . . ." (Benc, 1969:7).

2. Levels of statistical significance are not reported in Table 5.1 or in the other tables of this chapter because the data constitute the universe of cases, rather than a sample. The coefficients presented in analyses of variance are correlation ratios (eta's), or in the case of two or more factors, partial correlation ratios (beta's). They are analogous to standardized partial regression coefficients and represent the importance of each factor in accounting for the variance in the dependent variable.

3. This is fortunate since the degree of overlap between region and republic is such that both variables could not be entered simultaneously as factors in analyses of variance.

4. The correlation coefficients between the same variables based on the 120 constituencies of the 1960s (where constituencies could be matched across election) turned out to be very similar to the ones cited in Table 5.3. On this evidence, the distorting effect of the regional classification as a unit of analysis can be assumed to be minimal.

5. A number of studies (Zaninovich, 1970; Bertsch, 1976; Clark and Johnson, 1976; Jacob, 1971) using survey data on popular attitudes in the late 1960s, have attributed the emergence of "modern value sets" in Yugoslavia (especially noticable among party members and leaders) to the impact of economic development. In addition to focusing exclusively on a very short, and in many respects atypical, phase of Yugoslav political history, these public opinion surveys ignore the rich body of electoral data entirely and by-pass fundamental system-level questions relating to trends in political cohesion.

6. Since the basic ethnic make-up of Yugoslavia in 1971 had changed only very slightly from 1953, the analysis of all elections in this chapter employs ethnic data from 1953 only.

7. This test could not be performed for mean income because that variable was not reported at the commune level before the 1960s. Moreover, by that time the communes were defined differently, and were much more numerous, than in 1953.

8. Some survey research studies (Jacob, 1971; Clark and Johnson,

1976) dealing with the political impact of modernization in Yugoslavia as revealed through individual attitudes at one particular point in time, have utilized a composite indicator of economic development factoring together income per capita with other items such as education per capita, literary rates, radio sets per capita, etc. Our own approach, which employs one aggregate indicator of economic development, was determined by the accessibility of data on mean income per capita for both 1955 and 1971, and the fact that income has been found to be highly correlated with other indicators of economic development (Jacob, 1971:225; Clark and Johnson 1976:15).

9. A cut-off point was needed because the introduction of too many independent variables into the regression would lead to problems of overdetermination, which is not surprising given the nature of the variables and the small number of cases.

10. This transformation was effected by generating a linear combination of the relevant variables in each category, using the unstandardized partial regression coefficients from the regression equations of Table 5.6 as weights.

11. To have included in the analysis the proportion of the workforce employed in agriculture, and the change between 1953 and 1971 in this proportion, would not have altered this basic finding. These two variables do enter the regression and cause the income variables to appear with negative coefficients as well, suggesting countervailing forces of higher urban invalidation and higher invalidation in less developed or poorer regions. But the net effect is the same; ethnicity is weaker as a factor in 1969 and invalidation is uniform across regions of differing levels of prosperity.

6
One Party, Many Choices: Pluralist Socialism in the 1960s

The reorientation of the Yugoslav regime toward a more liberal or pluralistic brand of socialism during the 1960s implied the recognition of the legitimacy and "natural" character of group conflict, including conflict among the country's diverse regions and nationalities. From that recognition, it was only a short step to the question of how such interests might be articulated and politically accommodated. "The essential aspect of political pluralism," wrote a prominent Yugoslav theoretician of regime-strategy changes (Djordjević, 1967:78), "is the institutionalization of pluralism." One means to achieve this end, the development of a multi-party system, was clearly unacceptable to the regime, even if, as some commentators suggested at the time, all of the parties were socialist. In the opinion of the political elite, however, the absence of competing parties did not rule out the existence of "socialist alternatives," provided such alternatives did "not deny the socio-political premises of the socialist society":

> ... these alternatives confront one another but are not opposed to each other; they are open to discussion [dijalogične] but are not conflicting; they are in a certain sense friendly and not hostile to each other. No one is a priori a great Marxist and socialist if he accepts one of them rather than another. (Djordjević, 1967:80)

A number of channels and arenas for the expression of "socialist alternatives" were proposed. They included: (1) the various territorial units (commune, republic, federation) which comprise the federal structure; (2) the multi-cameral organization of legislative assemblies providing for representation by function and territory as well as by population; (3) market competition among self-managing enterprises; and (4) the plurality of organizations specializing in one or another socio-political task (the League, trade unions, associations for women, youth and veterans, etc.) or sphere of professional activity (the Union of Writers, Society of Engineers, etc.). Sounding more like Madison than like Marx, certain Yugoslav constitutional specialists even suggested that the supremacy of "assembly government" in their country did not preclude a "healthy" separation or division of powers among relatively autonomous legislative, executive, and judicial branches of the governmental structure (Gerškovic, 1967:37-38; Djordjević, 1971:409; Nikolić, 1969:129).

Increasingly in the mid-1960s, attention was focused on the parliamentary system as an acceptable and reasonably manageable site for the institutionalization of socialist alternatives. The reduced intervention of both the League of Communists and the state security apparatus as direct actors in the process of political decision-making also contributed to the emergence of legislative assemblies as focal points for the active consideration of important social and economic issues over which they had previously exercised only nominal control. As the political influence and status of the parliamentary system grew in significance, the composition of legislative bodies, and consequently the character of elections, naturally assumed greater importance. In June 1965, the Socialist Alliance (the successor to the People's Front as the mass socio-political organization with direct responsibility for the organization of legislative elections) passed a resolution urging more extensive use of plural-candidate electoral contests for legislative assemblies: "under present conditions the nomination of several candidates is an expression of the creative possibilities for broader selection of people who can perform public functions in socio-political life. It is the right of people to nominate one or more candidates." The position was put even more bluntly by Edward Kardelj (Institut Društvenih Nauka, 1967:329) -- at that time President of the Federal Assembly -- when he addressed a conference held specifically to discuss the electoral system in October 1966, just a few months after the purge of the secret police:

> It seems to me that we are still arguing a great deal about whether it is better to have one or more candidates. Everyone knows that it is better to have more candidates than one, to have more freedom in the process of nomination, etc. The essential question is, however, what conditions do we need to create so that we really can secure a more or less uninterrupted process of growth, and so to speak, the quantitative accumulation of those conditions which allow the development of our society to unfold without difficult convulsions, explosions, and various anti-democratic tendencies?

Plural-candidate electoral contests within the single-party Yugoslav framework had already taken place during the 1950s, but on a very limited scale and almost exclusively on the communal and republican-provincial levels.[1] In 1963 and 1965 under the new constitutional system, there were no plural-candidate contests at all on the federal level and only a few on the republican level. More choice was offered in elections for local assemblies, but even at that level a report of the Socialist Alliance (Socijalistička Savez, 1969:219) indicated that "several candidates for one mandate occurred in an insignificant number of electoral districts, and where several candidates were proposed, many withdrew for fear of not being elected, or at the suggestion of the political leadership." Gradually however, the full impact of the 1963 constitutional reform, together with the economic reforms of 1965, the purge of the secret police in 1966, and the reorganization of the League of Communists in 1967 which was designed to "divorce the party from power" (Crvenkovski, 1967), conveyed the necessary momentum for more fundamental changes in the electoral system. In 1967, there were several plural-candidate races for seats to the Federal Assembly, and also a striking increase in the number of candidates nominated and slated for seats in the republic and commune-level assemblies. This trend is shown in Table 6.1, which also indicates that a

TABLE 6.1
Candidate Choice for Popularly-Elected Legislative Chambers, by Level of Government and Stage of the Nomination Process, 1963-1969

Level of Government	Year of Election	Total Candidates Proposed at Voters' Meetings	Total Candidates Nominated	Total Candidates Slated by Electoral Commissions	Total Candidates on Ballot[a]	Total Candidates Elected (Seats Available)	Mean Candidates/ Constituency
Federal	1963	158	142	120	120	120	1.00
	1965/67[b]	943 (398/565)	758 (303/455)	161 (64/97)	139 (58/81)	118 (58/60)	1.18 (1.00/1.35)
	1969	n.a.	237	183	183	120	1.35
Republic[c]	1963	797	753	650	650	650	1.00
	1965/67[b]	3098 (1334/1764)	2674 (1141/1533)	2231 (482/1749)	789 (360/429)	650 (325/325)	1.21 (1.11/1.32)
	1969	n.a.	2737	1167	1167	620	1.88

Source: Yugoslavia (1964, 1965, 1967, 1969) "Predstavnička Tela Društveno-Političkih Zajednica," Statistički Bilten, Savezi Zavod za Statistiku, 266, 372, 491, 590.

[a] After indirect election by communal assemblies.
[b] Figures in parentheses represent totals for 1965 and 1967 elections separately.
[c] Data on the provinces of Vojvodina and Kosovo not available.

far more drastic expansion in the numbers of candidates took place at all levels in 1969. Clearly, at this point, the experiment in pluralist socialism was in full swing.

One important consequence of the opening-up of the system in the late 1960s was the very substantial rise in invalidation levels after 1966 at the federal level as was analyzed in Chapter 5. Our analysis also demonstrated that a modest countervailing tendency for the offering of candidate choice to be associated with lower-than-average invalidation levels had begun to make itself felt by 1969 (Table 5.9). Unfortunately, the combination of a small number of federal constituencies (120) in the 1960s, and a relatively restricted offering of candidate choice at the federal level (Table 6.1), meant that the number of competitive races was far too few to explore a major aspect of our inquiry: the potential for electoral choice to discourage ballot invalidation and thereby enhance the level of political incorporation in the system. In this chapter we shall explore this and related issues using data from popular elections to the republican assemblies, which provide both a much larger number of constituencies and a much more extensive application of the principle of competitive elections.

The use of republic-level electoral returns quite naturally raises questions concerning their value for reaching conclusions about the political system as a whole. This is especially true because, despite our best research efforts in Yugoslavia, we have been unable to acquire a complete set of republican electoral data. In particular, three republics -- Serbia, Montenegro, and Kosovo -- are totally unrepresented in our data set,[2] and two others -- Vojvodina and Slovenia -- are incomplete for the elections of 1963 and 1965/67. Table 6.2 presents a synopsis of the available data over the three elections.

No claim could be made that the five republics for which data has been gathered can be assumed to be representative of the whole country. On the contrary, it is clear that the sample is composed primarily of the non-Serbian areas. While in a certain sense this provides an exciting possibility for observing the behavior of the less influential and central ethnic groups and republics, it still leaves a void that must be taken into account. Some idea of how serious this void is, and how well republic-level electoral data reflect the same patterns as federal electoral data in general, can be gained from Table 6.3. This table presents an analysis of variance of 1969 constituency invalidation levels by republic and number of candidates for three different sets of data: (1) federal elections in all republics; (2) federal elections in the five republics for which republican data is available; and (3) republican elections in those same five republics.

The findings reported in Table 6.3 show a high degree of correspondence at the federal level between the five republics of the sample and the entire country in regard to these variables. Not only are the effects on invalidation of the two factors, republic and number of candidates, very similar in 1969, but the multiple classification analyses derived from the analyses of variance reveal a striking similarity in the overall invalidation rate for the country and in the patterning of the invalidation rates for the individual republics. Thus, the mean invalidation rate across the five sampled republics of 6.8 percent is virtually identical to the nation-wide mean of 6.9 percent; Croatia and Bosnia are shown to have invalidation levels below the mean in both cases; while Slovenia, Vojvodina, and Macedonia consistently rank above average in invalidation.[3] These findings provide some measure of confidence that the analysis of data from just five of the eight republics has not generated results which are

TABLE 6.2
Available Data by Constituency For Republican Elections of 1963, 1965/67, and 1969

Variable	Year	Bosn.	Vojv.	Croat.	Mace.	Slov.	Serb.	Koso.	Mont.	No. of Cases
Invalidation	1963	X[a]		X	X					338
	1965/67	X		X	X					331
	1969	X	X	X	X	X				504
Change in Invalidation	1963–1965/67	X		X	X					265
	1965/67–1969	X		X	X					284
Turnout	1963			X	X	X				340
	1965/67	X[b]	X	X	X					272
	1969	X		X	X	X				504
No. of Candidates	1963	X		X	X					340
	1965/67	X	X	X	X	X				451
	1969	X		X	X	X				504
Change in No. of Candidates	1963–1965/67	X		X	X					340
	1965/67–1969	X		X	X					322
Candidate–Choice Entropy	1969	X	X	X	X	X				291
Year of Election	1965/67	X		X	X	X				472
Ethnic Composition[c]	1971	X		X	X	X				504
Ethnic Entropy	1971	X		X	X	X				504
Mean Personal Income	1971	X		X	X	X				504
% Employed in Agriculture	1971	X		X	X	X				504
Total No. of Constituencies	(1969)	120	90	120	100	90	120	70	70	780

a"X" indicates available data.
b1967 only.
cPercentages of Montenegrins, Croats, Macedonians, Moslems, Slovenes, Serbs, Albanians, Hungarians, Turks.

unrepresentative of the system on a whole.

Equally important is the question of how representative republic-level electoral data are in respect to the patterns and relationships found at the federal level. A comparison of the results of the third analysis of variance in Table 6.3 with those of the first two analyses reveals a less-than-complete correspondence: the effect of the number of candidates on invalidation is quite similar, but the effect of republic is considerably weaker at the republic level. This conclusion should be tempered, however, with the knowledge that the mean invalidation rate is the same as at the federal level, and that the deviations by republic match the federal pattern quite closely, with Croatia and Bosnia again below average and the other republics at or above average in their mean invalidation levels. Apparently, the much greater number of constituencies at the republican level has resulted in a larger degree of within-republic heterogeneity in invalidation, but a very similar across-republic patterning. Moreover, when the same set of analyses of variance was recalculated using the "region" variable (introduced in Chapter 5) as a factor instead of republic, a similar series of findings emerged.[4] Indeed, the extent of correspondence in the republican and federal patternings according to the much finer regional classification is truly remarkable, and leaves little doubt that republic-level elections exhibit, to a very high degree, the same voting patterns and properties that underlie federal electoral results. It appears that on both counts -- the representativeness of the five republics and the representativeness of republic-level data for national patterns -- we are on reasonably safe ground to proceed in the proposed manner.

Although the electoral data for the individual republics is less complete than one would like, the linking of these data with the available demographic variables, also listed in Table 6.2, turns out to be much more direct; so direct in fact that the use of region as a unit of analysis to which all other units could be related was no longer necessary. It is still the case that census data was reported for communes and that communes were not necessarily identical with electoral constituencies. Nevertheless, through careful analysis we were able to match communes directly to constituencies for the five sampled republics with a substantial degree of accuracy. Occasionally this involved combining the data from two or more communes to match a single constituency, or in the reverse situation, assigning the data from one commune to two or more constituencies. But in almost every case, the matching up was effected at a low level and with a minimum of data aggregation.[5] In addition, it was possible to match constituencies across the three elections on a one-to-one basis, since few changes were made to constituency boundaries during the 1960s.

In the analyses that follow, we shall treat the five republican elections as if they can be pooled to form a representative sample of electoral behavior of the entire country. We shall be mindful that these are separate elections in formally separate political units, however, and use "republic" as a control factor at every appropriate stage in the analysis. The electoral phenomena we shall attempt to explain go beyond the virtually exclusive focus of Chapter 5 on invalidation levels to encompass both the degree of candidate choice taken up by the electorate and the amount of candidate choice offered by the authorities. By examining each of these three aspects of electoral behavior separately and relating them to background characteristics, both cross-sectionally and over time, a more complete understanding of the electoral dimension of pluralist socialism will be pursued. The ultimate objective, of course, is the best possible

TABLE 6.3
Comparative Analysis of Federal and Republic-Level Invalidation Levels, 1969 Elections

A. ANALYSIS OF VARIANCE

| Dependent Variable | Analysis No. | Factors | | Multiple Correlation |
		Region	No. of Candidates	
Invalidation per Constituency, 1969	1. All Federal Constituencies (n=120)	.46	.30	.50
	2. Federal Constituencies in Five Sampled Republics (n=71)[a]	.53	.28	.58
	3. Republican Constituencies in Five Sampled Republics (n=499)	.33	.25	.39

B. MULTIPLE CLASSIFICATION ANALYSIS

| Dependent Variable | Analysis No. | Grand Mean | Deviations from Grand Mean by Republic | | | | |
			Slov.	Croat.	Vojv.	Bosn.	Mace.
Invalidation per Constituency, 1969	1. All Federal Constituencies	6.9%	1.2%	-0.1%	1.3%	-2.1%	0.2%
	2. Federal Constituencies in Sampled Republics	6.8%	1.4%	-0.1%	1.4%	-1.9%	0.5%
	3. Republican Constituencies in Sampled Republics	6.9%	0.0%	-0.8%	2.4%	-1.8%	1.0%

[a]They are: Slovenia, Croatia, Vojvodina, Bosnia, and Macedonia.

assessment of the effect of pluralist socialism, the most interesting and unique of communist regime-strategies, upon Yugoslav political incorporation and cohesion.

CHOICE OFFERED: THE NATURE AND NUMBER OF CANDIDATES

The official encouragement of competitive electoral processes was, like other aspects of the new regime-strategy, not without its inherent limitations, if not contradictions. Without question, the Yugoslav leaders were intent upon moving beyond the completely safe single-candidate elections typical of Soviet-type "mobilization regimes," but they also sought to avoid any challenges to single-party dominance or to the "socialist self-managing" character of the political system. Thus, while the nomination process was considerably "democratized" in this period, efforts were still taken, albeit of a more informal and persuasive character than in the past, to ensure that the final list of candidates and those ultimately elected would have the characteristics and views deemed appropriate by the regime.

The general character of this type of electoral "guidance" can be seen in Table 6.4 which presents occupational background data on candidates proposed, nominated, and ultimately elected in the 1969 legislative assembly elections in a sample of communes covering all republics. Despite the frequent exhortations to recruit more "direct producers," young people, and women as political decision-makers, pressures were exerted to prevent any "uncontrolled" influx of these groups into legislative bodies. For example, while workers, peasants, students, and others (housewives, pensioners) made up about 16 percent of those candidates nominated in the first stage of the nomination process for the important "political chambers" of regional assemblies, representatives of those groups constituted less than 2 percent of those finally elected (actually there were no workers or peasants at all in those chambers, a pattern also found on the federal level at that time). Conversely, the percentage of party and mass organization functionaries chosen to sit in the political chambers was nearly twice the number proposed at the beginning of the process (although there was a gradual reduction of party functionaries, especially those from the revolutionary generation, in the overall composition of legislative bodies during this period).

In addition to maintaining some control over the occupational background of candidates, and thereby the character of different interests represented in the republican assemblies, a number of novel precautions were taken to dilute the potential impact of ethnic dissidence in the electoral process. For instance, competition among candidates of different ethnic backgrounds was strictly avoided. In ethnically mixed areas where some degree of proportional representation of ethnic groups in the political system was deemed essential, the complexity of the "assembly system" was used to advantage. Thus, the entire electoral process was structured so that candidates from one ethnic group would compete with one another for a seat in a legislature at one level of the federation while members of another ethnic group in the same electoral district competed among themselves for a seat in a legislature at a different level, or in a different chamber of the same legislature. With legislative assemblies in the 1960s being composed of three or more chambers at each level of governmental authority, there were ample possibilities for the engineering of an overall ethnic proportionality to political representation in this manner. Another measure sometimes used to curtail the possibility of overt ethnic confrontation was to gerrymander multi-ethnic communities into relatively homogeneous electoral districts so as to facilitate intra-ethnic candidate contestation. As one Yugoslav author pointed out, "an emphasis on several

TABLE 6.4
The Occupational Composition of Candidates and Elected Deputies to the Republican Assemblies in 1969[a]

Occupational Sector of Candidates and Elected Deputies	Political Chambers[b]			Functionally-Specialized Chambers[c]		
	First Stage: Candidates Proposed	Second Stage: Candidates Slated	Third Stage: Candidates Elected	First Stage: Candidates Proposed	Second Stage: Candidates Slated	Third Stage: Candidates Elected
Party (LCY) and Mass Organization Functionaries	27.5	42.3	48.1	9.1	11.1	12.3
Managerial Personnel in Economic Enterprises and Non-Economic Institutions	26.4	25.2	25.9	33.9	34.8	46.0
Professional Intelligentsia-Specialists (Technicians, Engineers, Economists, Doctors, Lawyers, Professors, etc.)	29.5	18.9	24.0	45.6	40.0	33.6
Workers, "Direct Producers"	4.5	4.5	--	7.5	9.7	5.3
Peasants, "Agriculturalists"	2.7	3.6	--	0.9	2.3	2.6
Students	1.8	0.9	--	1.5	1.4	--
Others (Pensioners, Housewives, etc.)	7.6	4.6	2.0	2.1	0.7	0.2
Total	100.0	100.0	100.0	100.0	100.0	100.0
	(N=443)	(N=111)	(N=54)	(N=1142)	(N=215)	(N=113)

Source: Sergije Pegan, (1970) "Socijalni sastav predstavničkih tela" in Milan Matić, et al., (eds.), Skupštinski izbori, 1969, Belgrade: Institut Društvenih Nauka.

[a] Based on data for candidates and elected deputies to the Republican Assemblies in thirty Yugoslav communes.

[b] Political Chambers: The popularly elected Republican Chambers in the Republican Assemblies.

[c] Functionally-Specialized Chambers: The Educational-Cultural, Economic, and Social-Health Chambers. This designation includes the Chamber of Communes in Montenegro and Macedonia, the Organizational-Political Chamber in Croatia and Serbia, and the Socio-Political Chamber in Bosnia-Hercegovina.

candidates of different nationality groups for a single legislative seat could, without these measures, divide the electorate and make it unworkable to conduct the election" (Damjanović, 1972:64).[6]

The introduction of electoral choice in 1967 and 1969 was, then, a rather manipulated affair: not only was the option of competitive parties, or even competitive socialist parties, ruled out, but the occupational and especially the ethnic backgrounds of candidates were an object of scrutiny and control. The question of how many candidates would be allowed to contest a constituency election raised similar difficulties for a party whose commitment to a pluralistic electoral system was fraught with ambiguities and undefined, but very real, limitations. Should the determination of the extent of candidate choice be essentially a matter for the citizenry of each constituency to decide (subject of course to very general party surveillance), or should the party actively intervene to insure that choice was offered only in situations where the privilege might not be "abused" by discontented elements in the society? With the aid of the electoral data at our disposal, some light can be cast on this matter.

In statistical terms, the task of interpreting the nature of the process of offering candidate choice begins with the determination of which constituency characteristics are associated with greater or lesser numbers of candidates. The characteristics available for analysis are the same demographic ones used in Chapter 5, with the exception that the percentage employment in agriculture variable can now be included in the analysis. The procedure we employ begins with a multiple regression analysis of all potential independent variables on the number of candidates per district in each election year.[7] In these regressions, a standardized regression coefficient or beta weight value of .10 once again is taken as the standard by which an independent variable's effect on the dependent variable is considered to be important enough to merit the retention of the variable in the regression equation. Since we are dealing with a sample of cases (although not a probability sample), levels of statistical significance can also be taken into account in this regard. It turns out, however, that with the sample sizes at our disposal, no beta weight as large as .10 ever failed to achieve a .01 level of significance in any of the regression analyses in this chapter; therefore the operative criterion is in fact the size of the beta weight. The level of significance will be of greater value in the analyses of variance which comprise the second step in the procedure, but even in these instances, our attention will be focused more on the size of the coefficients themselves.

In the 1965/67 elections, only two of the thirteen available independent variables proved to have a significant relationship with the dependent variable according to the above-mentioned criteria: they are the year of election (1965 or 1967) for the split election of 1965/67 and the constituency's ethnic entropy or H(E). The intercept and partial regression (slope) coefficients for the final regression equation containing these two independent variables are given in Table 6.5, which also presents, in parentheses, standardized partial regression coefficients or beta weights associated with the independent variables. The beta weights indicate that the principal influence on the number of candidates is the year of election, with districts which held 1967 elections having more candidates than those which held 1965 elections. The tendency for the less ethnically diverse districts to have more candidates is a somewhat less important factor.

At this point, it is appropriate to introduce "republic" as a control factor, since these are separate republic-level elections. The analysis of variance technique has the important feature of permitting the simultaneous introduction of both nominal-level independent variables, such as republic, and interval-level independent variables into the analysis. Since the coefficients generated for the interval-level variables or covariates correspond to the (unstandardized) partial regression coefficients of the regression technique, our objective is to discover in what manner the regression coefficients associated with the independent variables are altered when republic is introduced as a factor in an analysis of variance. In the present case, it is evident from the first analysis of variance in Table 6.5 that there is a significant, although rather weak, grouping effect associated with republic (eta=.14); that is to say, the five republics differ significantly in their mean numbers of candidates per constituency. What is the effect of this relationship on the previously-discovered relationships between candidate numbers and the two independent variables, year of election and ethnic entropy? This question is answered by the second analysis of variance, in which these two variables are introduced as covariates. The first result to note is that the effects of both republic and ethnic entropy become weaker and statistically insignificant; the year of election, in contrast, carries the same weight as it did in the regression. The simultaneous reduction in the sizes of the coefficients associated with republic and H(E) indicates a degree of overlap in their effects on the dependent variable: in other words, a portion of the grouping effect of republic is due to the fact that it was to some extent the ethnically less diverse republics that averaged more candidates per constituency. Whether this is coincidental or part of an overall design to keep competition out of ethnically diverse areas is impossible to determine definitively, but there is a curious development to this relationship in 1969 which will be considered below. Apart from this, the only other factor affecting the number of candidates in 1965/67 is the fact that more candidate choice was offered in constituencies having elections in 1967.

Table 6.6 presents the corresponding analysis of the determinants of the number of candidates per constituency in the 1969 election. In this case, four main independent variables achieved sizeable and significant partial regression coefficients: mean income, which is related positively to the number of candidates, and the proportions of Moslems, Serbs and Slovenes, which are associated with lower candidate numbers. Unfortunately, the presence of the last-named variable in the regression equation raises a problem with respect to the introduction of republic as a factor in an analysis of variance. This is because the overlap (collinearity) between the presence of Slovenes and one of the republics, Slovenia, is so great that both variables cannot be entered simultaneously. The republic variable cannot be ignored, however, because the first analysis of variance in Table 6.6 clearly establishes that the number of candidates per constituency in 1969 is significantly related to the republic within which the constituency is located (eta=.21). We shall therefore proceed as before, but with the republic of Slovenia and the proportion of Slovenes (temporarily) deleted.

The second regression equation in Table 6.6 shows that the effect of the first three variables on the number of candidates, as indicated by their regression coefficients, scarcely changes when the Slovenian element in the relationship is excluded. In as much as those three variables are concerned, the deletions have not affected matters noticeably at all. Turning to the analysis of variance by republic with these three independent variables as covariates (Analysis No. 2), a very interesting pattern of findings emerges. With republic controlled, the effect of income remains significant and

TABLE 6.5
Explaining Choice Offered, 1965/67 Republican Elections

A. REGRESSION ANALYSIS

Dependent Variable	Intercept	Independent Variables		Multiple Corre-lation
		Year (1965 or 1967)	H(E)	
No. of Candidates per Constituency, 1965/67	-6.12	.11** (.24)[a]	-.12** (-.13)	.27

B. ANALYSIS OF VARIANCE

Dependent Variable	Analysis No.	Factor Republic	Covariates		Multiple Corre-lation
			Year (1965 or 1967)	H(E)	
No. of Candidates per Constituency, 1965/67	1.	.14*			.14
	2.	.10	.11**	-.09	.30

* Significant at .05 level.
** Significant at .01 level.
[a] Standardized partial regression coefficients (beta weights) given in brackets.

strong, but both of the ethnic variables show much weaker and insignificant partial slope coefficients; the coefficient associated with republic, on the other hand, scarcely changes at all. This pattern of findings is consistent with the interpretation that the ethnic variables are in fact surrogates, representing effects better attributed to differences between republics rather than to ethnic groups. Since the tendency for numbers of candidates to be lower in Slovenia can be attributed statistically either to the republic or to the ethnic group, what the analysis points to is the existence of just two principal influences on the dependent variable: mean income and republic. This is represented in the third and final analysis of variance in Table 6.6, in which the Slovenian cases are included once again and the effects of the two independent variables are assessed simultaneously over all available cases. It will be noted that the inclusion of Slovenia only slightly alters the size of the coefficients associated with the two variables, and both variables remain significantly associated with the number of candidates variable.

TABLE 6.6
Explaining Choice Offered, 1969 Republican Elections

A. REGRESSION ANALYSIS

Dependent Variable	Analysis No.	Intercept	Independent Variables				Multiple Corre- lation
			Income	% Mosl.	% Serbs	% Slov.	
No. of Candidates per Constituency, 1969	1. All Cases	2.03	.18** (.19)[a]	-.50** (-.10)	-.33** (-.10)	-.38** (-.15)	.24
	2. Slovenia Excluded	2.04	.22** (.18)	-.47** (-.10)	-.34** (-.10)	--	.25

B. ANALYSIS OF VARIANCE

Dependent Variable	Analysis No.	Factor Republic	Covariates			Multiple Corre- lation
			Income	% Mosl.	% Serbs	
No. of Candidates per Constituency, 1969	1. All Cases	.21**	--	--	--	.21
	2. Slovenia Excluded	.19**	.20**	-.22	-.14	.27
	3. All Cases	.20**	.18**			.27

** Significant at .01 level.
[a]Figures in brackets are the standardized partial regression coefficients or beta weights.

From the substantial number of possible influences on the extent of candidate choice offered in 1965/67 and in 1969, the actual number of variables shown to be related to candidate choice is surprisingly few. The fact that more candidates to be offered in 1967 than in 1965 was already known. There is, in addition, the curious finding that ethnic entropy is related to choice offered in 1965/67 but mean income fulfils this capacity in 1969. This suggests the possibility that government concern over the offering of choice in ethnically heterogeneous constituencies in 1965/67 might have given way to a locally-based push on the part of the more developed areas of the country for greater liberalization of the electoral process. Finally, there is evidence that the individual republics were adopting distinctive patterns of candidate choice.

TABLE 6.7
Multiple Classification Analysis of Choice Offered, Republican Elections of 1965/67 and 1969

Dependent Variable	Derived From	Grand Mean	Deviations from Grand Mean by Republic				
			Bosnia	Croatia	Mace.	Slov.	Vojv.
No. of Candidates per Constituency, 1965/67	Table 6.5 Analysis of Variance, No. 1	1.22	-.01	-.02	-.09	.10	n.a.[a]
No. of Candidates per Constituency, 1969	Table 6.6 Analysis of Variance, No. 1	1.84	-.30	.27	.09	-.05	.01
No. of Candidates per Constituency, 1969 adjusted for income	Table 6.6 Analysis of Variance, No. 3	1.84	-.24	.25	.14	-.18	.02

[a]not available

The nature of the republican patterning in the offering of candidate choice is indicated by the multiple classification analyses in Table 6.7. The 1965/67 findings, which were derived from the first analysis of variance in Table 6.5, show the principal deviators to be Slovenia, which tended to have more candidates per constituency than the overall average of 1.22, and Macedonia, which had a less than average number of candidates in that election. The pattern by republic, however, changed considerably in 1969. In that election, Slovenia ranked below the average of 1.84 candidates per constituency, while Macedonia ranked somewhat higher than the average. Moreover, Croatia and Bosnia, which were very close to average in 1965/67, deviated much more profoundly in 1969, with Bosnia falling behind and Croatia shooting considerably ahead of the mean. Vojvodina (for which the 1965/67 electoral data are not available), was about average in candidate numbers in 1969. Since income was an important influence on candidate numbers in 1969, the third row of Table 6.7 presents the 1969 deviations adjusted for the effect of income. It is evident that the overall pattern is affected only slightly by that variable: the deviations of Bosnia and Croatia are reduced somewhat, but those of Macedonia and Slovenia are actually enhanced once income levels are controlled. Evidently, the greater significance of republic in 1969 represented a trend toward distinctive republican patterns of candidate choice which, unlike the 1965/67 pattern, is not modified by other influences like income or ethnicity. In other words, a greater degree of republican autonomy is evident in the process of offering choice, with certain republics such as Croatia and Macedonia more prone to take advantage of this autonomy than others, for reasons we shall explore below.

Keeping in mind the differences in the offering of choice in 1965/67 and 1969, it now becomes instructive to examine the process of expansion in candidate numbers per constituency more closely. One possible hypothesis concerning the expansion of choice would be that it took place in a cumulative fashion: that is, those constituencies that introduced candidate choice in 1965/67, whether through official satisfaction with the results or through constituency pressures in its favor, tended to expand or at least to maintain that choice in 1969. Plausible though it seems, this hypothesis is not borne out by the data: there is virtually no correlation (r=.034) between the number of candidates offered in 1965/67 and the number offered in 1969. Indeed, the greater the number of candidates a district had in 1965/67, the less it increased its candidate numbers in 1969. This is indicated by a sizeable negative correlation of -.41 between the number of candidates in 1965/67 and the increase between 1965/67 and 1969,[8] a finding that is matched at the federal level by a correlation of -.58. This suggests that, at the very least, the distribution of multi-candidacies was such that no momentum was allowed to build up in particular constituencies across the two elections.[9]

We can incorporate this interesting finding into the analysis by taking as the dependent variable the change in candidate numbers per district between 1965/67 and 1969, and repeating the procedure that was used in the explanation of the number of candidates in 1969. There is no need to go into detail concerning the findings, for they parallel those of the earlier analysis very closely. Three of the same four independent variables -- income and the proportions of Moslems and Slovenes -- emerge as significant predictors of the change in candidate numbers, and the number of candidates in 1965/67 also enters the regression significantly. When republic is introduced as a factor in an analysis of variance with income, the number of candidates in 1965/67 and the proportion of Moslems as covariates (the proportion of Slovenes and the republic of Slovenia being excluded for the moment), only the former two covariates retain statistical significance. With the interpretation that the ethnic variables are functioning here as surrogates for republican differences as before, the Slovenian cases were re-introduced and a final analysis of variance showing the effect of just three variables -- republic, income, and the number of candidates in 1965/67 was produced. This is given as the third analysis of variance in Table 6.8, which also lists the intermediate steps in the analysis for the interested reader. It will be noted that the effect of income and republic are very much as they were in Table 6.6; the only difference is the very substantial contribution from the number of candidates in 1965/67, a variable which raises the multiple correlation to a respectable .47.

The presence of a "counter-cumulative" effect in the offering of candidate choice in these elections strongly implies an element of manipulation in the process: in order to keep the pluralist experiment under control, the enormous expansion of choice from 1965/67 to 1969 was carried out in a fashion that appears designed to minimize any possible accumulation of popular expectations. A manipulative dimension may also

TABLE 6.8
Explaining Change in Choice Offered, 1965/67 to 1969

A. REGRESSION ANALYSIS

Dependent Variable	Analysis No.	Intercept	No. of Cands.	Income	% Mosl.	% Slov.	Multiple Correlation
			Independent Variables				
Change in No. of Candidates, 1965/67 - 1969	1. All Cases (n=317)	1.84	-.90** (-.39)[a]	.18** (.15)	-.56** (-.11)	-.46** (-.13)	.46
	2. Slovenia Excluded (N=278)	1.88	-.95** (-.38)	.17** (.15)	-.50** (-.11)	--	.44

B. ANALYSIS OF VARIANCE

Dependent Variable	Analysis No.	Factor Republic	No. of Cands.	Income	% Mosl.	Multiple Correlation
			Covariates			
Change in No. of Candidates, 1965/67 - 1969	1. All Cases	.22**				.22
	2. Slovenia Excluded	.21**	-.96**	.17**	-.28	.46
	3. All Cases	.20**	-.90**	.17**		.47

** Significant at .01 level.
[a]Standardized partial regression coefficients (beta weights) given in brackets

lie behind the negative relationship in 1965/67 between ethnic entropy and candidate numbers. This can be seen more clearly with the aid of Table 6.9, which explores the relationship over the two elections. The left-hand column of the table presents the mean ethnic entropy values for districts according to their number of candidates in 1965/67. A distinct negative relationship is evident with one-candidate constituencies being nearly twice as ethnically entropic as three-candidate races. Of the 443 constituencies in 1965/67, 316 can be matched up with 1969 constituencies. The analysis of these matched cases is given on the right-hand side of the table. The first point to note is that these districts show a similar, if somewhat weaker, negative relationship in 1965/67 (Column A), indicating that this sample is fairly representative of the larger set of cases. If we examine the

TABLE 6.9
Mean Ethnic Entropy, 1965/67, by Number of Candidates, 1965/67 and 1969

		All 1965/67	Matched (1965/67-1969) Districts			
		Districts	(A) Overall	(B) By No. of Cands., 1969		
				1	2	3
No. of Candidates, 1965/67	1.	.90 (356)[a]	.97 (257)	1.00 (127)	.94 (77)	.86 (36)
	2.	.78 (77)	.86 (52)	.78 (22)	.88 (25)	.92 (5)
	3.	.59 (10)	.67 (8)	--[b]	--	--

[a]Figures in parentheses refer to number of cases.
[b]Too few cases for the breakdown.

experience of these constituencies in 1969 (Column B), we note a curious divergence in pattern: among the more entropic districts that had single candidates in 1965/67, a similar pattern is reproduced in 1969 whereby the less entropic among them received more than one candidate. The ethnically less diverse and hence less "sensitive" districts which were allowed two candidates in 1965/67, however, follow the opposite pattern in which the more ethnically diverse districts offered more candidates. These tendencies are not so strong that we can unequivocally infer the presence of a deliberate design to restrict choice in more ethnically mixed and potentially troublesome areas, but it does show, at the very least, that the absence of an effect by ethnic entropy in 1969 can be attributed to two opposite patterns relating ethnic diversity to candidate numbers, rather than to no pattern at all.

If the tendencies to by-pass ethnically diverse areas and to increase candidate numbers less in those districts that were competitive in 1965/67 provide evidence of manipulation in the offering of choice, there are also indications of other processes at work. These apparently are of two sorts. First, there is the tendency in 1969 for the various republics to move towards greater divergence and distinctiveness in their levels of candidate choice. This finding accords with other evidence, to be discussed, concerning the assertion of degrees of autonomy on the part of republican party organizations which disturbed the central party leadership, and that most probably contributed to the abolition of the system of electoral pluralism itself. As for the effect of popular pressures, the clearest evidence from our data is the relationship between choice offered in 1969 and mean income: independent of republican patterns, higher income districts across the country tended to have more candidates. Whether this relationship is due to the behavior of local party organizations or to the populace itself cannot be determined from the data alone, but there are other indications that the citizenry was not a passive spectator in the pluralist experiment. For instance, even as early as the 1967 elections, individuals in a number of electoral districts were able to get proposed, nominated, and even elected without official support, and sometimes in direct opposition to the local or more superior party authorities.[10] Reacting to the surprises of the 1967 elections as well as to other manifestations of unmanaged political pressure from below, such as the Belgrade student rebellion in 1968, party leaders did attempt to assert more control over events. In preparation for the 1969 elections, a new law gave the Socialist Alliance even greater leeway to influence the nomination and composition of candidates, and made it more difficult for non-official or unorganized political forces to get their candidate on the ballot. In effect the threshold of recruitment for the legislative elite, which had never been open very wide, was again narrowed. Nevertheless, the 1969 election demonstrated that it was still possible for a small number of officially unacceptable candidates to get a foot in the door. As in 1967, there were cases involving the appearance of "private candidates" who had not received local party sponsorship. In fact, in several instances candidates and their supporters even crossed the boundary of what the regime regarded as tolerable conflict among socialist alternatives and engaged in a so-called "struggle for power." It was even officially alleged that these practices sometimes aroused unsavory remnants of bourgeois pluralism such as "canvassing" (korteštvo, or campaigning by means of group-oriented appeals and attacks on fellow candidates) and "cheap demagogy" (electoral promises) -- very distressing developments indeed.

We therefore conclude that the offering of candidate choice at the republic level was an ambiguous undertaking at best. It is true that the number of candidates increased enormously in a very short period of time and that great care was taken to ensure that no ethnic group was slighted in the candidate selection process. Moreover, the divergence in the extent of choice offered in the various republics suggests that central political control had diminished, and popular pressures at the local level in favor of competition may have been evidenced in the tendency for the more developed and affluent districts to come up with greater numbers of unofficial candidates. Yet, there is no dearth of evidence to point to official manipulation at every stage in the process: in the backgrounds of candidates, in the allocation of plural candidacies across the electoral districts, and the counter-cumulative method by which choice was expanded. It therefore becomes of critical importance to determine how the Yugoslav electorate responded to the implementation of the regime-strategy. Two aspects of that response are relevant here: the extent to which the invalidation option was used to express dissatisfaction and the manner and extent that the choice was taken up by the electorate. In the next section, we shall deal with the first of these aspects.

BALLOT INVALIDATION IN A COMPETITIVE ELECTORAL SYSTEM

The analysis of political incorporation in Chapter 5 relied heavily upon the tendencies of invalidation levels in federal elections to be patterned geographically, and to be negatively related to turnout levels. Both findings were essential to the utilization of invalidation rates as indicative of the state of political incorporation across the system. We also speculated that if invalidation in republic-level elections possessed these same characteristics, the more widespread experimentation with candidate choice at that level might be a very instructive object of investigation for purposes of assessing the overall effect of electoral pluralism on political incorporation. In Table 6.10, these points are explored by means of analyses of variance of republic-level constituency invalidation rates in the 1960s by region, number of candidates, and turnout levels. Concerning the first point, the findings reveal that invalidation does group by region and is associated negatively with turnout in all three elections. Following the logic of the last chapter, we take these two findings to mean that invalidation (and turnout) in republic-level elections reflects a society-wide patterning of levels of political incorporation rather than simply the expression of dissent by individual voters.

The similarity in the interpretation of elections at the two levels of analysis makes it meaningful to pose the question that inspired this chapter, namely, how is dissent influenced by the offering of more extensive candidate choice in the republic elections? Much of the answer is contained in the multiple classification analysis (MCA) of Table 6.10, which shows that the effect is generally negative in direction -- the more the candidates, the lower the invalidation level -- and that, for the overwhelming majority of constituencies that had one or two candidates, the effect is much stronger in 1969 than in 1965/67. These findings are reminiscent of the corresponding results at the federal level, reported in Table 5.9, which showed a weak positive relationship in 1965/67 that was reversed in 1969. Apparently, the effect that the expansion in multi-candidacies had in lowering invalidation rates began earlier at the republic level, perhaps because at that level a higher proportion of constituencies had more than one candidate in 1967. In any case, it is very clear that the effect in 1969 is much more pronounced at the republic level. Comparing the MCA deviations by number of candidates in Tables 5.9 and 6.10, we see that in 1969 one-candidate constituencies at the federal level averaged 0.5 percent above the mean invalidation rate of 6.9 percent, while one-candidate constituencies at the republican level were fully 1.4 percent above the 6.9 percent average. Conversely, two and three-candidate federal races were 0.8 percent and 0.2 percent below the mean on invalidation, while at the republican level they were 1.2 percent below the (same) mean in each case. Our speculation that more widespread introduction of plural candidacies at the republican level may have resulted in its having a greater effect on invalidation is thus supported by the data.

The relationship is not, however, perfectly monotonic. The multiple classification analysis in Table 6.10 also shows that the four- and five-candidate constituencies in 1969 are somewhat exceptional in that their mean invalidation rates were above the overall mean. Upon careful examination, it becomes evident that these rather high means are due entirely to just two four-candidate constituencies and one five-candidate constituency that had particularly high invalidation rates -- presumably for reasons specific to those constituencies. These exceptions apart, the overall pattern is one that points to an even greater incorporating effect at the republican level of the experiment in pluralist socialism.

A clearer picture of the relationship between choice and dissent may be derived from an examination of the effect of changes in the number of candidates on the expansion of invalidation across these elections. The shifting of attention towards the process of change in these variables permits us to evaluate the effect of the non-cumulative pattern of candidate expansion more carefully, and also to investigate the possibility

TABLE 6.10
Invalidation per Constituency by Region, Number of Candidates, and Turnout, Republician Elections of 1965/67 and 1969

A. ANALYSIS OF VARIANCE

| Dependent Variable | Factors | | Covariate | Multiple Corre- |
	Region	No. of Candidates	Turnout	lation
Invalidation, 1963	.63**	--	-.08**	.56
Invalidation, 1965/67	.43**	.11	-.32**	.52
Invalidation, 1969	.48**	.30**	-.11**	.50

B. MULTIPLE CLASSIFICATION ANALYSIS

| Dependent Variable | Grand Mean | Deviations from Grand Mean by No. of Candidates | | | | | |
		1	2	3	4	5	6
Invalidation, 1965/67	5.3%	0.2% (221)[a]	-0.7% (42)	-2.4% (6)	--	--	--
Invalidation, 1969	6.9%	1.4% (211)	-1.2% (200)	-1.2% (62)	0.5% (17)	1.6% (8)	-1.3% (2)

** Significant at .01 level.
[a] Numbers of cases given in brackets.

that the expansion of invalidation was a two-step process, with the year of the 1965/67 election being the critical factor. The findings of this analysis are presented in Table 6.11. The principal effect in the Table is the one produced by the year of the 1965/67 elections. The multiple classification analysis in the lower part of the Table shows that constituencies which held elections in 1967 experienced average increases in invalidation levels of 6.5 percent (4.6% + 1.9%) over their 1963 levels, while constituencies that went to the polls in 1965 showed invalidation gains averaging just 2.9 percent (4.6% - 1.7%). From 1965/67 to 1969, the situation was almost

TABLE 6.11
Changes in Constituency Invalidation Levels by Year of Election and Change in Numbers of Candidates, 1963 to 1965/67 and 1965/67 to 1969

A. ANALYSIS OF VARIANCE

Dependent Variable	Factors		Multiple Correlation
	Year (1965 or 1967)	Change in No. of Cands.	
Change in Invalidation, 1963-1965/67	.43**	.15*	.42
Change in Invalidation, 1965/67-1969	.30**	.26**	.40

B. MULTIPLE CLASSIFICATION ANALYSIS

Dependent Variable	Grand Mean	Deviations from Grand Mean by			
		Year		Change in No. of Candidates	
Change in Invalidation, 1963-1965/67	4.6%	1965	-1.7% (137)[a]	0	0.3% (214)
		1967	1.9% (126)	+1	-0.9% (43)
				+2	-3.0% (6)
Change in Invalidation, 1965/67-1969	2.1%	1965	1.7% (163)	-2	2.3% (3)
		1967	-1.8% (158)	-1	3.0% (22)
				0	0.8% (160)
				+1	-1.1% (83)
				+2	-2.6% (36)
				+3	-0.3% (11)
				+4	-1.6% (5)
				+5	-6.0% (1)

** Significant at .01 level.
[a] Number of cases given in brackets.

exactly reversed, as the deviations attest, producing a uniform overall increase across the constituencies from 1963 to 1969. It is evident that the key liberalizing steps taken by the regime between 1965 and 1967 had the same effect in stimulating increases in invalidation at the republic level as they had at the federal level, although invalidation rates had already risen more substantially before 1966 at the republic level than at the federal level. The importance of this series of findings is that the countervailing tendencies of greater candidate choice depressing invalidation and greater liberalization stimulating it, findings which were already evident in the federal election data, were even more strongly present at the republic level. It is interesting to examine the way in which the two factors interacted. The MCA deviations in Table 6.11 show that constituencies which lost candidate numbers between 1965/67 and 1969 had greater than average increases in invalidation. In particular the constituencies that lost one candidate experienced a very large invalidation increase of 3.0 percent above the mean increase. The plurality of constituencies that did not change their candidate numbers (most of them having just one candidate in both elections) were also somewhat above average in their invalidation increases (0.8 percent). On the other hand, constituencies that had increased numbers of competing candidates experienced substantially less growth in invalidation. The only exception, a partial one at that, is the group of eleven constituencies that gained three candidates, but this group contains two of the three deviant constituencies noted above. It seems apparent from the findings reported in this Table that the widespread experimentation with electoral choice at the republic level did indeed have a rather striking effect in suppressing the expansion of invalidation provoked by the change in the political climate; conversely, the counter-cumulative manipulation in candidate numbers whereby some constituencies actually lost candidate numbers in 1969 was greeted by the electorate with marked disapproval. Since the overall trend was towards higher candidate numbers, it would appear at this point that the offering of electoral choices could be viewed as a rather successful incorporation strategy.

The factors affecting invalidation levels that have been considered thus far are essentially political; both the year of the 1965/67 election and the number of candidates reflect changes in official policy which we have categorized under the label of pluralist socialism. Before drawing further conclusions, it would be appropriate to introduce economic and ethnic variables into the analysis in order to determine where these types of influence, which were so important at the federal level, fit into the picture. Our data presentation will be the same as in the proceding section: first a regression equation containing the major predictor variables will be given, then the effects due to differences between republics will be taken into account by means of an analysis of variance with republic as a factor. We will depart from the standard format here by concerning ourselves solely with the 1969 election and the process of change from 1965/67 to 1969. We have made this change because the main explanatory variables that enter into regressions of invalidation in 1965/67 and change in invalidation between 1963 and 1965/67 were ethnic, and we have a particularly small and ethnically unrepresentative sample of republics for those elections. There is no reason to expect that any relationships found would hold up if a larger range of data had been available.

The 1969 electoral data present a very different picture, but one which is not immediately apparent from the regression analysis reported in Table 6.12. Of the five independent variables in the regression of invalidation (1969), three are ethnic: the proportions of Macedonians, Hungarians, and Moslems. The number of candidates also enters the

TABLE 6.12
Explaining Invalidation Levels, 1969

A. REGRESSION ANALYSIS

Dependent Variable	Intercept	Independent Variables						Multiple Correlation
		No. of Cands.	Income	% Mace.	% Hung.	% Moslem		
Invalidation per Constituency, 1969	.080	-.008** (-.18)	.004** (1.0)	.020** (.14)	.053** (.19)	-.032** (-.14)		.32

B. ANALYSIS OF VARIANCE

Dependent Variable	Analysis No.	Factors		Covariates					Multiple Correlation
		Republic	No. of Cands.	Income	% Mace.	% Hung.	% Moslem	Turnout	
Invalidation per Constituency, 1969	1.	.30**							.30
	2.	.33**	.27**	.004*	.013	.007	-.016	-.119**	.43
	3.	.38**	.27**	.004*				-.120**	.43

regression with a negative coefficient, as one would expect from the previous findings, and income figures in the regression are the weakest of the five independent variables. The main difference between the 1969 and the (unreported) 1965/67 results appears with the introduction of republic as a factor by means of analyses of variance. Unlike 1965/67, 1969 invalidation groups quite well by republic, as is shown in the first analysis of variance in Table 6.12. More important, however, is the second analysis of variance. In that analysis, the number of candidates and republic are entered as factors, and turnout (shown in Table 6.10 to be related to invalidation) is entered along with the four independent variables from the regression equation as covariates.[11] The result is quite surprising: the slope coefficients associated with all three ethnic variables are substantially reduced in size and become statistically insignificant because of the presence of the republic variable, while income, the least important independent variable in the regression, survives intact. The fact that republic eliminates the effects of the ethnic variables indicates that their relationships to invalidation levels are better attributed to differences among the separate republics than to ethnic phenomena. This tendency did not show up in the 1965/67 data because republic itself had a very weak influence on invalidation levels, nor did it appear in the 1969 federal electoral data. This finding does, however, bear a strong resemblance to the analysis of the number of candidates in 1969, reported in Table 6.6. In both cases, there is a strong grouping effect by republic that eliminates all significant ethnic effects, and, apart from this, a cross-republic effect caused by the income variable. Although the effect of income on invalidation is much weaker than it is on choice offered, it is interesting to note that the more economically developed (higher income) constituencies experienced both higher numbers of candidates and, controlling for this factor, higher invalidation levels as well, even though the two dependent variables are themselves negatively related.

Table 6.13 presents the results of a corresponding analysis of the change in invalidation between 1965/67 and 1969. We have already seen that the year of the 1965/67 election and the change in the number of candidates are significantly related to changes in invalidation (Table 6.11). Both of these variables enter the regression significantly, as do income and the proportion of Macedonians. The two other variables present in the regression of invalidation in 1969 -- the proportions of Hungarians and Moslems -- were also statistically significant predictors of the dependent variable, but are excluded because their beta weights were less than the cut-off level of .10. The analysis of variance follows a pattern very similar to that of the analysis of variance of invalidation in 1969: there is a grouping effect by republic: this effect eliminates the association between the sole ethnic variable, the proportion of Macedonians, but does not alter the coefficients associated with income, year of election, or the change in the number of candidates. Had the two other ethnic variables, Hungarians and Moslems, been included, their effect on the dependent variable would likewise have been reduced substantially and rendered insignificant by republic. Thus, in the process of invalidation expansion, as well as in the end result of that process, it is republican differences (to be examined below), income levels, and the impact of the two indicators of regime-strategy change, the year of election and the number of candidates, that influence invalidation levels.[12] As we have seen, of these four variables, the first three also determine the fourth.

There is one final aspect of the connection between candidate choice

TABLE 6.13
Explaining Change in Invalidation Levels, 1965/67 to 1969

A. REGRESSION ANALYSIS

Dependent Variable	Intercept	Change in Cand. Nos.	Year (65 or 67)	Income	% Mace.	Multiple Corre- lation
			Independent Variables			
Change in Invali- dation, 1965/67- 1969	1.29	-.011** (-.22)[a]	-.019** (-.34)	.009** (.14)	.025** (.15)	.44

B. ANALYSIS OF VARIANCE

Dependent Variable	Analysis No.	Republic	Change in Cand. Nos.	Year (65 or 67)	Income	% Mace.	Multiple Corre- lation
		Factors		Covariates			
Change in Invali- dation, 1965/67- 1969	1.	.17*					.17
	2.	.17	.27**	-.019**	.009*	.002	.47
	3.	.18**	.27**	-.019**	.009*		.47

* Significant at .05 level.
** Significant at .01 level.
[a] Beta weights given in brackets.

and ballot dissent that can be investigated with the data at our disposal. It is conceivable that invalidation levels could have varied not only according to the number of candidates but also according to competitiveness of the race among those candidates. One might speculate that in districts where the electoral race was highly competitive and the outcome close, voters may have taken much more interest in the election and may have been more likely to perceive it as a valuable institutional innovation. In such instances, an additional effect of candidate choice on invalidation levels, a bonus, as it were, may have acted to reinforce the regime's quest for legitimacy and support.

This hypothesis, however consistent with the interpretation presented thus far concerning the incorporative impact of electoral choice, turns out to be well off the mark. Indeed, the opposite is nearer the truth. There is actually a <u>positive</u> correlation of .21 (p<.001) across the multi-candidate districts between the invalidation level and the closeness of the election, as measured by a "candidate competitiveness" variable (candidate-choice entropy divided by its maximum possible value, as in Chapter 3). Moreover, the correlation increases with the number of candidates involved: among two candidate races the correlation is .16 (p<.01), among three candidate races, it rises to .26 (p<.02), while among the (admittedly few) four candidate races, it becomes .48 (p<.02). Voters were not deserting the invalidation option as candidate competition became closer, they apparently were resorting to it more.

The effect of candidate competitiveness is considered in conjunction with the effects of the other variables previously shown as related to 1969 invalidation levels (republic, the number of candidates, turnout, and income) in Table 6.14. Since candidate competitiveness is defined only for districts that have two or more candidates, the analysis of variance is confined to a subset of 291 competitive districts. The findings indicate that the positive relationship between invalidation and candidate competitiveness holds up when the other predictor variables are included in the analysis and their influences controlled. Moreover, a corresponding analysis of variance of the federal electoral data, also presented in Table 6.14, shows that a very similar, positive relationship between candidate competitiveness and invalidation in 1969 exists at that level as well. These findings reinforce the conclusion that invalidation tended to be more commonly resorted to in districts that had closer races among candidates.

There are two plausible interpretations of this relationship. One is that the closeness of competitive electoral races bred confusion among some voters that resulted in spoiled ballots. Given the meaning of ballot invalidation in the Yugoslav context, however, one would expect that this confusion, if it existed, would be more likely to find expression in abstention from the polls altogether. Is there a connection between competitiveness and low turnout? In fact, as we shall discover in the next section, there is an association between these variables in the suggested direction. However, this association, while consistent with the notion that close races engendered confusion and hence abstention, is also consistent with Coleman's entropy hypothesis, which provided the theoretical basis of Chapter 3. We shall explore this question more fully when we examine the determinants of electoral-choice entropy, but for now we simply point out that it would seem unlikely that an electorate which in other respects responded positively to the offering of choice should tend to abandon the electoral process altogether in situations where the choice turned out to be a meaningful one.

We are left with one other possibility, namely, that invalidation was not merely an alternative to be used when there was dissatisfaction over the limited extent of choice, but rather that it may have been perceived in competitive situations <u>as part of the choice spectrum itself</u>. In other words, under this interpretation invalidation did not decline or disappear when the candidate choice was attractive enough to cause the vote to be spread out more evenly among those choices because in those districts some voters may have perceived invalidation as part of the legitimate range of alternatives from which they could choose. If this interpretation is correct, it would mean that no amount of "socialist choice" would eradicate the invalidation problem; further liberalization, on the contrary, might actually have encouraged greater use of this outlet.

Such a startling conclusion cannot be proven by the evidence of a positive relationship between these two variables, or indeed by any other evidence generated from aggregate voting statistics. But consider another finding that appears in Table 6.14. The analysis of variance reveals that income and republic are significant determinants of invalidation in 1969, as before, but the effects produced by both the number of candidates and turnout are statistically insignificant and much weaker than they were in Table 6.12. This means that the tendencies over the entire set of districts for turnout and invalidation to vary together and for invalidation to decline as candidate numbers increased must have been due in large measure to the one-candidate constituencies. In competitive constituencies, on the other hand, invalidation does not appear to have functioned as a protest mechanism related to the other protest mechanism, abstention. Moreover, consistent with the idea that it was no longer a means of indicating non-incorporation, invalidation is not affected by how much candidate choice was actually present (the remaining effect of the number of candidates on invalidation appears from the MCA deviations in Table 6.14 to be due almost entirely to the three exceptional four- and five-candidate constituencies noted earlier). In other words, the data strongly support the idea that what really mattered to the electorate was that there be choice; once choice was present, resorting to invalidation as a protest device in conjunction with abstention was largely abandoned and invalidation rates began to respond positively to the taking up of candidate choice. Since invalidation does not decline with increasing candidate numbers (above two), it would seem reasonable to conclude that no future extension of choice within the one-party format would have caused it to diminish or disappear.

Thus, the experience with electoral choice turns out to be a strategy that had a profound effect on voting behavior, but not precisely the one the regime desired. In several ways electoral behavior broke out of the parameters that the electoral engineering of the regime had set up: it curtailed but did not roll back invalidation in constituencies that had candidate choice; it led to large increases in invalidation in constituencies that lost their choice or had never had it; and in general it appears to have functioned as part of a choice spectrum that the regime would have wished to restrict to the official candidate choices alone. Perhaps the pluralist socialism the electorate endorsed included just one choice too many for the regime, that is, the choice to reject the regime's choices entirely. The implication of these findings and conclusions will be more fully developed in the next chapter when the overall effect of the strategy of pluralist socialism on political incorporation is assessed.

CHOICE TAKEN UP

The electoral choice available to Yugoslav voters in 1969 may be conceived of either as the official choice among two or more candidates on the ballot or, more broadly, as the candidate choice together with the alternative of ballot invalidation. The analysis of invalidation in 1969 has indicated that the choice spectrum which the voters responded to was the broader one. Accordingly, the dependent variable in this section shall be the extent to which the vote in each 1969 constituency is distributed evenly among all voting options save that of abstention. This is measured by an

TABLE 6.14
The Effect of Competitiveness on Invalidation Levels, Republican and Federal Elections of 1969 Compared

A. ANALYSIS OF VARIANCE

Dependent Variable	Factors		Covariates			Multiple Corre- lation
	Republic	No. of Cands.	Turnout	Cand. Choice Entropy	Income	
Invalidation in Multi- Candidate Republican Races, 1969 (N=291)	.44**	.15	-.047	.060*	.006**	.50
Invalidation in Multi- Candidate Federal Races, 1969 (N=49)[a]	.28	.26	.013	.046	--	.43

B. MULTIPLE CLASSIFICATION ANALYSIS

Dependent Variable	Grand Mean	Deviations from Grand Mean by No. of Candidates				
		2	3	4	5	6
Invalidation, in Multi- Candidate Republican Races	6.2%	-0.1% (202)	-0.2% (62)	1.9% (17)	0.6% (8)	-1.6% (2)
Invalidation, in Multi- Candidate Federal Races	6.3%	-0.1% (43)	1.0% (5)	-0.2% (1)	--	--

* Significant at .05 level.
** Significant at .01 level.
[a]Significance levels not calculated for federal races.

entropy calculation of the fragmentation of the vote across all voting choices, and shall be referred to as "total-choice competitiveness."

Since invalidation functions primarily as a means of protest or dissent in single-candidate districts, in this section we shall concentrate exclusively on plural-candidate districts. While a great many factors that cannot be taken into account statistically, such as the personalities of the candidates, must have affected the final distribution of votes in these districts, we are assuming that more general tendencies and relationships will appear in the data. In particular, we shall explore the possibility that total-choice competitiveness is patterned geographically and related to turnout in a fashion that reflects our findings from the elections of the 1920s and 1930s.

Table 6.15 presents the results of the analysis of this variable. Six independent variables entered the regression significantly and with beta weights above .10. Of the six, five (the proportions of Hungarians, Moslems, Albanians, Croats, and the ethnic entropy of the constituency) are ethnic in nature. This finding suggests a tendency toward an ethnic patterning in competitiveness; however, in order to establish such a conclusion, it is necessary first to introduce republic as a control factor. This is implemented in the first analysis of variance in Table 6.15, which reveals that republic has an important and significant grouping effect. Moreover, only two of the five ethnic variables now entered as covariates survive that effect, namely the proportion of Albanians and the ethnic entropy of the district. The number of candidates, entered as a factor, is also an important influence, reflecting a general tendency for districts with larger numbers of candidates to be less successful at evenly distributing the vote among all of their choices.

The second analysis of variance is designed to test the entropy hypothesis that turnout entropy is related positively to choice entropy. The findings indicate that there is indeed a small but significant relationship of this sort. This relationship holds up when the other two significant covariates, the proportion of Albanians and ethnic entropy, are included as well (Analysis No. 3). In fact, in the third analysis of variance there are two ways in which traces of an entropy hypothesis effect are evidenced: directly via the relationship of turnout to competitiveness and indirectly via ethnic entropy. This latter relationship fits the theory because social complexity is hypothesized by Coleman to be the root of the political complexity that entropy is designed to measure, and social complexity in Yugoslavia has always meant first and foremost, ethnic diversity.

We do not wish to exaggerate the entropy theory interpretation of electoral behavior in 1969 as the coefficients, after all, are small, especially in comparison with the findings from the interwar elections. Moreover, it seems likely that part of the relationship between total-choice competitiveness and turnout entropy is due to the inclusion of invalidation as a choice, since invalidation and turnout are related (although weakly) in multi-candidate races (Table 6.14). The recalculation of the analysis of variance with invalidation removed as a choice in the competitiveness variable resulted in the fourth analysis of variance in Table 6.15. Clearly, the relationship of turnout to what may be termed as candidate competitiveness is weaker; the slope coefficient decreases from .06 to .04, which is significant only at the p=.092 level. This reduction in the strength of the relationship may be the result of the more restricted variance of this particular dependent variable which averages 94.8 percent of its maximum possible value.[13] Whether a further or even continued liberalization of the electoral process would have led to a more pronounced indication of the

TABLE 6.15
Explaining Choice Taken Up, 1969 Republican Elections

A. REGRESSION ANALYSIS

Dependent Variable	Intercept	Independent Variables[a]						Multiple Correlation
		No. of Cands.	Hg.	Ms.	H(E)	Al.	Cr.	
Total-Choice Competitiveness	.64	-.06** (.63)	.05** (.11)	-.09** (.19)	.03** (.19)	-.13** (-.17)	-.03** (-.13)	.66

B. ANALYSIS OF VARIANCE

Dependent Variable	Analysis No.	Factors		Covariates						Multiple Correlation
		Republic	No. of Cands.	H(T)	Hg.	Ms.	H(E)	Al.	Cr.	
Total-Choice Competitiveness	1.	.40**	.66**		-.01	-.00	.02*	-.10*	.03	.70
	2.	.40**	.64**	.06*						.70
	3.	.38**	.65**	.06**			.02*	-.11**		.71
Candidate Competitiveness	4.	.22**	.20**	.04						.33

[a]Hg., Ms., Al., Cr. refer to the proportions of Hungarians, Moslems, Albanians, and Croatians respectively.

presence of an entropy effect is impossible to know.[14] It is highly interesting and suggestive, nonetheless, that candidate numbers and invalidation levels turn out to be affected by income, while choice taken up is related to ethnic complexity, echoing the pattern of the prewar era despite the fact that ethnic competition per se was not permitted.[15]

One final aspect of the experience with electoral pluralism at the republic level that should be discussed is the republic patterns themselves. We have seen that each of the three main dependent variables considered here groups significantly by republic in 1969. In Table 6.7, the deviations by republic on mean numbers of candidates per district were listed. In Table 6.16, these data are supplemented by the corresponding deviations that were produced by the analysis of invalidation (Table 6.12), and the analyses of both total-choice competitiveness and candidate competitiveness in 1969 (Table 6.15).

The deviations by republic on these variables, considered together, paint a rather interesting picture of the 1969 election. Consider the case of Bosnia. Bosnia was the one republic that lagged behind in invalidation at the federal level in 1969; the data in Table 6.16 indicate that at the republic level, Bosnia fell behind the other four republics of our sample on all counts: fewer candidates were offered, invalidation once again was lower, and choice was less eagerly taken up. One gets the impression of a republic, troublesome in the pre-Communist period, but now firmly held in check. The situation is somewhat different for Croatia. The Croatian party organization, in particular, took an increasingly independent line in the late 1960s which caused the central party leaders much concern and, as will be elaborated in Chapter 7, probably contributed to the abandonment of the experiment with pluralist socialism. The enthusiasm with which the Croatian party embraced the more liberal political climate of 1969 would seem to be reflected in its offering the electorate the highest mean numbers of candidates of any republic; yet at the mass level this choice was less completely taken up than elsewhere, and invalidation rates were below average. Exactly the opposite pattern appears to be true of Vojvodina, where the mean numbers of candidates offered was about average, but both invalidation and choice taken up were very high. For Vojvodina, unlike Croatia, it appears that the electorate outdistanced the party in terms of its eagerness to exploit the expanded opportunities for choice.

Finally, we consider the cases of Macedonia and Slovenia. At geographically opposite ends of the country, the two republics have represented extremes in economic development and, to some extent, electoral dissent. Yet Slovenia, which was well ahead of the other republics in the offering of choice in 1967, fell behind in 1969; its traditionally high invalidation levels are no longer in evidence, and the extent to which choice was taken up is no more than average. If Slovenia no longer appears in the forefront, it is in part due to the catching-up of Macedonia, which was above average in levels of invalidation and numbers of candidates offered, although its degree of choice taken up appears not to have greatly suffered for it.

The patterns displayed by Slovenia and Macedonia echo the enormous levelling-off process that we noted in invalidation levels in the federal elections of the 1960s. But this is perhaps the only indication, because over the five republics whose voting behavior we have investigated, there is no evidence of a more general disappearance in republican differences. It seems that the rising degree of incorporation exhibited in federal voting behavior was not duplicated at the level of the republics,[16] despite the very

TABLE 6.16
Multiple Classification Analysis of Choice Offered, Invalidation, and Choice
Taken up by Republic, 1969 Republican Elections

Dependent Variable	Derived From	Grand Mean	Deviations from Grand Mean by Republic				
			Bosnia	Croatia	Mace.	Slov.	Vojv.
Number of Candidates	Table 6.6 No.3	1.84	-0.24	0.25	0.14	-.18	0.02
Invalidation Level	Table 6.12 No. 3	6.9%	-2.1%	-0.7%	0.7%	-0.0%	2.9%
Total Choice Competitiveness	Table 6.15 No. 3	.80	-.04	-.02	.00	.00	.05
Candidate Competitiveness	Table 6.15 No.4	.95	-.01	-.01	-.01	-.01	.03

extensive similarities between their voting patterns in other respects, and it
is this fact in particular that concerned many party leaders. As we have
seen, the results of the experiment in electoral pluralism were uncertain in
other respects as well: the lower invalidation levels that came with
increased candidate numbers turned out to be due more to large increases in
invalidation where choice was taken away or never provided; invalidation
looked much less like something that a sufficiently broad, but controlled,
candidate choice could eventually eradicate and more like a manifestation
that could become more popular as voters became accustomed to the
expression of preferences; and the process of candidate selection itself
might not always be controllable, as the occasional success of maverick
candidates and the apparent dissatisfaction over the counter-cumulative
pattern of plural-candidacies showed. The entire experiment, in short,
could be interpreted as being much more dangerous than was indicated
through analysis of the federal elections in Chapter 5. How the experiment
was in fact interpreted, by whom and with what purposes, forms a central
element of the next and final chapter, which looks at Yugoslavia in the
post-halcyon days of the 1970s and 1980s, the country's present state of
incorporation and cohesiveness, re-emergent ethnic problems, and the
search for direction in the post-Tito era.

NOTES

1. The initial commentaries on the limited choice for regional
assembly seats in the 1950s did not seem very approving:

in 31 districts in Croatia, two or more candidates were nominated. It is well known what kind of political life developed in these districts. We won't go into the fact that sometimes certain conceptions emerged from this political activity which our system of socialist democracy places on a level with a campaign struggle for soliciting votes. But it is worth mentioning that at least in the majority of these districts, there was a very poor percentage turnout in elections, generally below the overall average. This can perhaps be attributed in certain cases to unprincipled propaganda which disoriented a certain portion of the electorate. (Borba, 31 December 1953:6)

2. All official reports of electoral results were examined. However, the officially published results of the elections to the Republican Chambers of Serbia and Montenegro offered only data on the number of votes received by the winning candidate. One might speculate that the absence of more complete returns in Serbia is the result of political sensitivity due to the relatively large number of upsets against regime (League) sponsored candidates and other negative manifestations in electoral behavior, which occurred in this republic in both 1967 and 1969. It also may reveal a more cautious stance toward political data and "scientific" inquiry by administrators of the Serbian and Montenegrin documentation services. Unfortunately, the election results reported in the press were too partial to compensate for the deficiency of the official sources. In the case of the province of Kosovo, the uniqueness of the electoral system prevented comparability with the other regions of the country.

3. The roughly similar deviations by republic above and below the mean did not occur automatically since the mean itself could have changed because of the absence of the three republics.

4. These data are not presented; however, a good indication of this similarity can be seen from a comparison of Tables 5.9 and 6.10, which analyze invalidation by region at the federal and republican levels respectively.

5. This process of matching communes to republican constituencies is described in detail in Appendix C.

6. The same observer pointed out that regime's efforts to avoid ethnic confrontation often led to the

creation of a certain artificial harmony, in a sense really fictional, an idealized picture, conflicts appeared to be solved, transformed in such a manner to lose some of their basic characteristics to create the impression that it is a question of different aspects of the same views and attitudes, making their presence less subjective, appearing as an influence which comes from the side, which isn't an expression of their community, etc. (Damjanović, 1972:64).

Although inter-ethnic contestation was discouraged in voting for the popular elected chambers in Yugoslav assemblies, the central legislature in the period (Federal Assembly) included a Chamber of Nationalities composed of deputies "delegated" by the assemblies in the republics and provinces. During the late 1960s, the Chamber of Nationalities became an important site for the expression of sectional and ethnic interests (Cohen, 1977). There are indications that everyone may not have been satisfied or understood the regime's ethnic arthmetic. An empirical study in one Bosnian electoral district revealed that few people acknowledged voting for representatives on the basis of ethnicity or locality (neighborhood), but that in informal conversations the question often arises: "why aren't our people also on the nomination list?" (Mujačić, 1971:1086-1089).

7. Since the dependent variable is not continuous, discriminant function analysis might be considered a more appropriate technique (although the dependent variable is not nominal in level, either). As it happens, discriminant analysis produced essentially the same predictor variables as regression analysis for both the number of candidates in 1965/67 and in 1969.

8. The number of candidates in 1965/67 variable was used to compute this correlation rather than the change in number of candidates from 1963 to 1965/67 because the two variables are equivalent (the number of candidates in 1963 being invariably one in those republics for which we have data), while the former variable is available for a larger number of cases.

9. This finding is consistent with the data in Table 6.7 which show that there is no continuity in the republican patterns of candidate offerings across the two elections.

10. It is interesting to note that the so-called "private candidates" in 1967 were not anti-communist or even always non-communist (the latter circumstance was permitted), but in some cases, popular communist war-heroes with a local following large enough to be elected without official backing. Ironically, most of these maverick candidates were either members or supporters of the conservative wing in the party, that is, the group that had opposed the recent series of economic and political reforms, including the liberalization of the electoral process. It appeared that the new electoral system, as one of a growing number of centers for political influence, offered itself to those best equipped to use it, irrespective of their underlying commitment to democratic norms.

11. The number of candidates variable, although (necessarily) treated as an interval-level variable for regression purposes, is entered in Table 6.12 and subsequent Tables as a factor in order to maintain continuity with previous Tables. The findings would be essentially the same if it had been entered as a covariate. As for turnout, since it is considered as a correlate rather than a cause of invalidation, it was not included as an independent variable in the regression analysis. It can, however, be included as a covariate of invalidation in the analysis of variance, a step which also enhances continuity with previous (and subsequent) Tables.

12. A "change in turnout" variable was not included in this analysis of variance although it is related negatively to change in invalidation because turnout data are not available for Bosnia in 1965 and these cases would have had to be excluded from the analysis.

13. This percentage shows that the candidate choice offered the electorate, however limited or manipulated, was amply embraced at the polls.

14. It is interesting that the main entropy effect occurs in three-candidate, rather than two-candidate races, mirroring a finding that Warwick (1983) found in U.S. Presidential elections, and suggesting that more extensive candidate choice might have produced a more pronounced entropy relationship.

15. Choice taken up is also related to the proportion of Albanians, but since the main center of Albanian concentration, the province of Kosovo, is not included in the analysis, we are unable to probe this relationship further. That all other ethnic relationships, except that of ethnic entropy itself, are eliminated by the republic variable appears to be the main point.

16. The decline in the grouping effect of republic on invalidation at the federal level in the 1960s, shown in Table 5.1, is not matched by any decline at the republic level. The corresponding eta coefficients are .10 (1965/67) and .30 (1969).

7
Consolidation Without Cohesion: Political Stability in a Fragile Mosaic

The fascinating political dynamics which characterized the 1969 elections represented the culmination of the experiment in pluralist socialism and a major watershed in Yugoslav political development. During the first fifty years of the state's existence (1918-1968) successive political elites utilized what was, arguably, the most varied repertoire of regime-strategies for coping with ethnic diversity ever attempted in a single country. In contrast, the period after 1969 has been marked by an uncharacteristic hesitancy and uncertainty over the future course of regime policy in this domain. The objective of this study has been to elucidate, to the fullest extent possible given the available sources of information, the effect on political cohesion of the various regime-strategies. In the next section, we shall briefly review the history of Yugoslavia's political cohesion derived from our analyses in order to set the context for a consideration of the developments and prospects of the 1970s and 1980s.

THE QUEST FOR POLITICAL COHESION: AN OVERVIEW OF THE FINDINGS

The most striking finding revealed by the analysis of voting patterns for the first decade of the country's history was the inability of the liberal-democratic regime to construct a cohesive polity. Admittedly, the odds were heavily against the regime's leaders from the beginning. In a political process marked by the recalcitrant opposition of almost all major ethnic groups to the strategy of charter-group hegemony employed by the Serbian elite, the multi-party majoritarian system merely articulated the strong nationality-based political commitments present in each region of the country. Lacking an earlier history of common experience as citizens of a single state, and with vivid memories of past rivalries and animosities, the country's diverse ethnic groups increasingly offered their support to a variety of sectional and separatist movements, each promising their respective audiences a better alternative than the new regime was willing to provide.

Many writers have portrayed the 1920s as another chaotic episode in Balkan history, colorfully describing the spectacle of ethnic conflict or enumerating the names of ethnic parties (Rabushka and Shepsle, 1972:199-202). The application of the entropy hypothesis to the analysis of successive legislative elections enabled us, however, to determine precise changes in the degree of political incorporation during this period. In this manner we were able to identify an overall trend toward non-incorporation that was not significantly inhibited by the regime's attempts to interfere with the electoral process. Our analysis of the elections indicated that after a decade of political hegemony and manipulation by the dominant ethnic group and the ensuing alienation of most other nationalities, the political system was even less cohesive than at the time of formation of the state (when pan-South Slavic sentiments and general optimism about newly won independence served as a temporary bond among ethnic groups and regions). The unbroken centrifugal pattern of party divisions and voter fragmentation resulted in a persistent syndrome of political obstruction, policy stagnation, and crisis on the elite level, finally precipitating the complete abandonment of democratic institutions by the monarchy at the beginning of 1929. The intensification of inter-group conflict and distrust caused by the failure of the first and most "liberal" Yugoslav regime and its hegemonic strategy created a legacy that was to haunt all subsequent efforts at political incorporation.

The decade of authoritarian rule after 1929 magnified the divisions which had burgeoned in the preceding period of political development. Although the King's dictatorial regime unveiled a new pan-ethnic strategy designed to transcend traditional cultural and regional loyalties, the highly exclusivist character of the new approach (large non-Slavic minorities and officially assimilated Slavic groups such as the Montenegrins and Macedonians were left out of the formula), and the realities of political power, betrayed the continuation of Serbian elite hegemony. The prohibition of overtly ethnic and regional political parties resulted in an artificial dualism between the official government-sponsored party on the one side, and an Opposition Bloc composed of all other forces alienated from the regime, on the other side. Within the latter camp each group or regional organization simply consolidated its parochial constituency, banding together only for the shortlived and blatantly manipulated elections held by the regime. Our analysis of voting data in this period revealed that the enormous reduction in the fragmentation of the party system imposed by the regime, as well as officially sponsored electoral corruption, failed to alter in any fundamental sense the underlying pattern of profound political non-cohesiveness in the system. Ironically, the regime's exclusivist and highly centralized strategy actually strengthened the resolve and popular base of most nationalist and sectional movements placed uncomfortably together in the Opposition Bloc. This combination of anxious constraint by the regime and persistent non-incorporation within the electorate became a vicious circle which prevented any real solution of the other serious problems facing the state.

In 1939, as international tensions mounted and political inmobilism and economic stagnation continued domestically, the regime finally changed its strategy and negotiated a compromise agreement with the leadership of the Croatian Peasant Party, the largest and strongest organization in the opposition camp. The new elite-focused consociational strategy underlying the agreement established a quasi-federal state structure, including the proportional allocation of central political offices and grants of limited regional autonomy to the country's two major groups (the implication was that the Slovenes would soon share in the arrangement with the Serbs and Croats). Unfortunately the new arrangements, which only had a modest chance of success, were adopted at an extremely inauspicious historical moment. The outbreak of the war in Europe, only days after the signing of the agreement, shifted attention almost exclusively toward military security and foreign relations, offering little opportunity for domestic political experimentation. It is worth mentioning, however, that the consociational strategy toward cultural diversity, although shortlived, was the most promising approach used in the interwar period. Given the deep divisions in the general population, partially fostered by the inept regime-strategies employed earlier, it is not surprising that an elite model of conflict regulation (presaging the "vanguardist" or one-party elite experiments that were soon to come) was perceived as offering an attractive method to maintain stability in the Yugoslav mosaic. Before that model could be fully implemented, however, the mosaic was shattered by a host of foreign and internal forces who had little fear that the young and still seriously divided Yugoslav state could repel their assault. The next "strategic" efforts to construct a more incorporated and durable political system would be in the hands of a new regime and a new revolutionary generation.

The World War II conflagration in Yugoslavia saw centrifugality and deadlock replaced by separatism and reciprocal massacre as twenty years of frustration and anger exploded in a bloody ethnic and political civil war. While each ethnic and regional movement implemented its special brand of ultra-nationalistic purification designed to liquidate or reduce its enemies, the Communist Party, in sharp contrast, promised all nationalities and regions in the country a new deal based on ethnic equality and the establishment of a federal system after the war. Although Serbs constituted the core of the communist-led partisan movement, the leadership consisted of a relatively unified and young group of revolutionaries from all the major ethnic groups and regions.

Once in power the Communists delivered on their promise to create a federal and more ethnically representative state. Most seasoned party leaders considered, however, that their recognition of "progressive" nationalist aspirations and their institutional accommodation of traditional loyalties would only be a temporary and largely symbolic gesture. Confident that revolutionary economic development would gradually erode pre-socialist forms of identity and result in the rather imminent fusion of groups on the basis of new ideological bonds, little attention or overt recognition was given to the serious ethnic problems still festering below the surface of the political process. Regional modernization and a transformation in consciousness through political indoctrination were seen as the best way to eliminate all "residual" values and difficulties. Unfortunately the belief that the national question had been solved in the wartime struggle was belied by the evidence from the early postwar elections which indicated that a number of important ethnic groups and regions were less than perfectly incorporated into the new political system. In the election of 1950, political non-incorporation was strongest in those areas and ethnic groups which had shown the greatest opposition or lack of support to the wartime partisan movement and its communist leadership.

Strains on regime cohesion deriving from ethnic factors continued into the next phase of Yugoslav political development (1951-1961). Although the regime underwent a fundamental political reorganization and political liberalization in the wake of the Tito-Stalin rift, the regime's strategy toward cultural diversity in this phase continued to stress the erosion of traditional ethnic and regional bonds, albeit through a more gradual and less administratively heavy-handed process than practiced earlier. This strategy of evolutionary merger was aimed at the creation of a new ethno-ideological identity -- socialist Yugoslavism -- which would replace existing loyalties to

142

cultural groups. The underlying basis or pre-condition for such Yugoslavism -- increasing economic equality and satisfaction among all groups and regions -- did not, however, develop in the anticipated manner. On the contrary, the economic gap between the more and less developed regions of the country actually widened as the overall industrialization of the country rapidly moved ahead. This economic imbalance led to serious divisions in the party elite regarding the distribution of power and regime's further development. As differences in regional economic development coincided closely with ethnic differences, it is not surprising that those more liberal party leaders (heavily concentrated in the northwestern areas of the country) who favored greater economic and political decentralization should also have opposed any centralized strategy of gradual cultural amalgamation. Although the overall levels of ballot invalidation declined through the elections of 1963, closer analysis of these elections revealed a pattern characterized by a substantial element of non-incorporation centering on the Hungarian and Slovenian sections of the country. Admittedly, the problem of distinguishing between ethnically based and economically based political behavior is very complex when using aggregate data, but it appears that at least up to the late 1950s, ethnic factors were still at the heart of electoral protest and non-incorporation.

By the early 1960s, the ascendancy of more liberal views in the party led to the abandonment of evolutionary merger as a strategy and the disappearance of socialist Yugoslavism as an officially endorsed concept. Convinced that economic equality and the elimination of tensions among the ethnic groups and regions would be a much longer process than earlier anticipated, the regime now endorsed a more pluralistic strategy which permitted the confrontation of distinct socialist alternatives within and outside of the electoral system, provided that the League of Communists remain the sole party organization and overall guardian of the country's cohesion.

The experiment with pluralist socialism was an ambitious and innovative undertaking which rendered results that were not altogether discouraging. For example, during the second half of the 1960s there emerged a degree of electoral uniformity never before seen in Yugoslavia, a development sharply suggestive of a general enhancement in overall political incorporation. It is true that invalidation was rising in response to the more liberal political climate, but more importantly, the standard ethnic patterning of that dissent had broken down, and the increases in invalidation seemed to be largely confined to districts which denied citizens an opportunity to choose among candidates. Those districts that were offered candidate choice not only manifested lower increases in levels of invalidation, but appeared to distribute their votes quite evenly among the candidates. This suggests that the provisions for political choice were very appealing to most voters, or at least seriously stimulated their attention, despite the absence of ethnic or party competition. The appearance of greater political incorporation is supported, moreover, by public opinion surveys that pointed to widespread satisfaction with electoral pluralism (Damjanović, 1967:146-149; Milosavlevski and Nedkov, 1968:130-133).

Despite certain positive features of the pluralist strategy there are reasons to question its long-term success. While invalidation declined where candidate choice was available, the evidence suggests that choice in itself could not have eliminated invalidation as a manifestation of dissent. It would be unwise to attribute too much significance to findings from an electoral experiment that had barely got off the ground before it was suppressed, but there are indications that the continuance of pluralist elections and the increased familiarity of citizens with the expression of their personal preferences might have encouraged the greater use of ballot invalidation as a political choice. We also discovered traces which suggest that the emergence of the interwar entropy pattern with its threatening basis in ethnic rivalry was not out of the question, although here the electoral evidence is (necessarily) very slight.

What the analysis indicates, in essence, is that electoral pluralism enhanced incorporation significantly, but at the risk of creating expectations for a wider expression of preferences that would probably not be compatible with a one-party state. Whether such emergent expectations might have eventually threatened the cohesion of the country would have itself depended on the extent to which ethnicity formed the basis for political choice, but it seems likely that popular demands for greater electoral competition would at least have posed a threat to the control and orthodoxy that any communist party, including the League of Yugoslav Communists, must insist upon. The leadership of the League, schooled in the maelstrom of Yugoslav ethnic history, was probably attuned to such ominous prospects. If so, it would help to explain the degree of conservatism with which they responded to the events of 1969, a response that seems surprising at first glance in view of the very modest rise in invalidation to 6.9 percent encouraged by the less repressive political climate. Fourteen years after the 1969 election, a prominent Yugoslav social scientist (NIN, 8 May 1983:15) shed some interesting light on what may have influenced the regime's thinking about the need to scrap the experiment with limited electoral pluralism:

> When during the struggle against Stalinism there emerged the slogan "democratization" and also the idea that it needed to be not only formal but real, a determination was made to offer more candidates in elections. The election of 1953 showed, however, that this led to conflicts among close comrades in the Party, and the emergence of pressure groups around individual candidates that resembled the seeds of new mini-parties. And so such a course was energetically resisted. We returned in most cases to the practice of appointing legislators [i.e., single rather than plural-candidate races].

> Only in the second half of the 1960s when there appeared a particular "movement of democratization" did the political leadership of the country again offer the slogan "more candidates," "more democratization of the elections." Once more, however, a tendancy toward political pluralism was expressed in the elections of 1967 and later in the elections of 1969. Immediately after the 1967 election the federal political leadership undertook an analysis of this phenomena, after which it adopted the political decision (unknown to the public) to introduce the delegate system. . . .

Our findings also suggest other causes for the regime's concern about the course of political development. When the more extensive republic-level experimentation in pluralist socialism is considered in all its apsects -- choice offered, invalidation, choice taken up -- it is evident that beneath the enhanced territorial uniformity in federal invalidation rates lies a substantial divergence among the five republics under study. Part of this divergence may be attributable to the increasingly independent behavior of certain republican party elites whose actions and utterances gave rise to anxiety among the central leadership that ethnic nationalism might once again be let loose. The basis for these concerns and the central leadership's actions to curb them forms the point of departure for the next section which deals specifically with the resurgence of ethno-regional dissidence.

PLURALISM REAPPRAISED: ELITE ANXIETY AND THE CROATIAN CRISIS

The political climate surrounding the election of 1969 provoked an important change in the direction of Yugoslav communist development. Although some political measures taken in the immediate aftermath of the election seemed to indicate a continuation of the pluralist strategy which burgeoned in the mid 1960s (for example, an influx of new party leaders at the Ninth LYC Congress in 1969, and the strengthening of legislative institutions), there were also ominous signs on the horizon. Increasingly throughout 1969 and 1970, Tito and a small number of seasoned party leaders from the partisan generation voiced strong reservations concerning the course of political development. The most disconcerting trend in the view of the older and more conservative wing of the party was the growing expression of nationalist sentiments by members of the intelligentsia in various regions of the country, a situation which seemed to be tolerated and sometimes even encouraged by regional party leaders.

As early as 1967, for example, a group of Croatian intellectuals had published a "Declaration" which complained about the domination of the Serbian literary language as a "state language" citing arguments and evidence which stirred up old emotions relating to the national question. In November of the following year widespread street demonstrations occurred in Kosovo during which members of the Albanian majority in that province rallied against the political domination of the Serbian and Montenegrin minorities in their midst. The Albanian demonstrators, including many students and members of the intelligentsia, called for the creation of an Albanian republic in Yugoslavia or in some cases even the union of Kosovo with Albania. Although the demonstrations were suppressed, the central party leadership feared (with good reason as events a little more than a decade later were to reveal) that the escalating demands for greater regional autonomy and the broadened recognition of minority ethnic groups might threaten the stability and survival of the political system. A week-long strike of Belgrade University students, only six months earlier, added to such anxiety concerning dissident behavior. When federal authorities cancelled a major road building program in Slovenia during the summer of 1969, the vocal public opposition of officials in that republic revealed the growing atmosphere of distrust and competition which had begun to impede seriously the formulation and implementation of public policy throughout the country. The successful action of the party leadership in Croatia in first ostracizing and the purging (April 1970) a delegate from their own republic (a Serb and Vice-President of the federal legislature) who had chosen to side with the viewpoint of the central authorities, also demonstrated the extent to which power had devolved to the regional level of the political system. When Tito placed renewed emphasis on "Yugoslav socialist patriotism" as a means to counteract the increasing regional divisions, Croatian leaders tauntingly referred to "Tito's Yugoslavism" (Pavlowitch, 1971:356) as if it were an initiative having little to do with daily political practice. In the face of such developments, the central party leadership, although certainly not devoid of either authority or leverage to influence events, appeared unable to formulate a coherent and forceful response to developments in the country. Indeed, the League of Communists seemed to function more like an association of eight regional party machines rather than a single monolithic organization.

Faced with this situation, one segment of the top political leadership concluded that the 1967 decentralization of the League of Communists which had followed the defeat of Ranković and the so-called "unitarist" or "statist" faction in the party, had gone too far and that steps were now needed to reunify both the party and the political system. In this context, it is easier to see how the elections of 1969, held only four months after the Kosovo "disorders," and characterized by features such as increased ballot invalidation (especially where choice was denied), decreased turnout rates, and the appearance and even the success of candidates not endorsed by the party, could be regarded as a divisive and negative development by the more conservative and anxious portion of the party leadership. While the character and outcome of the elections in 1969 did not, in their own right, present serious impediments to the stability of the political system, and indeed displayed indications of greater political incorporation (Chapter 5), in the minds of some party leaders the electoral process and voting patterns were undoubtedly symptomatic of a much broader disintegration of the political system along the lines of "bourgeois pluralism."

Failing to reverse the centrifugal pattern of political development by means of both private meetings with regional party leaders and a public campaign against the evils of nationalism (1968-1971), Tito decided to take matters into his own hands. The reappearance of nationalism and particularly the intensity of the national question in Croatia threatened, Tito later was to explain, nothing less than a major political "crisis" verging on "civil war" (Vjesnik, 8 October 1972). The growth of nationalism both within and outside of party ranks, together with such other negative phenomena as "rotten liberalism," "bureaucratism," and "technocratism" had fostered, it was argued, the development of "monopolistic groups" or "elites" opposed to the system of self-managed socialism. The "unprincipled jockeying for power" by these elites, and especially the so-called "techno-managerial centers of power" (frequently criticized during the 1969 legislative elections and in the work of the assemblies) were seen as having eroded the unity and authority of the party, paralyzing the process of political decision-making in the government, and pushing the country to the brink of political and economic disaster (Savez Komunista Jugoslavije, 1975). On 1 December 1971, in a landmark address to the Presidency of the League of Communists in Belgrade, Tito, reporting on his conversations with the top party leadership of Croatia only the day before, stressed that earlier (1966-1970) criticisms of central party activity or elite manipulation designed to regulate or transform relations among the country's regions and nationalities — a practice conventionally tagged with the pejorative label of "unitarism" — may have been carried too far:

> I said that I do not approve of all the talk about unitarism and I
> demanded once and for all what kind of unitarism is in question.
> If it is a matter of the unitarism of Versailles Yugoslavia
> [1918-1941], I am also, it goes without saying, most strongly
> against it. If, however, it is a matter of the unity of our country
> of Yugoslavia as an indivisible whole — then I am for such

"unitarism," for such a unified Yugoslavia. And then that is not unitarism, but simply our unity. (President Tito's . . . 1972:92)

Thus, pre-communist "unitarism" connected with the interwar strategies of charter-group hegemony and authoritarian exclusion was to be avoided as was, Tito also explained, the centralized and bureaucratic brand of unitarism associated with the communist strategies of revolutionary fusion and evolutionary merger. He left no doubt, however, that it was "nationalism and chauvinism," not unitarism, which had become "the basic danger" to the survival of the current regime. In his view, and that of other party leaders who shared his outlook, the reappearance of nationalism could be traced directly to the excessive liberalism stemming from the pluralist strategy adopted in the mid-1960s.

In early 1972, with the support of the military, Tito boldly engineered an extensive purge of the League of Communists in Croatia, expelling both prominent party leaders and rank and file members accused of "nationalist" and "techno-managerial" sentiments. Arrest and criminal prosecution were employed, although on a very selective basis and primarily against the most outspoken advocates of nationalism and opposition to the existing regime. Later in 1972, similar purges and political measures were undertaken in Serbia, Macedonia and (to a somewhat lesser extent) in the other republics, thereby reasserting the control of party conservatives and also enabling the central party leadership to deny any particular ethnic or regional basis in the suppression of nationalism and liberal activity. Although Tito and his allies vigorously denied foreign and domestic accusations that they had returned to the use of repressive "administrative methods" or to the "statist-bureaucratic model" of socialism which had existed immediately after the war, it was clear that the political dynamics and development of the regime had been altered, at least temporarily.

PRAGMATIC CONSOLIDATION WITHOUT A STRATEGY, 1972-1980

The purge of nationalists and liberals from regional party organizations during 1972 officially signalled the termination of the pluralist strategy used to foster political cohesion. It did not, however, herald the introduction of a new strategy to deal with the problem of ethnic and regional diversity. In retrospect, the entire period from the Croatian crisis to the death of Tito in May 1980, appears to be characterized less by a coherent strategy than by a very eclectic effort to maintain the most notable and distinctive features of Titoism (for example, self-management, a quasi-market economy, non-alignment, etc.), while simultaneously controlling some of the more deleterious and unintended consequences of Yugoslav political development relating to the still unresolved national question (regional loyalties, economic nationalism, and various forms of ethnic chauvinism). This approach, which may be termed a policy of pragmatic consolidation, included general elite support for the notion that Yugoslavia would and should remain a highly diverse country of many nations, minorities, and regions. Recognition and acceptance of such diversity included the expectation that different ethnic and regional interests would sometimes come into conflict, and that it was the political system's responsibility to channel, accommodate, and reconcile such divergent interests, albeit within a one-party framework. Thus, there was to be no return to pre-1960 theoretical formulae suggesting the imminent fusion or gradual merger of "peoples" on the basis of some new state identity or cultural amalgam. The continued official celebration of <u>ethnic</u> pluralism in the period after 1971 was explicitly disassociated, however, from notions supporting increased <u>political</u> pluralism, and especially any hint of genuine political choices or serious competition in the recruitment of state and party leaders. In a partial throwback to formulations and practices which had been more popular during earlier stages of socialist development, the regime placed renewed stress on the need for "revolutionary unity" and increased "consciousness" of the "general interests of the entire Yugoslav community."

For analytical purposes, the decade of political consolidation can be divided somewhat roughly into two stages. During the period from 1972 through 1974, regime policy included a far more centralized approach to relations among the nationalities and regions than had prevailed in the preceding period of pluralist socialism. During this stage, any advocacy of Yugoslav political development along more pluralistic lines was criticized as a "reactionary and bourgeois" perspective arising from "anarcho-liberalism" or "narrow techno-managerial" mentality. After 1974, and up to the death of Tito in May 1980, the regime's leaders invested more energy in finding "a new equilibrium" (Wilson, 1979:208-224) or "conciliational" policy (Zimmerman, 1977:41-42) which would combine a solid institutional and normative basis for regime unity with a return to at least some limited forms of one-party political pluralism. Elite anxiety concerning the possible reappearance of another nationalist "crisis," and the related impact which Tito's departure from political power might have on ethnic relations, gave the entire decade after 1972 more the flavor of a transitory holding action -- almost an interregnum between the period of Tito's active governance and the post-Tito era -- than a theoretically coherent phase of political development. A sharp but largely covert dissensus between advocates of a more conservative and a more liberal approach to political control and the maintenance of political cohesion contributed to a certain tactical ambiguity and oscillation in the regime's policies throughout the period, especially with respect to issues such as the treatment of political dissent and the expression of nationalist feeling. It was not until the late 1970s that fundamental issues of political organization and behavior -- such as how far limited pluralism might extend -- again became the subject of lively and more open debate among political activists.

The institutional basis for a more centralized and "co-ordinated" approach to relations among the regions and nationalities had begun to take shape even before Tito moved to "settle accounts" with the nationalists and liberals in the political elite. Superficially, a package of constitutional amendments adopted during the highpoint of regional demands for greater political autonomy in mid-1971 had organized the state on a more "confederal" basis by formally giving the republics and provinces responsibility for certain tasks previously handled by federal agencies. The 1971 amendments had also, however, reflected the growing disenchantment of more conservative party leaders with the constant failure of the recently strengthened (1967-1969) legislative institutions to resolve inter-regional conflicts concerning some very serious economic questions (for example, foreign exchange and monetary policy, aid to the less developed regions, etc.). As Edward Kardelj (1970:25-26) explained, the use of the "republican 'veto' (is) already infiltrating itself into our assembly life in an 'uncontrolled' manner through the force of pressure. History has shown that systems based on the right of 'veto' have been an historical failure."

After barely two years of experience, the Yugoslav regime abandoned the use of the parliamentary system as a mechanism for the management of regional and ethnic problems. The formal structure of the Chamber of Nationalities was retained intact, but in an effort to forestall the probability of continued legislative paralysis, an entirely new framework of five "inter-republican committees" was introduced within the federal executive branch and given primary responsibility for working out agreements among the republics and provinces. Hoping to negotiate between the Scylla of minority veto and the Charbydis of majority rule as alternative methods for making decisions, the Yugoslav leadership established an elaborate procedure for the "co-ordination" of regional interests and the achievement of unanimity prior to the formulation of policy by the central government (Federal Executive Council) and its consideration by the Federal Assembly. The burden of such co-ordination would be undertaken by members of the republican and provincial executive councils and their representatives working more or less outside of direct public view in the various inter-republican committees at the federal level (Cohen, 1977b:149-153).

The 1971 amendments also created a rather novel collective presidency (following up on one of Tito's initiatives in September 1970), composed of representatives from each republic and province and having special powers to break inter-regional deadlocks in policy-making. The new Presidency together with the creation of the inter-republican committees shifted the major responsibility for inter-regional conflict management from elected deputies in the assemblies (who were frequently rotated and included an increasing number of amateur political activists) to smaller groups of "delegated" political professionals in the executive and administrative branches of the state structure. When, as a result of Tito's "coup" in 1972, the more regionally and ethnically oriented political leaders were removed from positions of power, the new executive arrangements offered an excellent vehicle for the relatively rapid co-ordination of views and the resolution of earlier conflicts. Some participants in the lively and influential legislative process of the late 1960s worried that the Federal Assembly was again becoming a virtual rubber stamp for detailed agreements worked out in advance by professionals, political executives and bureaucratic elites, but their objections carried little weight (Cohen, 1977:150-151). The new political atmosphere and official policy after 1971 favored the efficient management of regional conflicts rather than an open and often futile process of pluralistic consensus-building.

The enlarged role of the federal-level executive and administrative bodies in the formulation of public policy was accompanied by efforts to counteract "tendencies toward the ideological and political disintegration of the League of Communists" (Savez Komunista, 1975). In what amounted to a sweeping indictment of party reforms adopted over the preceding two decades, Tito sponsored a campaign beginning in late 1971 to re-establish "discipline" and "unity" by means of a "strengthened party center." The long-neglected concepts of "democratic centralism" and the "dictatorship of the proletariat" were now resurrected as the proper terminology and operational principles for a "revolutionary and unified organization." As a prominent Croatian member of Tito's old guard (FBIS, 4 November 1971:15) claimed just prior to the bold stroke of the central apparatus against nationalists and liberals in his own republic, "until the society becomes classless, a kind of dictatorship must exist. Do I believe a dictatorship of the proletariat is ruling now? It rules, but it is a little slack, however. This slackness has been used by those who want to use the present situation in society." The preference for the pre-1952 term "party" rather than "League" in speeches by Tito and his supporters was also a cue to political activists of the change in policy. Earlier criticisms of the party and especially its central organs for unnecessary "meddling" in various societal activities such as the media, publishing and education, as well as in other political spheres such as the legislative assemblies and state administration, were now considered to have been unjustified. According to the new policy, the party's "leading role" as an essential political actor "in the system" needed to be reaffirmed and further developed as a basis for political cohesion.

The adoption of a new constitution in 1974 (incorporating the general features of the 1971 amendments) together with the programmatic and personnel changes adopted at the 10th Party Congress a month later, provided a more complete theoretical and institutional synthesis of the new course in Yugoslav political development. The Central Committee elected at the 10th Congress included a large number of political leaders, who, although new to the 1974 Committee, were veteran professional politicians from the partisan generation (some of whom had even been dropped from high office during the liberal 1960s and were now "recalled" for elite service). Such personnel changes provided a source of "revolutionary" continuity and signalled a partial return to the old politics. Another significant change in elite composition was the increase in military representation on the Central Committee. In 1974, the proportion of military officers doubled to form 10.8 percent of the total Central Committee membership. Moreover, the new military contingent (sixteen of the eighteen officers) was made up almost entirely of members of the prewar and wartime political generation, many of whom (as was the case the large contingent of newly elected professional politicians) had served in higher party bodies in the 1950s and had been retired during the heyday of pluralist socialism. The increase of military representation in the Central Committee, and particularly of older more conservative military personnel, was clearly related to the support of Tito and the "party center" by the armed forces during the political crisis of 1971-1972. In terms of its ethnic composition, the Central Committee elected in 1974 continued the trend begun in the 1960s toward relatively balanced "parity" representation of the principal ethnic groups, as well as a proportional increase in the number of members from the smaller nationalities and minorities. Sensitive to charges of "great-nation hegemony" especially during a time of expanded central control, the regime's ethnic mathematicians thus saw to it that the percentage of Serbs in the Central Committee was lower than at any time in the post-war period (Cohen, 1979:467-468). Superficially, the keen attention of the regime to ethnic and regional balance in the composition of party and other political elites revealed a certain continuity with the pre-1971 approach toward cultural diversity. However, in contrast to the pluralistic strategy underlying recruitment at the Ninth Congress of the League in 1969, the members of the 1974 party elite were selected primarily for their loyal support of the "party center," rather than for their responsiveness to ethnic and regional constituencies. While the bargaining among the still powerful elite spokesmen from the different ethnic and regional groups resembled aspects of the consociational strategy used from 1939 to 1941 and similar practices in many other multi-national states, the salience of central elite control in the mid-1970s, and the climate of contrived attitudinal unity made it a very spurious, or at least extremely artificial, consociational variant.

The departure from the pluralist strategy of the late 1960s was also clearly revealed in new electoral and legislative procedures designed to eliminate remaining "vestiges of classical bourgeois parliamentary democracy." The complex electoral mechanism introduced in 1974 is based on the delegate principle whereby each tier of the assembly system (federal, republican-provincial, and communal) is composed of delegates elected by legislative bodies at lower levels of the structure. The entire system emanates at the bottom of the structure from delegations elected by citizens in individual "self-managed" enterprises, organizations, and communities that comprise the basic electoral constituencies. Although the new legislative structure proved rather ingenious in terms of its organizational novelty and ideological paternity (inspired by Marx's comments on the Paris Commune of 1871), in operation it has tended to enhance the political control of the party organization and constrain the more participatory and genuinely self-managing evolution of the Yugoslav system (Cohen, 1980). The indirect character of elections for legislative bodies above the base of the delegate system completely eliminates popular voting for assembly chambers on the important republican-provincial and central levels of the federal system. The new electoral system provided some elements of choice to the voters for local assemblies, with the number of candidates in excess of the number of delegates to be elected, but the new procedures almost totally eliminates choice in elections for assemblies at higher levels.[1] Moreover, any competitive features in the new electoral process are also dampened by a political climate far less tolerant of divergent opinions than during the period from 1966 to 1971, and by the determination of the party elite to exercise greater guidance over candidate selection according to "precisely established and socially negotiated criteria" (Trajkovski, 1974:785).

Given these new arrangements, the first three elections for the delegate system in 1974, 1978 and 1982 appeared similar, at least in their effect, to a much earlier phase of Yugoslav communism, namely, closely controlled or "safe" elections aimed at the symbolic legitimation of the regime through the near perfect mobilization of all eligible voters. Thus, data available on the elections of 1974 and 1978 reveal that the regime was able to achieve a noticeable success, compared to 1969, in the mobilization of voter turnout and the reduction of ballot invalidation throughout the country (Figure 5.1).

Although the changes in the structure of the assembly system and electoral procedure greatly limit the value of aggregate voting data as a useful indicator of political incorporation and political cohesion, there is another data source that can be employed which offers an alternative means of measurement. Using officially published, but hitherto unanalyzed aggregate statistics which report the number and characteristics of persons prosecuted (charged and convicted) for crimes against the state (or what are usually referred to as "political crimes") it is possible to get some indication of both the pattern of repression by the Yugoslav regime, as well as regional levels of dissidence against the current political system.[2] Years in which there are a large number of convictions for political crimes indicate the increased zealousness of the regime in supressing anti-state dissidence, and therefore also a more authoritarian tilt in the course of political development. Periods exhibiting a lower number of convictions for political criminality reflect a more open political system in which the authorities are less inclined or less well organized to combat political dissidence through the use of penal sanctions. Thus, a period in which there is a noticeable reduction in the number of convictions for political crime does not signify that manifestations of anti-regime behavior have diminished, but only that for some reason the regime has probably chosen to tolerate such behavior and adopt a more benign definition of political criminality. Indeed, it is precisely during such periods of liberalization that we witness an intensification of activity by the more dissatisfied and politically non-conformist segments of the community, a development which usually precipitates another round of arrests and convictions by the regime.

Figure 7.1 illustrates general trends in the magnitude of political criminality between 1966 and 1980, based upon the number of persons either charged or convicted for crimes against the state considered as a percentage of the total number of individuals charged or convicted for all crimes. Keeping in mind that there is about a one or two year lag between arrests and statistically recorded indictments and convictions, the figure shows that between 1966 and 1971, when the strategy of pluralist socialism was at its apex, convictions for political criminality reached one of the lowest levels in the postwar period. For example, political crimes constituted approximately 0.1 percent of convictions for all crimes in 1967, as compared to 7.7 percent in 1947, 3.0 percent in 1951, and 0.3 percent in 1961. The November 1968 nationalist demonstrations in Kosovo and other manifestations of anti-state protest (closely paralleling the growth of ballot invalidation in legislative elections and most likely for closely related reasons) contributed to a noticeable increase in convictions for political criminality in 1969, during what otherwise was a relatively non-repressive period. Convictions for anti-regime dissidence soared dramatically, however, as a result of a campaign against nationalists and liberals at the end of 1971. By 1973, convictions for political crimes reached a level of 0.8 percent of all criminal convictions or about the same level recorded just prior to the emergence of a more liberal model of Yugoslav communism in the early 1950s, (e.g., 1.1 percent in 1953 and 0.7 percent in 1954, resulting from regime measures against dissidents during the more authoritarian period which ended in 1952). By 1974, with the adoption of a new constitution and other steps to allegedly "democratize" and systematize the pattern of political development, convictions for political criminality began to drop off noticeably. Although complete data is not yet available on convictions for the period after 1977, the closely related statistics on persons charged for political crimes, also shown in Figure 7.1, indicate that by 1978, anti-state dissidence had been reduced to levels approximating the pre-1971 pluralistic stage of development. The striking reversal of this downward trend which occurred during 1979 and 1980, has been attributed by the Yugoslav federal public prosecuter -- who describes himself as having responsibility for the overall management of "repression" (NIN, 12 July 1981:17) -- to the subversive activities of emigré circles who have been stimulated by the "worsening world situation due to a sharpening in relations between the superpowers" and "the illness and death of President Tito" (NIN, 29 June 1980:21).

Although aggregate data on the rate of political criminality reveals more about the intensity of regime control and prosecutorial zeal in any given year than it does about the precise magnitude of anti-state dissidence in the country, such data can, nevertheless, also shed considerable light on when and how persistently such dissent becomes troublesome to the regime. Moreover, when the political authorities are prompted to take such

152

FIGURE 7.1
Indictments and Convictions Reported as "Political Offenses" by Year,
1966-1980

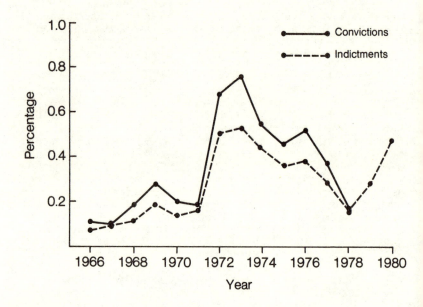

punitive measures in the same regions or against any of the same groups
fairly frequently, it offers a more systematic geographic and demographic
picture of past and potential points of political instability. An investigation
of the republican-provincial breakdown of political crimes from 1966-1978,
presented in Table 7.1, indicates that Croatia, Kosovo, and Bosnia -- all
areas of high ethnic fragmentation -- have been persistent hotbeds of
political criminality, with the latter republic being consistently above the
country-wide mean in every year. Complete information on the ethnic
identity of "political criminals" is not available for the entire period under
discussion here, but on the basis of the partial data which is available
(Cohen, 1981) and also official statements, (NIN 12 July 1981:17; Danas, 6
June 1982:10-13) it is reasonable to conclude that most of the political
criminality in Bosnia and Croatia involves ethnic Croats, while in Kosovo
such crimes are committed in large part by ethnic Albanians. Albanian
dissidence in Macedonia and Montenegro is also responsible for the sporadic
rise of political criminality in those regions (along with the discovery and
prosecution of an ideologically-based neo-Stalinist movement in Montenegro
during the 1970s). Regional differences in the level of political criminality
can additionally provide a rough indicator of political division and cohesion
among the different sections of the country. Viewed from this perspective,
the very large differences between regions of high and low anti-state

TABLE 7.1
Convictions for Political Criminality as a Percentage of all Convictions, by Republic (Province), 1966-1978a

Republic	Year												
	1966	1967	1968	1969	1970	1971	1972	1973	1974	1975	1976	1977	1978b
Bosnia-Hercegovina	.21	.29	.70	.58	.47	.37	1.42	2.56	1.22	.86	1.39	.87	.50
Montenegro	--	--	--	.19	--	.14	.34	.34	.67	.46	.25	.45	.02
Croatia	.23	.08	.17	.33	.23	.33	1.68	1.17	.91	.79	.74	.60	.24
Macedonia	.09	--	.17	.59	.43	.08	.10	.21	.14	.11	.09	.08	.06
Slovenia	.01	.08	.06	.07	.03	.07	.15	.12	.22	.23	.29	.24	.10
Serbia	.01	.02	.02	.03	.06	.04	.05	.12	.10	.08	.11	.08	.04
Kosovo	.17	.27	.16	1.84	.67	.77	.18	1.15	.86	1.49	1.36	.79	.12
Vojvodina	.04	.14	.17	.18	.13	.03	.35	.43	.46	.31	.43	.19	.17
Total	.11	.09	.18	.28	.20	.18	.68	.76	.54	.46	.52	.37	.17
Difference between highest and lowest level	.22	.27	.68	1.81	.64	.74	1.63	2.44	1.12	1.41	1.30	.79	.48

Source: Yugoslavia (1967-1979) Statistički Godišnjak Jugoslavije. Savezni Zavod za Statistika: Belgrade.
aNoteworthy regional percentages are underlined.
bConvicted not available. 1978 represents percent charged for political crimes.

dissidence, especially in the 1968-1969 and 1972-1973 periods, as well as shifts in the location of high dissidence, reflect the regime's persistent difficulty in maintaining a relatively uniform level of cross-regional support (the reappearance of serious Albanian nationalist agitation in Kosovo and Macedonia beginning in mid-1981, continues this non-cohesive pattern and will be discussed further below).

Although criminal prosecutions were one way of dealing with the most excessive manifestations of conflict, the regime's response to political and ethnic diversity in the second phase of pragmatic consolidation (1975-1980) showed signs of continued elite division and uncertainty about the best way to move forward. While the resolution and reports at the Tenth Congress of the League of Communists in 1974 and subsequent party meetings over the next several years condemned threats to "national equality" stemming from both "separatist-nationalist" impulses and "bureaucratic centralist forces," it was apparent that there was a lack of agreement in the party leadership about just which of the two problems constituted the greater danger. The political leadership was also divided between those anxious to quickly put the "firm hand" measures of 1971-1973 aside and move ahead with the democratic development of self-management now that the most volatile "anti-socialist elements" had been silenced, and another faction urging the need for continued vigilance, "discipline," and strict party control over the political system and society. A third but less clearly identifiable group in the elite tried to avoid what they claimed were the extreme consequences latent in both of the two previous perspectives (that is, either democracy leading to "anarcho-liberalism" or centralization leading to "statism"), by taking a more prudent middle course of action. Support for the latter position by Tito and certain members of the old guard resulted in a hesitant moderation of political control in the late 1970s, and was characterized by an ambiguous blend of political devolution and centralization, repression and tolerance. Political debates up to and following Tito's death, however, tended to reflect elite differences about the best way to maintain political cohesion. It was no longer a question, as in the earlier post-war period, of whether there was to be a long-term recognition of regional and ethnic difference, but rather the best methodology for the co-ordination and management of those differences.

One of the most important interventions in the discussion regarding the proper course of future political evolution was a long report presented by Edward Kardelj in June 1977 entitled Directions of the Development of the Political System of Socialist Self-Management. In essence, the Kardelj study represents a clever but strained effort to justify theoretically a model of socialism combining single-party guidance over society with certain limited aspects of political pluralism. While abhoring any emulation of bourgeois multi-party pluralism, and differentiating his own work from Yugoslav allusions to pluralism in the late 1960s, Kardelj argued (1978:110-116) for "the establishment of a democratic pluralism of self-management interests." Such a "self-managing pluralism" or "pluralism of the interests of self-management communities" growing out of Yugoslavia's social, economic, and cultural diversity can find expression, Kardelj claimed, through the new "delegational" legislative structure. Decision-making should reflect, he argued (1978:178-189), "a democratic struggle of views" which provides that "in the course of day-to-day decision-making working citizen self-managers can freely divide themselves into the majority and minority which constantly keeps changing in connection with every question on the agenda." This process of differentiation is, however, sharply distinguished from a "struggle for power" which "has inevitably given rise to a political division into parties" or "into the party in power and the opposition." Kardelj admitted (1978:218-223) that the practice of self-managing pluralism is often undermined by the tendency of some professional politicians to create "narrow groups which impose themselves as centers of power." Despite such distortions, he felt strongly that the single party system remains crucial to the operations and maintenance of the regime under present conditions and for the foreseeable future. "We would not be realists," Kardelj informed his audience, "if we did not see and recognize that our system of self-management democracy contains, and that it must contain elements of both political pluralism and a one-party system." If the legislative system, as he claimed, is the backbone of the entire social and political system, it is nevertheless the single party -- the League of Communists -- which is the brain and the central nervous system.

> . . . we are not in favor of the rule of the minority, although the League of Communists is a minority. It has to be a minority, because it is only as a minority that it can, under our conditions, be the vanguard of social progress, that is to say, to comprehend socialist practice in its entirety . . . the instability of the system is the source of nondemocracy (nedemokratija). . . . Only the stability of the key positions of the system which insure the leading role of the class in power makes possible the development of democracy. . . . The LYC has a special role in this, as it represents the powerful leading ideological and political cohesive force of the revolution and thereby also of our political system of socialist and democratic self-managing pluralism. (Kardelj, 1978:214-215)

Given the persistence of deep regional and ethnic cleavages within Yugoslav society as evidenced in the events of 1968 and 1971-1972, it is not difficult to understand the commitment by Kardelj and most other Yugoslav leaders to stability engineered by a political minority and the continuation of a single-party framework. Beyond simply their own personal stake in maintaining the present position and role of the party, it is also important to recall the party leadership's keen awareness that it was the failure of interwar pluralism and the multi-party system to resolve the national problem which had led to the violent confrontation of ethnic animosities during World War II, and the eventual collapse of the old regime. Since ineffectual and discredited pluralism had helped bring the Yugoslav communists to power, it would be the height of political naivete for them to repeat the mistakes of their predecessors. In an omission which was characteristic of the period in which he was writing, Kardelj did not spell out how the conflicts among Yugoslavia's various nationalities and regions fit into his overall concept of self-management pluralism. "This is not to say," Kardelj cryptically noted, "that in this respect there exist no problems. . . ." (Kardelj, 1977:29). Perhaps the unhappy experience with his previous endeavor to formulate a macro-strategy regarding cultural diversity (the notion of "socialist Yugoslavism" in the late 1950s) had made him hesitant to venture into this area again. It is more likely, in the climate of the late 1970s, that he felt it was wiser to temporarily postpone such matters. It was not until 1981, three years after Kardelj's death, that the public learned of his confidential remarks made in 1977 to the leadership of Kosovo, concerning the deterioration of ethnic relations and the possibility of a "counter-revolutionary" outburst in that province (NIN, 7 June 1981:10-13). The publication of Kardelj's ideas regarding self-management pluralism had little practical effect on the actual operation of the Yugoslav political system or on the distribution of political power, but it did spark a more open discussion about the current condition of the regime and its future development. Kardelj, unintentionally perhaps, also gave strong encouragement to the less conservative elements in the political elite who felt that the extent of centralization and party interference in society had gone beyond the point required by the "crisis" of 1971-1972. Enthusiasm for the latter view was displayed by only a small number of those who had supported the earlier pluralistic strategy; more often it simply attracted leaders who felt that restrictive measures had outlived their usefulness. As a leading Yugoslav political analyst claimed during a discussion of Kardelj's work:

> ... the difference between what the liberals said [1970-1971] and what we are discussing today is so great that no such comparisons are possible. Today [1977] we have a different historical situation ... the society is maturing and it is learning from its own victories and defeats. Do not forget the essentially different state of awareness that we have today and also the new institutional solutions. ... I have already said that the preliminary process has been mainly completed and the 'state of emergency' has mainly passed. But certain consequences have remained. It seems to me that certain structures oppose a democratization of the system. It is very difficult to determine the correlation of forces, because this cannot be measured, in view of the fact that all opposition forces are covert. But on the basis of experience I could agree with you that they are quite strong. (FBIS, 17 November 1977:I 5-I 6)

Kardelj's pronouncement on self-management and the discussion it spawned coincided with perhaps the most "liberal" point in the entire decade after the 1971 events. The policy of cautious and pragmatic consolidation continued with a decidedly authoritarian cast, but the boundaries of political dialogue were broadened and the more reform-minded political activists in society looked forward to a more tolerant and innovative climate just ahead. As Figure 7.1 indicates, prosecutions for political criminality dropped to their lowest point since the earlier crisis in Croatia. The political leadership was clearly more relaxed and convinced that they had restored stability,[3] but restrictive measures continued to be employed, if on a more selective basis. When intellectual dissent trespassed on the acceptable and rather hazy boundaries of political diversity, as in the case of the well-known Praxis group of writers, and the outspoken philosophers at Belgrade University, the authorities took punitive measures to deal with the situation. As the Croatian political activist Stipe Šuvar (Borba, 24 July 1979:4) aptly remarked: "the flourishing of the pluralism of self-managing socialist interests implies -- if you want -- the suppression of the pluralism of those social interests which are not organized in this way."

Throughout 1979 and the beginning of 1980, expectations of an imminent leadership succession arising from Tito's advanced age and prolonged illness shifted attention away from reform proposals and back toward the strategy of pragmatic consolidation. Regime sensitivity to anti-state dissidence and increased exploitation of the situation by opposition elements were again reflected in the statistics on political criminality. The public prosecutor reported that the "processing of political criminals" grew by 83 percent in 1980 compared to the previous year, mainly due to nationalist outburst of various kinds, and that approximately half of all such criminality occurred in Croatia (NIN, 17 May 1981:21).

Increasingly, however, the focus was on the capacity of the "new institutional solutions," and principally the collective state and party presidencies inspired by Tito himself, to carry the political system through the very difficult juncture in its development. By 1980, there was no question that the new executive structure (including the inter-republican committees and other federal administrative bodies composed of an equal number of officials from each republic and province) had become more effective sites for political decision-making than the more pluralistic framework used during the 1960s when, in Tito's own works, "the federation's legislative functions were over-emphasized" (FBIS, 1 May 1979:12). It was also apparent, however, that such success was due as much to the political climate and the personnel changes wrought by Tito, as to the intrinsic value and efficiency of the new constitutional structure. What remained to be seen was whether the new arrangements would prove to be sufficiently legitimate and workable under the management of Tito's successors.[4] Forty years after the fall of the old regime, the Yugoslav communists prepared to face the most serious test of their political skills.

POLITICAL COHESION IN THE POST-TITO ERA: TRENDS AND PROSPECTS

We have seen that Yugoslavia's unique experiment in pluralist socialism undertaken at the end of the 1960s was followed by a period of political consolidation which witnessed the resurgence of more centralized and active party guidance. The unity allegedly restored in this period, however, was more an artefact of party pronouncements, induced personnel rotation, and institutional reorganization, than an outcome of genuine political incorporation or enhanced cohesion among the different segments of the population. The regime's disavowal of the pluralist experiment had, of course, what many political leaders regarded as desirable consequences. For example, the indirect and less competitive system of voting for the new delegate system did not contain the disturbing "negative" electoral phenomena so troublesome to party conservatives in 1967 and 1969. For the time being, the nationalist flirtations of regional party barons, as well as the activities of even more extreme ethnic spokesmen (e.g., non-communist and anti-communist intellectuals), were also eliminated from the legitimate political arena. At the same time, party leaders during the 1970s, were deeply divided among themselves about the best way to proceed with political development now that the "state of emergency" had passed. Compared to earlier periods the political leadership appeared to lack a clear vision of what long term strategy to adopt toward cultural diversity (Šuvar, 1975). Fusion, merger, and pluralism had all been discredited, in the case of the first two strategies for being overly "unitarian," and in the later case for encouraging nationalism and liberalism.

By 1980, a still divided but essentially pragmatic and prudent political elite eschewed any schemes for major reform and pinned their hopes on the strengthened structure of executive institutions as the best chance for the regime to survive the difficulties expected to accompany Tito's departure from leadership. The relatively smooth transition to a new leadership group which followed Tito's death temporarily bolstered the regime's self-confidence and seemed to auger well for its survival. Indeed, there is no question that the political system was far more stable than a decade before when Tito had personally intervened to halt the drift toward the politicization of ethnic plurality. The problem still causing strains in the post-Tito leadership, however, was how long a program of pragmatic consolidation and contrived cohesion could be substituted for the more democratic and spontaneous, albeit more turbulent, mode of political compromise and incorporation which had been so obviously popular in the 1960s. While some leaders cautiously debated the best way to blend party control with Kardelj's new "self-management pluralism," others promoted the idea that a gradual expansion of electoral choice -- mainly at the local level -- might be a good idea as a means of regaining momentum and moving forward with the democratization of the political system (Nenadovic, 1980; Borba, 6 November 1980:6). Survey research conducted in the late 1970s also indicated that as in the earlier period of pluralist socialism, there was popular support for an expansion of election choice (Siber, 1980:172-176).

In March 1981, close to a year after Tito's death, the initial optimism surrounding the leadership succession was shattered as Yugoslavia once more found itself in the throes of a nationality crisis. Unlike the crisis of 1971, which started in one of the more developed sections of the country, this time the problem was in Kosovo, the most economically underdeveloped region. In 1979, Kosovo's income per capita was $676 U.S. compared to $4,936 U.S. in Slovenia and a national average of $2,400 U.S. (NIN, 14 June 1981:16). Although local feelings of relative deprivation relating to Kosovo's chronic underdevelopment were undoubtedly at the root of the crisis, the anti-regime protests quickly assumed a strongly nationalist and separatist character. A new surplus population of unemployed university graduates mainly in the social sciences -- and ironically produced by the rapid expansion of Kosovo's educational structure in recent years -- also helped fuel the demonstrations.

The protest began with Albanian students demonstrating about conditions at the university and gradually escalated into street demonstrations involving thousands of young people throughout the province. Led by anti-regime members of the Albanian intelligentsia and a small number of individuals occupying responsible positions of authority in the province (for example, in the media and education), the demonstrators demanded, among other things, the creation of a separate Albanian republic within Yugoslavia. After virtually sealing off the province from the rest of the country (a temporary information blackout, restricted travel and access, etc.), the regime quickly acted to quash the alleged "counter-revolution" and special "war strategy" of the ultra-nationalist forces (FBIS, 28 June 1981:I 5), a step which resulted in bloody confrontations between demonstrators and the militia. These initial measures have been followed (1981-1983) by a vigorous campaign of "political differentiation" in Kosovo designed to prosecute and purge those individuals exposing the cause of Albanian nationalism. In view of the broad popular support received by the Albanian demonstrators and the great anxiety raised within the provinces's influential Serbian and Montenegrin minorities (who see the events as a continuation of an ethnic struggle going back at least to the last war if not much earlier in Balkan history), the problem of "stablizing" Kosovo will very likely be a long and arduous task.[5] Although there was no question of direct negotiations with the demonstrators concerning their demands, regime spokesmen made it clear that in principle, the call for the creation of a new territorial unit expressing the interests of Yugoslavia's Albanian population was completely unacceptable. The fear was that such a measure would not only signal a capitulation to violent nationalist protest that could encourage other groups, but might potentially alter the entire shape of the Yugoslav federation (the presence of large and concentrated Albanian minorities in areas of Macedonia and Montenego adjacent to Kosovo implies such broader boundary adjustments), as well as strengthen the irredentist-secessionist movements (also present in the demonstrations) who called for union of the Kossovar Albanians with their brethren in the neighboring People's Socialist Republic of Albania.

The "counter-revolution" in Kosovo, occuring so soon after Tito's death and only a decade after what he described as a near "civil war" in Croatia, has again raised important questions about Yugoslavia's durability as a multi-national state. Our analysis indicated that major steps towards enhanced political cohesiveness were made in the first two decades of the communist regime's existence, and moreover, that the liberalization attempted in the latter 1960s in many ways aided in this process. The levelling-off of ballot invalidation at the relatively high level of 6.9 percent in 1969 could be viewed, for example, as a tolerable sacrifice to be made for the incorporative aspects of the election such as its cross-regional uniformity, its replacement of ethnic by economic and political factors in motivating voting behavior, and its popularity where candidate choice was offered. Despite such achievements, the elections of 1969 raised a fundamental dilemma for the future of the political system, namely, the possibility that even limited political choice, once provided and encouraged by a more pluralist and more democratic brand of socialism, might not be contained within the restricted options of the Yugoslav regime. The manifestations of independence and protest by regional intellectuals and party leaders may have presaged much wider manifestations of the same sort on a mass level that truly would have challenged the very basis of the regime. Thus, the incorporative strategy that seems to have been the most successful in Yugoslav history, and the one which we feel has the greatest hope for success in the future, is also the one deemed most dangerous by the party elite.

As for the future, we interpret the relatively cautious approach of the regime in the short period since Tito's death, and also the rather heavy-handed suppression of the 1981 Kosovo demonstrations (or what might be termed a counter-counter-revolution), to suggest that a continued period of pragmatic consolidation lies ahead. Sharp public polemics concerning policy questions, elite dissensus over past history and long-term objectives, and even quite pronounced party factionalism -- all facets of the post-Tito political landscape -- will certainly continue, but it is unlikely that the bold initiatives and experimentation with new forms of one-party pluralism which were so visible in the 1960s, will soon be repeated. Further reorganization of the electoral system, including a return to plural-candidate elections, should not be ruled out,[6] especially in view of the Yugoslav penchant for institutional engineering, but the indirect character of elections in the delegate system, as well as the greater care now taken to insure both the "moral and political suitability" of electoral contestants and to maximize participation (giving a kind of mobilization flavor to elections that was absent in the 1960s), should effectively constrain the more spontaneous and centrifugal features which can accompany a real exercise in political choice. Seeking expedient refuge in stability, the regime also appears unwilling to offer, as some Yugoslav specialists themselves observe, anything in the way of a new "vision" or strategy on the "national question" (NIN, 5 July 1981:18-20). Indeed, it would seem that there is little more Tito's heirs can do, firmly dedicated as they are to the continuation of single-party rule, desperately fearing a return of pluralist turbulence and ultra-nationalism, and no longer possessing a "historical personality" who can temporarily set things straight when they go wrong.

Barring external interference in their affairs, which appears very unlikely, there is a good chance that the present Yugoslav elite can "stablize" the situation in Kosovo, (or further incidents of the Kosovo type) and continue the Titoist pattern of control. Prosecutions for political criminality, routine popular compliance with the authorities, and the elimination of overt party factionalism can all be engineered with a reasonable degree of success. After all, the communist elite has demonstrated considerable skill in developing and implementing techniques of control, a capability now being exhibited vigorously against Albanian nationalists. Moreover, after nearly four decades of rule the Yugoslav communist system has acquired a good deal of genuine support throughout most segments of the country's population. The exceptionally large number of people who designated themselves as "Yugoslavs" in the 1981 census rather than as members of different ethnic groups may also indicate a growing trans-ethnic consciousness or commitment to the state that was not present in the past (see Appendix A). The relatively uniform and sustained political incorporation of Yugoslavia's diverse nationalities and regions, however, is a far more difficult task and one that seems to have eluded every Yugoslav regime thus far. This task has not been made any easier for the present political leadership by the severe and apparently long-term economic slump which beset Yugoslavia during 1982 and 1983.[7]

Thus, while the chances for a continuation of an "ambiguous stability" (Windsor, 1981) are reasonably good, the likelihood of achieving greater political cohesion in the near future seems far less encouraging. Clearly, in terms of its chronological durability and partial popular legitimation (Denitch, 1976:198), the communist regime has done better than their predecessors, but the kinds of extreme anti-regime and pro-regime forces (ultra-nationalist, anti-communist, and authoritarian marxist) which emerged in connection with the short-lived experiment in socialist pluralism, and again more recently in Kosovo, illustrates the great difficulties involved.

In an interview connected with the situation in Kosovo, Stane Dolanc, one of Yugoslavia's most influential politicians, indicated the dilemma faced by the regime and the skepticism that anything can quickly be done about it:

> We are a multi-national country, and at the same time economically underdeveloped. Differences among our republics, and provinces do exist. Regrettably the boundaries of development and underdevelopment coincide with nationality boundaries. The fact is that a pluralism of interests exists which must be coordinated constantly, patiently and on a long term basis. All this constantly forces us to a political reality. And it will force us tomorrow and the day after tomorrow until

we achieve the level of development that will enable us to have a really complete economic equality and prevent any kind of nationalist manifestations ... the Yugoslav communist party always had as one of its strategic tasks the solution of the national problem. ... It is a process which will last a long time. (FBIS, 13 April 1981:I 9)

The sober and cautious views expressed by Dolanc offer a sharp contrast with the post-revolutionary optimism and rather glib economic determinism of the new communist elite that took control of the country in 1944-1945. Rapid modernization is now recognized, even by most marxists, to have a far more complex and multi-sided impact on traditional loyalties than was perceived in the past. As with so many other "divided societies" where resurgent cultural impulses have challenged established or emerging political structures, Yugoslavia appears destined to continue as a fragile mosaic persistently in search of cohesion.

NOTES

1. Electoral choice at the communal level was almost entirely confined to the "chambers of associated labor" and the "chambers of local communities," rather than the more politically influential "socio-political chambers" composed of professional politicians. The number of plural candidate electoral contests at the local level and base of the delegational system declined in 1978 compared with 1974 while choice at higher levels of the federation was limited to only a few cases (Yugoslavia, Socijalistička Federativna . . ., 1974 and 1978).

2. A fuller elaboration of the data on political criminality used in this chapter is offered in Cohen (1981).

3. At the 11th Congress in June 1978, Tito assessed the current state of internationality relations: ". . . today our nations and nationalities are more united, and the cohesion of our federal community is firmer than ever in the past. We remember the very recent past when national forces tried to undermine and turn away from the self-managing course of our development ... toward bureaucratic nationalism, separatism or bureaucratic centralism. We decisively overcame those dangers to the further self-managed development of our federal community and more firmly solidified the equality, brotherhood and unity of our nations and nationalities. This, of course doesn't mean that we don't need improvement and further development in this area." (Yugoslavia, XI Kongres Saveza Komunista . . ., 1978:46).
At a meeting of one of the Congress Commissions, a leading official from Kosovo stated "thanks to the activity of the League of Communists and the solutions written into the SFRJ Constitution internationality and political relations in Kosovo are stable . . ." (FBIS, 22 June 1978:I 20).

4. The unsettled political climate of this period is reflected in a recent Yugoslav study (Stanić, 1982:27) of trends in party membership: "Socio-political conditions abroad and in Yugoslavia began to deteriorate after 1979. It was necessary to repay large foreign debts made from 1972 to 1980. The standard of living began to decline and unemployment to rise.

The position of the working class and young people kept worsening and social differences growing. In this period eligibility requirements for admission of new members stiffened. The inflow of new members gradually decreased but was still considerable. The process of leaving the League continued for varied reasons. During Tito's illness and after his death in 1980, there was a big increase in the number of new members."

5. According to official data, nine persons lost their lives in the Kosovo disorders, eight demonstrators and one member of the security service (FBIS, 8 May 1981:I 22). By the end of August 1981, some thirty trials had been held in the province resulting from the events of March and April, with 245 persons sentenced to serve up to fifteen year prison terms (FBIS, 15 September 1981:I 12).

Mainly as a result of the counter-revolution in Kosovo, the number of individuals charged with political crimes in 1981 increased 7.5 percent compared with 1980, thereby continuing the upward trend which began in 1979. Individuals from Kosovo made up only 4.7 percent of all those charged with political crimes in 1980, but 50.5 percent in 1981. Even more striking is the fact that 65 percent of the 594 people charged with political crime in 1981 were Albanians (Danas, 6 June 1982:10-13). Sporadic nationalist incidents continued to erupt in Kosovo throughout 1982 and 1983, including student demonstrations in March 1983, to mark the second anniversary of the 1981 events (FBIS, 14 March 1983:I 10). Political officials in Kosovo claim (FBIS, March 8, 1983:I 4, 6 April 1983:I 9) that small Albanian nationalist "sects" are regrouping into a movement calling for a separate Albanian republic in Yugoslavia.

6. A Yugoslav study (Pegan, 1982:59-60) of 366 political activists and functionaries before the 1982 election showed that two-thirds of the respondents wanted plural-candidate elections. There was less support for this idea among professional politicians and older respondents. Many Yugoslav political scientists have urged a return to plural-candidate elections, but only within the new delegate system (Borba, 6 November 1980:6; NIN, 8 May 1983:13-15).

7. In 1982, serious problems in the repayment of its large foreign debt forced the regime to adopt laws rationing gasoline and electricity, and also controlling the circulation of foreign currency. In addition, beginning in 1982, citizens were required to deposit a certain amount of money in a Yugoslav bank before receiving permission to take trips outside the country (the amount, which increases for each successive trip, is refundable after one year and does not apply to short cross-border visits). Serious shortages have also forced many Yugoslav communes to introduce ration coupons for coffee, edible oil, washing powder and certain other goods in early 1983. The impact of these economic problems (and many others, such as rising unemployment) on political cohesion is very difficult to gauge. Intellectuals, for example, a group that has often helped to spawn nationalist sentiment, may feel that restrictions which exist on the scope of their expression are a more serious reason for opposing the regime than economic difficulties. As one dissident writer (recently accused of fanning Seribian nationalism for having told of the genocide of Serbs by Croats in World War II) remarked: ". . . the country will not collapse just because there is no longer any coffee. But if we shroud past crimes in silence then we are in danger" (FBIS, April 1983:I 11).

Appendix A:
The Ethnic Composition
of Yugoslavia

According to the final results of the census taken on 31 March 1981, Yugoslavia has a population of 22,427,585, a growth of about 9 percent compared to the census taken a decade earlier. The census recognized six "nations" (Serbs, Croats, Slovenes, Macedonians, Montenegrins and Moslems), and eighteen "nationalities" (Albanians, Hungarians, Slovaks, Turks, etc.). The category "nations" includes the most influential and (except for the omission of Albanians), the largest ethnic groups in the country, while the "nationalities" are generally smaller groups which had been designated as national minorities in the precommunist and early communist periods.[1] As Table A.1 indicates, the Serbs constitute the largest ethnic group (8,140,507), followed by Croats (4,428,043), Moslems, who have been considered as an ethnic as well as a religious group since 1981 (1,999,890), Slovenes (1,753,571), Albanians (1,730,878), Macedonians (1,341,598), and Montenegrins (579,043). Although considered as a nationality rather than as a nation, the Albanians are the fastest growing ethnic group in Yugoslavia, their numbers having increased 230.6 percent between 1948 and 1981 (mainly as a result of a high birth rate, a reduced mortality level, and few mixed marriages to weaken group bonds). The absolute number of Macedonians and Moslems also grew significantly from 1971 to 1981, while Montenegrins and Slovenes increased their numbers only moderately, and the number of Serbs and Croats actually dropped off slightly. Serbs and Croats together constituted 65.5 percent of Yugoslavia's population in 1948, a figure which had decreased to 56.1 percent by 1981.

In addition to the officially recognized nations and nationalities, there is also a group of citizens who chose a supranational (or some might say a non-ethnic state identity) as "Yugoslavs." Although a Yugoslav "nation" as such does not exist under the Yugoslav Constitution, approximately 1.2 million citizens or 5.4 percent of the total population declared themselves as Yugoslavs in 1981, which is nearly five times more than in the census of 1971. Preliminary research indicates that the large increase in the number of Yugoslavs is most prevalent in some of the multi-national regions of the country (particularly in Croatia, Bosnia-Hercegovina and Vojvodina, all areas where many Serbs appear to be reclassifying themselves as Yugoslavs), as well as in urban centers, but detailed examination (Vušković, 1982; Raić, 1982) of this recent phenomenon in trans-ethnic commitment is only just beginning. In 1981, approximately 46,000 (0.2 percent) citizens of Yugoslavia exercised their constitutional prerogative to remain silent about their ethnic identity and another 25,000

TABLE A.1
The Percent Ethnic Composition of the Yugoslav Population by Republic and Province (31 March 1981)

Ethnic Groups	Yugoslavia Total Population	Republics and Provinces								
		Total Republic	Serbia			Mont.	Mace.	Slov.	Croat.	Bosnia-Herce.
			Serbia "proper"	Vojvo.	Kos.					
Serbs	36.3	66.4	85.4	54.4	13.2	3.3	2.3	2.2	11.5	32.0
Montenegrins	2.6	1.6	1.4	2.1	1.7	68.5	0.2	0.2	0.2	0.3
Macedonians	6.0	0.5	0.5	0.9	0.1	0.2	67.0	0.2	0.1	0.1
Slovenes	7.8	0.1	0.1	0.1	-	0.2	-	90.5	0.6	0.1
Croats	19.8	1.6	0.5	5.4	0.5	1.4	0.2	2.9	75.1	18.4
Moslems[a]	8.9	2.3	2.7	0.2	3.7	13.4	2.1	0.7	0.5	39.5
"Yugoslavs"[b]	5.4	4.7	4.8	8.2	0.2	5.3	0.7	1.4	8.2	7.9
Albanians	7.7	14.0	1.3	0.2	77.4	6.3	19.8	0.1	0.1	0.1
Hungarians	1.9	4.2	0.1	19.0	-	-	-	0.5	0.6	-
Other Nationalities	3.6	4.5	3.2	9.2	3.2	1.4	7.7	1.3	3.1	1.6
Total	100.0	100.0	100.0	100.0	100.0	100.0	100.0	100.0	100.0	100.0
(number in thousands)	(22,427.5)	(9,313.6)	(5,694.4)	(2,034.7)	(1,584.4)	(584.3)	(1,912.2)	(1,891.8)	(4,601.4)	(4,124.0)

Source: Yugoslavia, (1982) "Nacionalni Sastav Stanovništva po opštinama, Konačni Rezultati," Statistički Bilten, Savezni Zavod za Statistiku, 1295 (May).
[a] Moslems have been considered as an ethnic group since 1961.
[b] A supranationality designation discouraged by official policy during the 1960s and 1970s.
Levels less than 0.1 percent are not recorded.

(0.1 percent) chose a regional rather than ethnic label to characterize themselves.

Since 1945, Yugoslavia's diverse ethnic groups have resided within a federal state which today consists of six socialist republics and two "socialist autonomous provinces." The territorial distribution of nations and nationalities in Yugoslavia does not, however, coincide precisely with the administrative divisions of the country's federal system. For example, 97.7 percent of all ethnic Slovenes live in the republic of Slovenia, and 95.5 percent of the Macedonians live in the republic of Macedonia, but only 59.8 percent of the Serbs live in the core area of the republic of Serbia (that is, "Serbia Proper" without the provinces of Kosovo and Vojvodina), and only 69.2 percent of the Montenegrins reside in Montenegro. Thus in 1981, 16.2 percent of the Serbs lived in Bosnia-Hercegovina, 19.6 percent in Vojvodina, and 6.5 percent in Croatia (the diffusion and influence of Serbs outside of Serbia Proper is an important historical phenomena which is touched upon in different sections of this book, and which continues with certain changes in the present-day Yugoslav state). Moreover, the configuration of ethnic groups is quite different in each administrative unit of the federal system. For example, Slovenia is a highly homogeneous republic (90.5 percent of the citizens are ethnic Slovenes, with the remaining groups each being very small), while the ethnic group symmetry of Bosnia-Hercegovina (the only one of the six republics which does not have a name resembling the largest ethnic group within its borders) is far more multi-polar (39.5 percent Moslems, 32 percent Serbs, 18.4 percent Croats, 7.9 percent Yugoslavs etc.). The pattern of ethnic diversity in Yugoslavia's 510 communes -- the administrative unit directly below the republican and provincial level of government -- also varies considerably from one section of the country to another, with some communes almost completely homogeneous (even in otherwise very multi-national regions) and other communes exhibiting extreme ethnic heterogenity.

Beyond the plethora of nations and nationalities registered in the census, the citizens are also divided along linguistic lines (Slovene, Macedonian, Albanian, Serbian, and Croatian, as well as the so-called Serbo-Croatian or Croato-Serbian variants of the latter two, to mention only the most widely spoken languages), by religious traditions (mainly Roman Catholic, Eastern Orthodox, and Islamic), and the use of two alphabets (Cyrillic and Latin). As in the case of other categories of ethnic affiliation mentioned above, the concentrations of one or another linguistic, religious or alphabetic persuasion are not neatly co-terminous with the parts of the federal administrative framework. In this book terms such as "ethnic diversity," "cultural diversity," "multi-national structure," and the "national question" (the last formulation found more frequently in the Marxist and Yugoslav political lexicons) are used very generally and interchangeably to refer to any or all of those aspects of identity, allegiance, or tradition which are mentioned in this appendix.

NOTES

1. The 1963 Yugoslav Constitution replaced the old term "national minority" with the broader term "nationality-national minority," but a Constitutional Amendment (XIX) in 1968 simply used the term "nationality." A technical distinction is sometimes drawn in Yugoslavia between nationalities and ethnic groups. A "nationality" refers to members

of a people who are already organized with their own written language and other features, and usually also form states outside of Yugoslavia. An "ethnic group" refers to a people at a lower level of organization whose collective consciousness and traditions are transmitted through oral history or story-telling rather than by means of a developed written literary language and with primarily an oral tradition such as the Vlachs and Romanies (Jončić, 1982).

Appendix B:
Entropy Tests of Interwar Yugoslav Elections

Perhaps the most striking feature of the entropy hypothesis advanced by Coleman (1975) is that it runs counter to a very basic proposition in political science which holds that, other things being equal, voter turnout increases with electoral competitiveness. Strictly speaking, this proposition involves two sorts of considerations. First, turnout should be higher in constituencies in which more than one party is running for office (Dahl, 1971:25). Second, within competitive constituencies, turnout should rise as the expected outcome of the election becomes more and more uncertain (Milbraith, 1965:96). Thus, in single-member districts with two competing candidates, the more it seems likely that each candidate will receive close to 50 percent of the vote, the greater voter turnout will be. The same may be said for districts with larger numbers of competing parties: the smaller the winning candidate's margin of victory over his opponents is expected to be, the greater will be the voter participation.

The reasons for holding the expectation that competitiveness will lead to higher turnout are well-known. Where parties face serious competition in their quest for electoral victory, they must attempt to "reach out" to the voters, especially to those who normally might not vote, and stimulate their interest in the election (Dahl, 1971:25). The individual voter, by the same token, tends to be susceptible to such appeals. Since the act of voting entails a certain amount of effort, the voter will be more disposed to vote the more likely it seems that his vote will matter in determining the outcome of the election (Campbell et al., 1966:411).

The policy issues at stake in the election may also be part of the equation. The anticipated closeness of an election may not affect the propensity to vote unless the issues raised in the election are salient to the potential voter (Key, 1949:523). This idea has been conceptualized by Downs (1957:260-76) as an interaction effect between the likelihood that the individual voter's vote would determine the election and the expected benefit in policy terms of the voter's preferred party or candidate winning. In this formulation, voting will occur only if the product of these two terms exceeds the "costs" associated with voting. Since the likelihood of determining an election with a single vote is small and tends to reduce the value of this product to miniscule proportions, Riker and Ordeshook (1968) have suggested that a fourth factor, citizen duty, be added to the equation in order to make it come out positive (i.e. predict that voting will occur) with some degree of regularity.

168

Empirical evidence gathered in the United States in support of this proposition is considerable. At the individual level, Campbell et al. (1966:54) reported that among those respondents of the Michigan Survey Research Centre's 1956 presidential election survey who had medium or strong partisan preferences (two-thirds of the sample), those who felt that the 1956 presidential election would be close were more likely to vote than those who did not. The same result was reported by Riker and Ordeshook (1968) for the S.R.C.'s 1952 and 1960 surveys as well. Discordant notes were provided by Ferejohn and Fiorina's (1975) demonstration that the effect of closeness on turnout in the 1952, 1956, 1960, and 1964 S.R.C. surveys were generally insignificant and Sander's (1980) demonstration of the same result for 1972. Aldrich (1976) has pointed out, however, that if respondents who erroneously reported voting are excluded from the analysis and if a question concerning the closeness of the presidential election in the respondent's state rather than in the nation as a whole is used, the relationship becomes stronger.

At aggregate levels, Dawson and Robinson (1963) found that a rank ordering of American states on inter-party competitiveness in congressional and gubernatorial races produced a Spearman rank-order correlation of .807 with a ranking of the states on turnout. Milbraith (1965:96) reported similar results for gubernatorial and senatorial elections in the 1950s. Barzel and Silberberg (1973) employed multiple regression analysis to show that the closeness of elections was a very powerful determinant of turnout among U.S. states in the gubernatorial elections of the 1960s; and Silberman and Durden (1975) reflected this finding for the congressional elections of 1962 and 1970. Finally, Kim, Petrocik, and Enokson (1975) found that, once the effects of the individual-level factors of race, age, income, and education are removed, turnout levels among states in the 1960 presidential election correlate at .785 with the authors' index of electoral competitiveness.

None of these studies gives any indication that the hypothesized relationship is meant to apply to the United States alone, and even in the studies that confine themselves to American data, the theoretical rationales are couched in what would appear to be very general terms. The hypothesis, if valid, should therefore be evidenced in other political systems, such as the Yugoslav democratic regime of the 1920s. In Chapter 3, we pointed out that party-choice entropy or H(P) represents a reasonably good measure of the competitiveness of elections, provided that the number of competing parties is controlled for. The hypothesis can therefore be tested quite easily by computing constituency-level partial correlations of H(P) with turnout controlling for the numbers of parties for each of these elections. If competitiveness encourages turnout, we would expect positive coefficients. The coefficients obtained are: -.343 (1920), -.456 (1923); -.020 (1925), and .042 (1927). Clearly, the standard or "common-sense" hypothesis relating competitiveness positively to turnout is not affirmed for any of these elections, and in fact a substantial negative coefficient is produced in two of them.

These findings represent the first clue pointing to the validity of the Coleman hypothesis. That hypothesis predicts that H(P) will be related to turnout entropy or H(T) according to the formula:

$$H(P) = \log_2 k \, H(T) \quad (Coleman, 1975:41)$$

where k is the number of competing parties in the constituency and both entropy measures incorporate logarithms to the base 2. The most basic test

TABLE B.1
True and Estimated Values of Entropy Hypothesis log k Coefficients, 1920
to 1927 Elections

No. of Parties (k)	True log k	Estimated log k Coefficients			
		1920	1923	1925	1927
2	1.00	.72(1)[a]	--	1.29(1)	1.05(6)
3	1.58	1.41(4)	1.56(8)	1.30(4)	1.47(2)
4	2.00	1.82(17)	1.95(12)	1.84(9)	1.72(14)
5	2.32	2.15(10)	2.16(10)	2.29(19)	1.93(8)
6	2.58	2.27(5)	2.27(12)	2.30(6)	2.45(7)
7	2.81	2.39(9)	2.77(4)	2.44(9)	2.21(11)
8	3.00	2.65(6)	2.58(6)	2.43(5)	3.00(1)
9	3.15	2.70(3)	2.54(2)	--	2.61(3)
10	3.32	--	3.44(2)	2.97(2)	2.89(3)
11	3.44	--	--	--	3.11(1)

[a]Number of cases given in brackets.

of the hypothesis is to determine whether the empirically-derived coefficients linking H(P) and H(T) resemble the logarithms of the numbers of competing parties. The results for the Yugoslav national elections of the 1920s are given in Table B.1. It is evident from the Table that many of the estimated coefficients, especially in the earlier elections, are reasonably close to their predicted values, although there is a general tendency for the estimated values to be lower than the predicted values. This tendency is most likely a function of the arbitrary manner by which the number of parties per district was determined. Following Coleman (1975:149), all parties receiving 1 percent or more of the vote were counted as distinct parties, with all vote totals less than 1 percent pooled into an "other" category. With so many small parties in the elections, this procedure, although as reasonable as any, could have quite easily assigned a district to an orbit that is too high for its "effective" number of competing parties, thereby making its H(P) level appear too low. There is, in addition, the undeniable fact that most coefficients were estimated from a very small number of cases. Even if a surer method of knowing in which orbit a district should be located were available, situations such as this one in which there are relatively few districts and many distinct orbits cannot be expected to provide good indications of the validity of the entropy hypothesis.

Some idea of how orbits derived from the coefficients in Table B.1 fit a data array of H(P) against turnout can nevertheless be gained from Figure B.1, which fits orbits calculated from the coefficients in the Table to the data for the 1923 election. In the figure the orbits do appear to follow the shape of the data quite well, suggesting that the data conforms in a general manner to an entropy-type pattern. The one major irregularity is the positioning of the seven-party orbit above the eight-party and nine-party orbits, which themselves are virtually coincident. This could, of course, be

FIGURE B.1
Estimated Entropy Orbits, 1923 Election

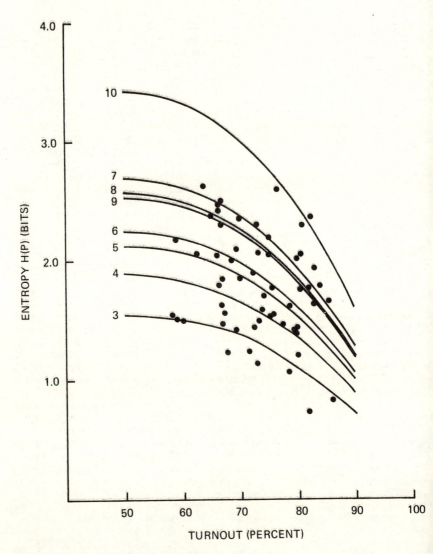

a consequence of faulty estimation of the coefficients due to the use of a small number of cases or to misplacement of districts into orbital categories.

It was because of these drawbacks that the polynomial-fit test was employed as the first test of the hypothesis in Chapter 3. This test was performed in two stages. First, a single second-degree polynomial of the form $f(t) = a_0 + a_1 t + a_2 t^2$ was fitted to the data for each election as arranged in Figure B.1, in order to determine if it takes on the approximate shape of an entropy curve, concave downwards and with a maximum at around 50 percent turnout. Since there are a rather large number of orbits, the data for each election were then divided into two groups, districts with six or more parties and districts with less than six parties, and the test was re-applied. This dividing line was chosen for the simple reason that it provided the most even division of the districts over the four elections. Because of the probability -- likely to be great in a new political system with a large range of orbits -- that many districts will be in the process of orbital change (i.e. increasing or decreasing their numbers of competing parties) at any one time, it is expected that the upper contour of the data survey will fit the hypothesized form better (Coleman, 1975:99-102).

The results of these tests were given in Table B.2. A polynomial of the hypothesized form would have a positive 'a_1' coefficient and a negative 'a_2' coefficient. For the first stage of the test -- the fitting of a single polynomial to all districts in each election -- parabolas of the expected shape are produced in three of the four elections (1920, 1923, and 1927). The maxima of these fitted parabolas are somewhat above the 50 percent turnout level, but since the range of turnout levels is rather restricted in these data (no districts in any of the elections had turnouts as low as 50 percent), errors in estimating the shape of the curve outside of this range are to be expected. Nor should too much emphasis be placed on the multiple correlations generated by this polynomial fitting. Their generally low values reflect the fact that the data-points are spread out over a large number of orbits in all of the elections.

In the remainder of Table B.2, the findings of the separate polynomial fits to the two halves of the data distributions for each election are presented. It is immediately apparent that the upper halves of the data arrays (those with six or more parties) do conform to the hypothesized shape much better than the lower halves. In the 1920, 1923, and 1927 elections, parabolas of the correct shape are again produced for the upper halves with maxima at turnout levels closer to 50 percent turnout and larger multiple correlations than before. In the 1925 election, the distribution of data-points conforms more closely to a straight line; however, the slope of the line is negative, indicating that H(P) decreases with turnout as the hypothesis predicts. Thus, all elections exhibit, at their upper levels of party numbers, relationships that are basically consistent with the entropy hypothesis, although the 1925 election demonstrates this perhaps less than the others. In contrast, among districts of five or fewer parties, only one election (1927) took on the hypothesized form.

The other test that was employed in Chapter 3 consisted of a regression of electoral competitiveness (H(P) divided by the logarithm of the number of competing parties) on H(T) for each election. This test involved relating each data-point to its predicted orbit as did the test in Table B.1, but with the difference that just one coefficient, expressing the overall conformity of the data to the hypothesis, is produced. In this test, reported in Table 3.1, the 1920 and 1923 elections produced results in reasonable conformity with the hypothesis but the 1925 and 1927 elections showed high degrees of error, even if the upper contours of their data arrays did exhibit an entropy pattern.

If we are to accept the validity of the entropy hypothesis in accounting for these electoral data, it would be desirable to have some indication that the error discovered for 1925 and 1927 can be attributed to

TABLE B.2

Polynomial Fit Test of Entropy Hypothesis, 1920 to 1927 Elections

A. ALL DISTRICTS

Dependent Variable	Election	Polynominal Fit with Turnout			Turning Point	Multiple Corre- lation
		a_0	a_1	a_2		
H(P)	1920	0.5	4.4	-3.4	65.7%	.07
	1923	-0.5	8.3	-7.1	59.0%	.32
	1925	14.3	-32.8	21.2	--	.29
	1927	-7.7	28.1	-20.8	67.6%	.22

B. DISTRICTS WITH SIX OR MORE PARTIES

Dependent Variable	Election	Polynominal Fit with Turnout			Turning Point	Multiple Corre- lation
		a_0	a_1	a_2		
H(P)	1920	-4.2	21.8	-18.1	60.2%	.41
	1923	-2.7	17.0	-14.3	59.4%	.56
	1925	2.7	-1.2	--	--	.18
	1927	-1.7	2.2	-2.4	45.8%	.23

C. DISTRICTS WITH FIVE OR FEWER PARTIES

Dependent Variable	Election	Polynominal Fit with Turnout			Turning Point	Multiple Corre- lation
		a_0	a_1	a_2		
H(P)	1920	5.2	-10.8	8.2	--	.23
	1923	3.6	-4.1	1.9	--	.26
	1925	18.4	-44.2	28.8	--	.46
	1927	4.1	16.4	-11.8	69.9%	.15

processes of change. In Chapter 3, we employed two tests for this purpose. The first test correlated the residual error in H(P) at any one election with the amount of orbital change from that election to the next. A tendency for districts that were distant from their predicted orbital positions at one election to have changed orbits in the next election was indeed found for the 1923-25 and 1925-27 periods. The second test correlated changes in

H(P) levels with changes in turnout controlling for changes in party numbers or orbits for 1923-25 and 1925-27. This test, too, produced correlation coefficients consistent with the hypothesis.

There is one further test of the hypothesis that processes of change were taking place in these years that follow the lines of the entropy hypothesis. A district's party-choice entropy may change either within its own orbit or between orbits; however, Coleman (1975:106) specifies that inter-orbital changes are more likely to occur at turnout rates of or near to 0 percent, 50 percent, and 100 percent, while intra-orbital changes tend to occur closer to 25 percent and 75 percent turnout rates. The reason is that a district that lies near the maximum (50 percent) or the minima (0 percent, 100 percent) for its orbit will find it easier to change its H(P) by changing orbits because in that manner it need not alter its turnout rate. A district that falls in between these extreme points, on the other hand, will tend to change its H(P) by moving within its own orbit because, although it must change its turnout rate, it can make smaller H(P) changes than would be required for a leap from one orbit to another. Accordingly, if orbital change (taken as the absolute value of the change in the number of parties between consecutive elections) is plotted against initial turnout, one should find a non-linear relationship with orbital changes tending to occur at turnouts closer to 50 percent and 100 percent, and reaching a minimum around 75 percent turnout. To test this expectation, a second-degree polynomial curve was fitted to the data for the two electoral periods, 1923-25 and 1925-27. In both cases the polynomial curve fit the data better than did a straight line, and multiple correlation coefficients of .183 and .469, respectively, were produced. These coefficients indicate that the polynomial fit is poor for the first period, and fairly good for the second period. Thus, for the latter period at least, inter-orbital changes did tend to occur at turnout values predicted by Coleman's theory. Figure B.2 presents the scattergram with the estimated polynomial curve for the 1925-27 data.

The finding that the 1925-27 pattern of inter-orbital change fits the hypothesis better than the 1923-25 pattern is most likely related to earlier findings that single out 1925 as the most deviant election of the four. In Chapter 3 we noted a particularly pronounced geographic patterning to the 1925 errors in H(P) levels, and suggested an interpretation in terms of governmental interference in the electoral process. We shall consider some further aspects to the error in 1925 and 1927 in due course; first, let us turn to the even more manipulated election of 1935, when just four electoral choices, two of them very minor, were permitted to appeal to the electorate.

In Table B.3, the results of two tests of the entropy hypothesis, the polynomial-fit test and the estimates of the log k coefficients in the entropy equation, are presented. Because there were 353 constituencies in the 1935 election and just three orbits, these tests were performed separately for each orbit (twenty-eight constituencies had just one party and were excluded from the analysis). The polynomial-fit data indicate that the relationship takes on the expected concave parabolic shape for each orbit, but, as in the 1920s, the maxima occur at turnout levels well above 50 percent. As for the log k estimates, they are lower than the hypothesis predicts, particularly for the three- and four-party orbits.

That the log k estimates are especially poor for the three-party and four-party constituencies would seem to be a reflection of the fact that the two small parties in the election garnered so few votes (less than 2 percent in total). The regression test presented in Table 3.3 also indicated that the

174

FIGURE B.2
Orbital Change (1925-27) by Turnout (1925)

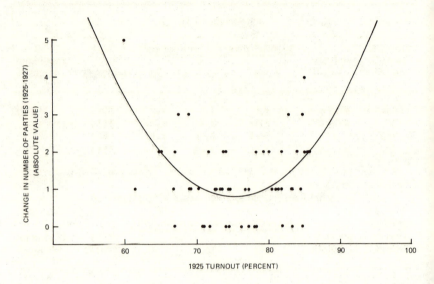

minor parties did not function as meaningful choices for the electorate, for when they were not taken into account, the test produced results much closer to the predictions of the hypothesis and to the findings for the 1920 and 1923 elections. On the assumption that the 1935 election should be treated as a two-choice election (Government bloc vs. Opposition bloc), the estimate of the log k coefficient derived from all 325 competitive constituencies becomes 0.96, remarkably close to the predicted value of 1.00.

This series of findings substantially bolsters the argument that the 1935 data conform to the general shape of the entropy hypothesis. Even so, the amount of error is relatively high: the explained variance on the regression test is between three and four times less than it was for the 1920 and 1923 elections. In addition, the turning-point or maximum for the fitted polynomial, which occurs at the 64.8 percent turnout level, is well above the predicted 50 percent mark, as it was for the elections of the 1920s. It is tempting to attribute the lower explained variance in 1935 to the nearly sevenfold increase in the number of constituencies, which undoubtedly introduced much more random error into the data. Yet there is a way in which both types of errors can be attributed, at least in part, to the geographic distribution of the H(P) residual errors discussed in Chapter 3.

One basic characteristic of this pattern is that the ethnically homogeneous regions to the northwest and southwest of the central axis formed by Bosnia, Vojvodina, and parts of Croatia tended to display exceptionally low constituency turnout levels, for reasons which, we suggested, were linked to governmental pressures and manipulations of various sorts. Since these constituencies were ethnically more

TABLE B.3
Entropy Hypothesis Tests, 1935 Election

A. POLYNOMINAL-FIT TEST

Dependent Variable	No. of Choices (k)	Polynominal Fit with Turnout			Turning Point	Multiple Corre- lation
		a_0	a_1	a_2		
H(P), 1935	2 (n=198)	-2.1	8.8	-6.7	65.7%	.37
	3 (n=111)	-0.1	2.8	-2.0	71.9%	.20
	4 (n=16)	-9.1	27.7	-18.5	74.8%	.45
	All (n=325)	-1.5	7.5	-5.8	64.8%	.33

B. ESTIMATES OF LOG K COEFFICIENTS

Dependent Variable	No. of Choices (k)	True log k	Estimated log k
H(P), 1935	2 (n=198)	1.00	0.85
	3 (n=111)	1.58	1.09
	4 (n=16)	2.00	1.32
	2 (All cases)	1.00	0.96

homogeneous, their H(P) levels would naturally have been low as well. The result is a concentration of constituencies which had turnout levels closer to 50 percent, yet H(P) levels lower than other constituencies in the country. The effect of this type of error is not just to weaken the goodness-of-fit of the data to the hypothesis but, more specifically, to prevent the polynomial curves from reaching their maxima at the 50 percent turnout level. This is because the presence of data-points with low H(P) levels and turnout levels closer to 50 percent than the hypothesis predicts would cause a polynomial curve which had been increasing in H(P) levels with declining turnouts to reverse itself at some point above 50 percent turnout and begin to decline with declining turnout thereafter. This explanation for higher than expected turning-points is equally valid for the elections of the 1920s and for the 1935 election, but in 1935 a second source of error is also evident. In that election, it appears that constituencies in the central high-entropy regions of the country, possibly frustrated by the artificial limitations imposed on maximum H(P) levels implicit in the limitation on the number of competing parties, were more prone to over-shoot predicted H(P) levels than they had been in the 1920s.

176

FIGURE B.3
Party-Choice Entropy Residuals by Region, 1935 Election

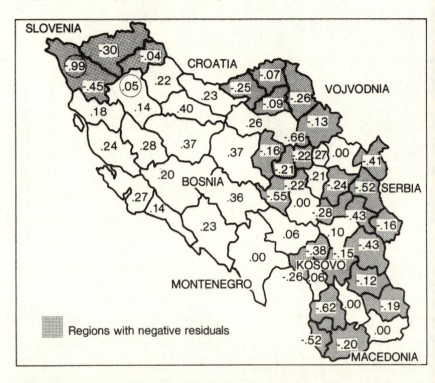

This can be seen clearly if Figure 3.4, which plots H(P) residuals for 1925, is compared with Figure B.3, which plots the mean 1935 residuals for the same fifty-six districts.

The most remarkable features that emerge from this analysis are (1) that the error turns out to be so highly patterned, and (2) that the data continues to conform to the basic pattern predicted by the entropy hypothesis, despite the increasingly heavy-handed manipulations of mass electoral behavior by the authorities in later elections. The hypothesis has demonstrated a certain degree of "robustness" which has allowed us to discover the reality of the state of incorporation in the system beneath the contrivances of the authoritarian regime. In none of the evidence considered here is there any support for the common assumption that competitiveness stimulates turnout. Rather, we would maintain, the evidence over the five elections provides substantiation enough to conclude that Coleman's hypothesis adequately describes electoral behavior in interwar Yugoslavia and can function as a valid theoretical base for reaching conclusions concerning political incorporation and cohesion in the system.

Appendix C:
Data Matching and the Definition
of Standardized Regional Units

The availability of statistical data on the voting behavior and the socio-economic characteristics of the Yugoslav population, and the ability to relate the one to the other, was a basic precondition of this book. In the postwar period, however, the task involved the analysis of electoral data covering five elections under three different constituency patterns at each of two levels of the federation and their connection with census data reported over three different categorizations of territorial units, none of which corresponded with constituency patterns. Clearly we were presented with a virtually insuperable task.

The procedures that we adopted to overcome these problems of non-comparability of units inevitably involved a fairly large ad hoc element. There exists no tried and true method of achieving equivalence between census and electoral data, or within either type of data over time, in a country that is disturbingly prone to frequent administrative re-organization. The device that ultimately allowed us to match up data on so many different territorial units was the classification of the country into fifty-five regions. These regions were adapted from a regional classification of Yugoslavia developed by specialists of the Federal Statistical Institute to assist Yugoslav authorities in planning at a level between that of the commune, the standard census unit, and the republic. This regionalization, which was based upon traditional ethno-cultural and geographic divisions in the country, is explained in detail in Macura, et al. (1963). It was first used as a classificatory scheme in the 1961 census.

The Federal Statistical Institute's regionalization scheme is in fact a dual one: both regions and sub-regions are indicated. Statistical problems relating to the combining of data into larger units of analysis (discussed in Appendix D) increase with the size of the grouping units, and for this reason we generally used the sub-regions as our unit of analysis. There were, however, difficulties in some cases where the sub-regional division was so fine that it was not clear that certain constituencies in some elections or certain of the administrative districts for which mean capita income in 1955 was reported did not cross sub-regional boundaries. Where such situations cropped up, we resolved the dilemma by by-passing the sub-regions and using the regions instead. In this manner seventy-five sub-regions created by the Federal Statistical Institute became the fifty-five regions that were ultimately used in this study.

The attribution of communes to regions posed few difficulties because the regions were generally defined on the basis of communes and commune maps for the 1953 and 1961 censuses are available (Simeunović, 1964). Unfortunately, constituency maps for any of the elections of the postwar years are not. Two clues provided the information needed to resolve the difficulty that the unavailability of constituency maps posed. The first was provided by the 1969 electoral law for Croatia which, more clearly than other republican electoral laws, indicated that constituencies were defined in terms of communes (Večerina and Paja, 1969). This was confirmed by a map of the republic-level constituencies of Croatia in 1969 superimposed on a map of Croatian communes (Benc, 1974), which also showed that constituencies followed the commune boundaries. The second clue was the very high extent to which the nomenclature of constituencies in all parts of the country matched commune nomenclature. This suggested that the practise of defining constituencies along communal lines was a general one. Since communes could be located within regions very easily from maps, this meant that constituencies could be so located as well.

One important difference in the regionalization of communes and constituencies is that while the regional electoral data used in the study are constituency means in each region, the regional census data represent not commune means but true regional means, i.e. commune means weighted by the populations of the communes in question. This procedure was followed whenever commune data had to be combined into larger units. Other occasions that called for the use of this procedure were the direct commune-to-constituency matchings effected for the 1953 federal election and for the republican elections of the 1960s; in each there were certain cases for which it was evident that two or more communes had been grouped together to form a single constituency. Incidentally, the 1953 election is extraordinary for the extent to which a one-to-one matching of communes to constituencies is possible, a fact essential for the ecological fallacy testing of the regional grouping that is discussed in Appendix D. For both the direct matching of the 1953 federal data and the 1963-69 republican data, the only significant potential for error occurred in the case of multi-constituency communes, i.e. cities, where census data for the entire commune had to be attributed to each of the constituencies in it. Since regions are much larger than multi-constituency communes, it affects the matching to regions much less than it does the direct matching of communes to constituencies. Nevertheless, there is the possibility for error that should not be forgotten, although difficult to estimate. We were even unsuccessful in our efforts in the field to determine how cities were divided into constituencies in order to be able to estimate the scope of the error incorporated in the assumption that all constituencies in any one city had the same ethnic make-up.

There was one other territorial categorization that had to be fitted into the regions: the 107 administrative districts defined in 1956 for which we obtained data on mean per capita income (Ivanović, 1964). No map or definitional material relating to the construction of these districts was found, but since they were undoubtedly constructed from communes and bear commune names, it was a relatively straightforward process to assign them to regions. In combining two or more 1956 administrative districts into a single region, however, there were no means by which the districts could be population-weighted. We therefore proceeded on the assumption that the districts were of equal population, and computed simple or unweighted averages of district income means to serve as the regional figures.

This procedure could incorporate a considerable degree of error. One means of verifying its accuracy would be to relate the pattern of regional mean incomes in 1955, so obtained, with the regional income pattern for 1971. The latter was derived from census data reported by commune and therefore was converted into regional means without difficulty. Despite the considerable economic change that took place between 1955 and 1971, one would expect that if the regional income means for 1955 are accurate, they should bear a substantial resemblance to the corresponding means for 1971. In Chapter 5, we noted that the two income variables correlate at .69, which goes a considerable distance toward providing the needed reassurance in this regard. Table C.1 provides even more reassurance. In the table two sets of correlations are presented, the correlations of income in 1955 and income in 1971, respectively, with invalidation for each postwar election for which electoral data were obtained. Since invalidation is the principal dependent variable in Chapter 5, a comparison of the two sets of income correlations with this variable is particularly appropriate. Table 6.1 shows that the two sets of correlations are indeed highly similar, implying that the regional income means for 1955 are most likely reasonably accurate.

The final area which required a complicated process of matching of data reported for different territorial units is the republic-level elections of the 1960s, which form the basis for Chapter 6. Because constituencies at the republic level were considerably more numerous than at the federal level, a much closer one-to-one correspondence between constituencies and communes existed at the republic level. This meant that there was no need to resort to the regions as an intermediary device to effect the linkage. For example, in the republic of Bosnia, a direct matching of communes to constituencies was possible in sixty-seven out of ninety-seven cases. A further eighteen communes contained more than one constituency, which necessitated attribution of the demographic characteristics for those communes to each of the constituencies they contained. This left just twelve communes that could not immediately be assigned to constituencies. In these cases careful cartographic analysis and some ad hoc judgements were required in order to effect the linkage. Similar situations characterized the other republics, with the exception of Croatia for which a commune-constituency map (noted above) was available to take the guesswork out of the procedure entirely.

If the matching of commune to constituency data at the republic level is more direct, the availability of electoral data at the republic level is considerably poorer than at the federal level. Not only were data on some republics not available (Serbia) or not comparable (Kosovo) even as late at 1969, but data on elections held before 1963 were for the most part unobtainable. The only election for which complete data for the five republics analysed in Chapter 6 were obtained is the 1969 election itself, as Table 6.2 reveals. Another complication is the fact that republic-level constituency boundaries were not invariate throughout the 1960s, as they were at the federal level. One of the sampled republics, Slovenia, underwent a very substantial restructuring of its electoral districting which reduced its 120 constituencies of 1965/67 to ninety constituencies in 1969. In addition, Macedonia, which maintained the same number of constituencies in both elections, used highly different nomenclatures in the two elections that made matching between the two elections difficult. The result was that of the ninety constituencies in Slovenia and the 100 in Macedonia in 1969, only thirty-eight and twenty-nine, respectively, could be matched directly to 1965/67 constituencies. As for the other republics, a straight

TABLE C.1

A Comparison Between Correlations of Income (1955) and Income (1971) with Invalidation per Region, 1950 to 1969 Federal Elections

Dependent Variable	Election	Correlation with	
		Mean Per Capita Income (1955)	Mean Per Capita Income (1971)
Mean Regional	1950	.12	.15
Invalidation	1953	.37	.35
Level	1958	.57	.53
(N=55)	1963	.61	.48
	1965/67	.61	.64
	1969	.08	.00

one-to-one matching across the 1960s was effected for both Croatia and Bosnia, while for Vojvodina data at the republic level for elections held before 1969 were unobtainable. It is remarkable that the inter-election relationships reported in Chapter 6 proved to be so similar to the corresponding cross-sectional ones for 1969, which were established on the basis of a considerably greater number of cases. It is also very fortunate, for otherwise we would not be able to know if the divergences were or were not merely due to the shortage of cases.

Appendix D:
Ecological Fallacy Tests
of Postwar Electoral
and Census Data

The difficulties in interpretation of statistical relationships that first attracted the label of "ecological fallacy" essentially concern multiple levels of analysis. Strictly speaking, a class of problems that might more accurately be referred to as cross-level fallacies of interpretation are involved. These complex matters have been analyzed with considerable sophistication and detail in the social science literature (Przeworski and Teune, 1970), but for our purposes we are concerned with just two relatively straightforward issues.

The first issue involves the classification of communes and constituencies into regions. It is well-known that grouping data into larger units of analysis enhances the size of statistical relationships because (a) part of the error variances are "averaged out," and (b) systemic variables at the higher level of analysis may be introduced surrepticiously into the analysis, creating relationships where none existed at the lower level or otherwise altering the association among the original variables. In order to relate demographic factors taken from census data on communes to electoral data reported on federal constituencies, we were obliged to group both sets of data upwards to the level of regions. The issue here is, has this grouping created or distorted statistical relationships in any significant way?

Fortunately, we can answer this question with some degree of assurance. This is because of a unique feature of Yugoslav territorial organization in the election year of 1953: the country was divided into very similar numbers of communes (301) and constituencies (282). The inference that constituencies and communes were defined similarly is a valid one, and permitted the direct matching of the two types of sub-units with a minimum of error (see Appendix C). A comparison of the correlations generated between ballot invalidation and the demographic variables calculated over the 282 constituencies in 1953 with the same correlations calculated after the data had been grouped into the fifty-five regions can afford an indication of the degree to which the grouping into regions distorts statistical relationships.

This comparison is presented in Table D.1, which lists the correlations for 1953 of invalidation levels with the percentage of the population belonging to each of the nine largest ethnic groups, with the ethnic entropy (fragmentation), and with the percentage of the workforce employed in agriculture for both the regional and constituency levels of analysis. (Mean income per constituency was not reported at this time.) It is clear from the Table that very little inflation or distortion in the ethnic relationships is

TABLE D.1

A Comparison Between Demographic Correlations with Invalidation Levels
for Constituencies and Regions, 1953 Federal Election

	Correlation with	
Demographic	Invalidation Level	Invalidation Level
Characteristic	(55 Regions)	(282 Constituencies)
% Serbs	-.13	-.04
% Hungarians	.61	.41
% Albanians	-.28	-.20
% Turks	-.13	-.11
% Yugoslavs (Moslems)	-.40	-.33
% Croats	.03	.08
% Slovenes	.28	.18
% Macedonians	-.07	-.02
% Montenegrins	-.20	-.17
Ethnic Entropy (H(E))	.03	-.02
% Employment in Agriculture	-.26	.00

evident at the regional level. True, the coefficients are uniformly larger
for the regions, but what matters more is that there is no instance where a
small correlation at the constituency level is inflated into a sizeable one at
the regional level; no matter which data-set we were working from, the
correlations with the percentages of Hungarians, Yugoslavs (Moslems),
Albanians, and Slovenes, in that order, would have stood out.

This is not the case, however, for the employment in agriculture
variable. Here it seems that although constituencies do not show a
connection between agricultural employment and invalidation, regions that
are more agricultural tend to have lower mean invalidation levels. It is
possible that there is, in fact, a broad tendency for the more agricultural
regions to exhibit lower levels of invalidation that the constituency unit of
analysis, being very low-level and susceptible to minor idiosyncratic
irregularities, could not pick up. But the base unit of behavior, strictly
speaking, is the constituency and we must abide by its findings. We
therefore proceeded in Chapter 5 on the assumption that this particular
variable is producing a relationship that is spurious at the constituency
level, and it was left out of the analysis. Apart from this one exception,
however, the degree of correspondence between variables at the two levels
of analyses is such as to permit the assumption that any results calculated
at the regional level may be accepted with a substantial degree of
confidence as applying at the constituency level as well.

The second cross-level problem concerns the need to make inferences
below the level of constituencies, using either constituency-level or
region-level data. Consider, for example, the correlations between the
presence of certain ethnic groups and invalidation reported in Table D.1.
We know the correlations exist at both the regional and constituency levels

of analysis, but what assurance do we have that they signify that those ethnic groups are in fact responsible for the ballot invalidations associated with their presence? For example, just because higher concentrations of Hungarians in certain constituencies coincide with the appearance of higher invalidation levels does not prove that it was the Hungarians that were spoiling ballots. The responsible ones could have been non-Hungarians in constituencies heavily populated by Hungarians, who were perhaps alienated by the presence of so many Hungarians in their community. Or the correlation could be the result of coincidence. Consider another ethnic group associated with high invalidation levels, the Slovenes. Slovenia, the home of most Slovenes, is a highly developed part of Yugoslavia. Is it because Slovenes, as an ethnic group, are not incorporated that their presence is associated with invalidation, or could it simply be that higher levels of economic development are more conducive to dissenting behavior, and Slovenes happen to inhabit a relatively developed region of the country?

There is no way to eliminate these alternative explanations short of conducting sample surveys of the electorate, but there are methods by which their plausibility can be tested. If it is some characteristic of the general region, such as the extent of Hungarian presence in Vojvodina or the economic development of Slovenia as a whole, that is at issue, then the ethnic correlations listed in Table D.1 should not appear if the correlations are calculated over constituencies within those republics only. In Table D.2, the four largest constituency-level ethnic correlations with invalidation in the 1953 election have been re-calculated for the relevant republics. It is clear that, despite the limited number of cases and the restricted variances of some of the variables (e.g. Slovenes are heavily concentrated throughout Slovenia), all relationships survive with the same sign and very much the same magnitude as they had in Table D.1.[1]

These findings strongly suggest that a straightforward ethnic interpretation of these correlations is justified. Unfortunately the analysis in Table D.2 can only be performed for the 1953 election, as only for that election is a direct commune-to-constituency match-up possible. The test can be approximated for all elections at the regional level, however, by means of the following test. For each election between 1950 and 1969, those ethnic variables that had beta weights of .20 or greater in the regression of invalidation for that election, given in Table 5.6, were selected.[2] These variables were then entered as covariates in analysis of variances of invalidation for the appropriate election, with republic as a factor. Controlling for republic in this manner is roughly equivalent, at the regional level, to the control for republic in Table D.2, which was simply to examine each relationship within the relevant republic. If an ethnic interpretation of the relationships in Table 5.6 is valid, one would expect the same outcome: the ethnic relationships should persist even when republic is controlled for.

The findings of this analysis are presented in Table D.3. In the multiple regression section of the Table, the regression equations from Table 5.6 are re-calculated to include as independent variables only those ethnic variables that met the .20 cutting-point. The coefficients entered in Table D.3 are, however, the unstandardized partial regression coefficients rather than the standardized coefficients or beta weights given in Table 5.6. The lower part of the Table contains the analyses of variance with republic as a factor. In the first analysis of variance for each election, the correlation ratios signifying the effect on invalidation levels achieved by republic alone are given. In the second analysis of variance, the appropriate

184

TABLE D.2
Within-Republic Correlations of Selected Ethnic Group Concentrations with
Invalidation Per Constituency, 1953 Federal Election

Ethnic Group (%)	Republic	Number of Constituencies	Correlation with 1953 Invalidation Level
Hungarians	Vojvodina	29	.45
Yugoslavs (Moslems)	Bosnia and Macedonia	69	-.44
Albanians	Kosovo	14	-.23
Slovenes	Slovenia	24	.44

ethnic variables are entered as covariates. If it is the ethnic groups that are responsible for invalidation levels, then the coefficients associated with these variables should remain sizeable and significant even when republic is entered as a factor; correspondingly, the coefficient associated with republic should be diminished. If some feature or features of the republic were responsible, on the other hand, its coefficients should survive relatively intact and the coefficients associated with the ethnic variables should suffer.

The actual results, although not as clear-cut as these alternative prescriptions might have led one to expect, do tend toward the former interpretation. In every election but one, the effect of republic is substantially reduced due to the presence of ethnic variables. Several of the ethnic variables are themselves reduced as well, but in general these reductions appear to be much less appreciable. Part of the reason that both the coefficients associated with the ethnic variables and with republic can be simultaneously reduced is that, over just fifty-five cases, it is difficult to separate out statistically the effects of each type of variable because of their very considerable overlap. In fact, in 1958 and 1963, the principal ethnic group associated with invalidation, the Slovenes, had to be excluded from the analysis, along with Slovenia itself, because the overlap is simply too great for the effect of the republic and the ethnic group to be differentiated. This blemishes the one case, 1963, where it appeared clear that republic rather than ethnicity was the root of the invalidation pattern, for in that election by far the largest ethnic relationship pertained to the Slovenes. That rather doubtful case apart, the general trend of the analysis in Table D.3 affirms the hypothesis that when ethnic correlations are present in the aggregate data, a straightforward ethnic interpretation is probably the correct one.

TABLE D.3
Ecological Fallacy Tests of Ethnic Correlates of Regional Invalidation
Levels, 1950 to 1969 Federal Elections

A. REGRESSION ANALYSIS

Dependent Variable	Election[a]	Intercept	% Hung.	% Alb.	% Mos.	% Serbs	% Turk	% Croat.	Multiple Correlation
Regional Invalidation Rates	1950	.05	.28	--	-.14	.03	--	--	.74
	1953	.05	.12	-.05	-.08	--	--	--	.75
	1958[b]	.01	.06	--	--	.02	--	.03	.70
	1963[b]	.02	.05	--	-.02	--	-.05	--	.65
	1969	.07	--	--	-.07	--	--	--	.43

B. ANALYSIS OF VARIANCE

Dependent Variable	Election	Factor Republic	% Hung.	% Alb.	% Mos.	% Serbs	% Turk	% Croat.	Multiple Correlation
Regional Invalidation Rates	1950	(1).67							.67
		(2).36	.27	--	-.14	.00	--	--	.79
	1953	(1).80							.80
		(2).50	.07	-.05	-.05	--	--	--	.85
	1958[b]	(1).71							.71
		(2).43	.04	--	--	.02	--	.04	.75
	1963[b]	(1).72							.72
		(2).51	.03	--	-.01	--	-.01	--	.74
	1969	(1).48							.48
		(2).29	--	--	-.06	--	--	--	.51

[a]Election of 1965/67 excluded as no ethnic variables had beta weights above
.19 (Table 5.6).
[b]Slovenia and % Slovenes excluded due to collinearity.

NOTES

1. The case of the Montenegrins within Montenegro is excluded from Table D.2 because of the very small number of constituencies (8). The correlation, at -.89, is nevertheless in the expected direction.

2. Only ethnic variables are used here because it is really only with respect to ethnicity that interpretation of the aggregate data analyses needs to be taken to the level of individual characteristics. If the income variables are not excluded, however, it does not substantially alter the conclusions reached concerning this analysis.

References

Adam, H. and H. Giliomee (1979) Ethnic Power Mobilized: Can South Africa Change? New Haven: Yale University Press.

Aldrich, J. (1976) "Some Problems in Testing Two Rational Models of Participation," American Journal of Political Science 20, No. 4 (November):713-734.

Allworth, E. (1971) Soviet Nationality Problems. New York: Columbia University Press.

Almond, G. and S. Verba (1963) The Civic Culture. Princeton: Princeton University Press.

Anderson, A. and J. Frideres (1981) Ethnicity in Canada: Theoretical Perspectives. Toronto: Butterworths.

Avakumovic, I. (1956) "The Communist Party in Yugoslavia," Occident 12(3):197-213.

--------------- (1964) History of the Communist Party of Yugoslavia. Aberdeen, U.K.: Aberdeen University Press.

Azrael, J. (1978) Soviet Nationality Policies and Practices. New York: Praeger.

Barnard, F. (1972) "Between Opposition and Political Opposition: The Search for Competitive Politics in Czechoslovakia," Canadian Journal of Political Science 5, No. 4 (December):533-552.

Barnard, F. and R.A. Vernon (1977) "Socialist Pluralism and Pluralist Socialism," Political Studies 25, No. 4 (December):474-490.

Barry, B. (1975) "The Consociational Model and Its Dangers," European Journal of Political Research 3:393-412.

Barzel, Y. and E. Silberberg (1973) "Is the Act of Voting Rational?," Public Choice 16 (Fall):51-58.

Bazler-Madzar, M. (1976) "Regional Development," in F. Horvat (ed.) The Yugoslav Economic System. White Plains, N.Y.: International Arts and Science Press.

Beard, C. and G. Radin (1929) The Balkan Pivot: Yugoslavia. New York: Macmillan.

Bell, W. (1974) "Ethnicity, Decision of Nationhood, and Europes of the Future," in W. Bell and W.E. Freeman (eds.) Ethnicity and Nation-Building. Beverly Hills: Sage Publications.

Benc, M. (1969) Demokratizaciji izbornog postupku i izborna apstinencija. Zagreb: Institut za društvena istraživanja sveučilišta u Zagrebu.

--------------- (1974) Izborno ponašanje gradjana. Zagreb: August Cesarec.

188

Bertsch, G. (1976) Values and Community in Multinational Yugoslavia. Boulder: East European Quarterly.

Blalock, H. (1972) Social Statistics. New York: McGraw Hill.

Breznik, D. (1982) "The Dynamics of Population in Yugoslavia," Eastern European Economics 20, No. 3-4 (Spring-Summer):215-249.

Campbell, A. et al. (1968) Elections and the Political Order. New York: John Wiley and Sons.

Clark, C. and K.F. Johnson (1976) Development's Influence on Yugoslav Political Values. Beverly Hills: Sage Publications.

Cohen, L. (1977a) "Political Participation, Competition and Dissent in Yugoslavia: A Report of Research on Electoral Behaviour," in J.F. Triska and P.M. Cocks (eds.) Political Development in Eastern Europe pp. 178-216. New York: Praeger.

--------------- (1977b) "Conflict Management and Political Institution-alization in Socialist Yugoslavia: A Case Study of the Parliamentary System," in A.F. Eldridge (ed.) Legislatures in Plural Societies pp. 122-165. Durham, North Carolina: Duke University Press.

--------------- (1978) "Political Science in Socialist Yugoslavia: The Regime-Management and the Self-Management of a Discipline," in S. McInnes et al. (eds.) The Soviet Union and East Europe into the 1980's: Multidisciplinary Perspectives pp. 69-99. Oakville, Ontario: Mosaic Press.

--------------- (1979) "Partisans, Professionals, and Proletarians: Elite Change in Yugoslavia, 1952-1978," Canadian Slavonic Papers 21, No. 4 (December):446-478.

--------------- (1980) "Politics as an Avocation: Legislative Professional-ization and Participation in Yugoslavia," Legislative Studies Quarterly 5 (May):176-209.

--------------- (1981) "Political Crime in Yugoslavia: The Ethnic and Regional Basis of Anti-State Dissidence, 1929-1980 (A Preliminary Report)." Unpublished paper.

Coleman, S. (1975) Measurement and Analysis of Political Systems: A Science of Social Behavior. New York: Wiley-Interscience.

Crvenkovski, K. (1966) "Divorcing the Party from Power," Socialist Thought and Practice 22:23-28.

Ćulinović, F. (1961) Jugoslavia izmedju dva rata (1). Zagreb: Jugoslavenske Akademije Znanosti i Umjetnosti.

Dahl, R. (1971) Polyarchy: Participation and Opposition. New Haven: Yale University Press.

Dahlie and T. Fernando (1981) Ethnicity, Power and Politics in Canada. Toronto: Methuen.

Damjanović, M. (1967) "Opravdanost usmeravanja izbornog procesa u uslovima društvenog samoupravljanja," Izborni sistem u uslovima samoupravljanja. Belgrade: Institut Društvenih Nauka.

--------------- (1972) "Konflikti u izbornom procesu," Revija za Sociologiju 2:61-69.

--------------- (1978) Subjekti izbornog procesa. Belgrade: Institut za Političke Studije Fakulteta Političkih Nauka.

Dawson, R.E. and J.A. Robinson (1963) "Inter-party Competition, Economic Variables, and Welfare Policies," Journal of Politics 25:265-289.

Denitch, B. (1976) The Legitimation of a Revolution: The Yugoslav Case. New Haven: Yale University Press.

Djilas, M. (1969) The Unperfect Society. New York: Harcourt Brace and World.

189

--------------- (1977) Wartime. New York: Harcourt Brace and World.
Djonlagić, A., Z. Atanacković, and D. Plenća (1967) Yugoslavia and the Second World War. Belgrade: Medjunarodna Stampa.
Djordjević, J. (1967) Demokratija i izbori. Zagreb: Informator.
--------------- (1971) O Samoupravnom i odgovornom društvu. Belgrade: Službeni list.
Djordjević, Ž. (1969) Skupštinski sistem. Belgrade: Centar za društveno-političko obrazovanje radničkog universiteta "Djuro Salaj."
Downs, A. (1957) An Economic Theory of Democracy. New York: Harper & Row.
Dzinić, F. (1967) Izborni sistem u uslovima samoupravljanje. Belgrade: Institut Društvenih Nauka.
Easton, D. (1975) "A Re-assessment of the Concept of Political Support," British Journal of Political Science 5 (October):435-457.
Elkins, D. (1974) "The Measurement of Party Competition," American Political Science Review 68:682-700.
Enloe, C. (1973) Ethnic Conflict and Political Development. Boston: Little Brown.
Ehrlich, S. (1981) Pluralism: On and Off Course. New York: Pergamon Press.
Esman, M. (1973) "The Management of Communal Conflict," Public Policy 21 (Winter):49-78.
Farer, T. (1981) "Reagan's Latin America," New York Review of Books 28, No. 4 (March):10-16.
Ferejohn, J. and M. Fiorina (1974) "The Paradox of Not Voting: A Decision Theoretic Analysis," American Political Science Review 68:525-536.
Friganović, M. (1980) "Changes in the Life of the Peasantry: The Yugoslav Model." Unpublished paper.
Geršković, L. (1967) "Problemi perspective razvoja skupštinskog sistema Jugoslavije," Rad Jugoslavenski Akademije Znanosti i Umjetnosti. Knjiga 347:1-66.
Gladdish, K.R. (1979) "The Political Dynamics of Cultural Minorities" in A. Alcock, et al. (eds.) The Future of Cultural Minorities. London: Macmillan Press.
Gligorijević, B. (1969) "Razlike i dodirne tačke u gledište na nacionalno pitanje izmedju Radikalne i Demokratske stranke 1919-1929," Jugoslovenski Istorijski Časopis 4:153-158.
Goldhagen, E. (1968) Ethnic Minorities in the Soviet Union. New York: Praeger.
Gordon, M. (1964) Assimilation in American Life. New York: Oxford University Press.
--------------- (1981) "Models of Pluralism: The New American Dilemma," Annals of the American Academy of Political and Social Science (March):178-188.
Graovac, I. (1974) "O proučavanju struktura sudionika NOB-e i socijalističke Revolucije u Hrvatskoj 1941-1945," Časopis za suvremenu povijest 6:7-64.
Gruber, H. (1974) Soviet Russia Masters the Cominterm. Garden City: Anchor.
Gurr, T. (1974) "Persistence and Change in Political Systems, 1800-1971," American Political Science and Review 68 (December):1482-1504.
Hechter, M. (1976) "Ethnicity and Industrialization: On the Proliferation of the Cultural Division of Labor," Ethnicity 3:214-224.
Hehn, P. (1979) The German Struggle Against Yugoslav Guerrillas in World War II, East European Quarterly. New York.

190

Hodnett, G. (1967) "The Debate Over Soviet Federalism," Soviet Studies 18:458-481.
Hondius, F. (1967) The Yugoslav Community of Nations. Mouton: The Hague.
Huntington, S. (1970) Authoritarian Politics in Modern Society: The Dynamics of Established One Party Systems. New York: Basic Books.
Hurewitz, E. (1973) "Contemporary Approaches to Political Stability," Comparative Politics 5 (April):449-463.
Ivanović, B. (1964) "Classification of Underdeveloped Areas According to Level of Economic Development," Eastern European Economics 2 (Fall-Winter):46-61.
Jacob, P. and H. Teune (1971) Values and the Active Community. New York: The Free Press.
Jončić, K. (1982) Nationalities in Yugoslavia. Belgrade: Jugoslovenska Stvarnost.
Kardelj, E. (1960) Razvoj Slovenačkog nacionalnog pitanja. Belgrade: Kultura.
--------------- (1967) "Remarks" in Izborni sistem u uslovima samoupavljanja. Belgrade: Institut Društvenih Nauka.
--------------- (1970) "Current Problems of Our Political System," Socialist Thought and Practice. (October-December):3-38.
--------------- (1977) "The Political System of Socialist Self-Management," Socialist Thought and Practice 18, No. 4 (November):25-42.
--------------- (1978) Pravci razvoja političkog sistem socijalističkog samoupravljanja. Belgrade: Komunist.
Key, V.O. (1949) Southern Politics in State and Nations. New York: Vintage.
Kidrić, B. (1948) On the Construction of Socialist Economy in the FPRY. Belgrade.
Kim, J.-O., J. Petrocik, and S. Enokson (1975) "Voter Turnout Among the American States: Systemic and Individual Components," American Political Science Review 69:107-123.
Kristan, I. (1980) "Intrafederal Relations in the Socialist Federal Republic of Yugoslavia," Yugoslav Survey 21 (August):3-28.
Liebman, L. (1982) Ethnic Relations in America. Englewood Cliffs: Prentice-Hall.
Lijphart, A. (1975) The Politics of Accommodation. Berkeley: University of California Press.
--------------- (1977) Democracy in Plural Societies: A Comparative Exploration. New Haven: Yale University Press.
--------------- (1978) "Majority Rule Versus Democracy in Deeply Divided Societies," in N. Rhoodie (ed.) Intergroup Accommodation in Plural Societies. London: Macmillan.
Linz, J. (1975) "Totalitarian and Authoritarian Regimes," in F. Greenstein and N. Polsby (eds.) Macropolitical Theory. Reading, Mass.: Addison-Wesley.
Low, A. (1958) Lenin on the Question of Nationality. New York: Bookman.
Maclean, F. (1957) Tito. New York: Ballantine.
Mačura, M., et al. (1963) Šema stalnih rejona za demografska istraživanja. Belgrade: Institut Društvenih Nauka.
McRae, K. (1974) Consociational Democracy. Toronto: McClelland and Stewart.
Milbraith, L. (1965) Political Participation. Skokie, Ill.: Rand McNally and Company.

191

Milosavlevski, S. and N. Milan (1968) Izborniot sistem i izbornata demokratija vo praktoka. Skopje: Institut za sociološki i političkopravno iztražuvanja.

Musil, J. (1980) "Yugoslavia," International Journal of Sociology. (Summer-Fall):141-147.

Mužić, I. (1969) Hrvatska politika i Jugoslavenska ideja Split: Franjo Kluz.

Nenadović, N. (1980) "Izbori ili cinovnička imenovanja," NIN 1530 (May 4):26-27.

Nikolić, M. and D. Atlagić (1967) O nacionalnom pitanju. Belgrade: Sedma Sila.

Nikolić, P. (1969) Savezna skupština u ustavnom i političkom sistemu Jugoslavije. Belgrade: Savez Udruženja Pravnika Jugoslavije.

Nordlinger, E. (1972) Conflict Regulation in Divided Societies. Cambridge, Mass.: Center for International Affairs, Harvard University.

Palmer, H. (1976) "Reluctant Hosts: Anglo-Canadian Views of Multi-culturalism in the Twentieth Century," in Conference Report, Second Canadian Conference on Multiculturalism. Ottawa: Canadian Consultative Council on Multiculturalism.

Parsons, T. (1978) "Cleavage and Conflict in Modern Type Societies," in N. Rhoodie (ed.) Intergroup Accommodation in Plural Societies. London: Macmillan Press.

Pavlowitch, S. (1971) Yugoslavia. London: E. Benn.

Pečujlić, M. (1963) Promene u socijalnoj strukturi Jugoslavije. Belgrade: Visoka Škola Političkih Nauka.

Pegan, S. (1982) "Od poželjnih ličnih osobina do stvarne uloge delegata," in J. Djordjević (ed.), Skupštinski izbori 1982. Belgrade: Institut za Političke Studije.

---------------- (1970) "Socijalni sastav predstavničkih tela," in Milan Matić et al. (eds.) Skupštinski izbori, 1969. Belgrade: Institut Društvenih Nauka.

Petranović, B. (1964) Političke i pravne prilike za vreme privremene vlade DJF. Belgrade: Institut Društvenih Nauka.

-------------- (1969) Politička i ekonomska osnova narodne vlasti u Jugoslaviji za vreme obnove. Belgrade: Institut za Savremenu Istoriju.

Popovic, N. (1968) Yugoslavia: The New Class in Crisis. Syracuse: Syracuse University Press.

Prelević, M. (1970) "Neki podaci o oružanim formacijama NOR-2 1941-1944 godine," Zbornik Radova: Politička Skola JNA 3:120-132.

Przeworski, A. and H. Teune (1970) The Logic of Comparative Social Inquiry. New York: John Wiley and Sons.

Pupić, V. (1969) "An Assessment of the Elections," Socialist Thought and Practice 34 (April-June):58-64.

Rabushka, A. and K.A. Shepsle (1972) Politics in Plural Societies: A Theory of Democratic Instability. Columbus: Charles E. Merrill.

Rae, D. (1967) The Political Consequences of Electoral Laws. New Haven: Yale University Press.

Raić, A. (1982) "Jugoslaveni u Vojvodini," Naše Time 26, No. 10.

Rakočević, M.F. (1937) "Slovenačko Selo," in Selo i Seljaštvo. Sarajevo: Pregled.

Reitz, J. (1980) The Survival of Ethnic Groups. Toronto: McGraw-Hill.

Rhoodie, N. (1978) Intergroup Accommodation in Plural Societies: A Selection of Conference Papers with Special Reference to the Republic of South Africa. London: Macmillan.

Riker, W. and P. Ordeshook (1968) "A Theory of the Calculus of Voting," American Political Science Review 62:25-42.
Rotenburg, G. (1966) The Military Border in Croatia 1740-1881. Chicago: University of Chicago Press.
Rothchild, D. and V. Olorunsola, eds. (1982) State Versus Ethnic Claims: African Policy Dilemmas. Boulder: Westview.
Rothschild, J. (1974) East Central Europe Between the Two World Wars. Seattle: University of Washington Press.
--------------- (1981) Ethnopolitics, A Conceptual Framework. New York: Columbia University Press.
Rusinow, D. (1977) The Yugoslav Experiment 1948-1974. Berkeley: University of California.
Sanders, E. (1980) "On the Costs, Utilities, and Simple Joys of Voting," The Journal of Politics 42, No. 3 (August):854-867.
Savez Komunista Jugoslavije (1975) Deseti kongress saveza komunista Jugoslavije. Belgrade: Komunist.
Seton-Watson, R.W. (1976) R.W. Seton-Watson i Jugoslaveni, korespondencija II, 1918-1941. Zagreb: Liber.
Shoup, P. (1968) Communism and the Yugoslav National Question. New York: Columbia University Press.
Šiber, I. (1979) Delegatski sistem i izborni procesi. Zagreb: Institut za Političke Nauke, Fakultet Političkih Nauka.
Silberman, J. and G. Durden (1975) "The Rational Behavior Theory of Voter Participation: The Evidence from Congressional Elections," Public Choice 23 (Fall):101-108.
Simeunović, V. (1964) "Stanovništvo Jugoslavije i Socijalističkih Republika 1921-1961," Studije, Analize i Prikazi 22 (December):1-135.
Simmonds, G. (1977) Nationalism in the USSR and Eastern Europe. Detroit: University of Detroit.
Skilling, G. (1976) Czechoslavakia's Interrupted Revolution. Princeton: Princeton University Press.
Socijalistički Savez (1969) Zbornik dokumenta, 1945-1969. Belgrade: Export Press.
Stanić, G. (1982) "Membership in the League of Communists of Yugoslavia," Yugoslav Survey 23, No. 4 (November):25-36.
Šuvar, S. (1970) "Marginal Notes on the Nationalities Question," International Journal of Politics 2 (Spring):42-77.
--------------- (1975) "Naciji i medjunacionalni odnosi," in N. Pasić and B. Spadijer (eds.) Društveno-Politicki Sistem SFRJ. Belgrade: Radnička Stampa.
Te Selle, S. (1973) The Rediscovery of Ethnicity. New York: Harper and Row.
Tito, J.B. (1948) Political Report of the Central Committee of the Communist Party of Yugoslavia. Belgrade.
--------------- (1963) Selected Speeches and Articles 1941-1961. Zagreb: Naprijed.
--------------- (1978) "Josip Broz Tito on the National Question," Yugoslav Survey 19 (May):3-24.
Tomasovich, J. (1975) The Chetniks. Stanford: Stanford University Press.
Trajkovski, T. (1974) "Prvi izbori na delegatskom principu i sastavu delegacija i skupština," Socijalizam 17:781-795.
Tudjman, F. (1978) Nationalism in Contemporary Europe. Boulder: East European Monographs.

Van den Berghe, P. (1981) Ethnic Phenomenon. New York: Elsevier.
------------- (1967) Race and Racism: A Comparative Perspective.
New York: John Wiley and Sons.
Večerina, M. and B. Paja (1969) Izbori 1969. Zagreb: Narodne Novine.
Verba, S. et al. (1971) The Modes of Democratic Participation: A Cross-
National Analysis. Beverly Hills: Sage Publications.
------------- (1978) Participation and Equality: A Seven Nation
Comparison. Cambridge: Cambridge University Press.
Vlajčić, G. (1970) "KPJ: Nacionalno pitanje 1919-1941," Socializam i
nacionalno pitanje. Zagreb: Centar za Aktualni Politički Studij.
Vrhovec, J. (1970) "Akualni politički aspekti nacionalnog pitanja,"
Socijalizam i nacionalno pitanje. Zagreb: Centar za aktualni politički
studij.
Vušković, B. (1982) "Tko su Jugoslaveni?," Naše Teme 26, No. 10.
Walzer, K. (1980) "Pluralism: A Political Perspective," in S. Thernstrom
(ed.) Harvard Encyclopedia of American Ethnic Groups. Cambridge:
Harvard University Press.
Warwick, P. (1983) "Competitiveness and Voting: Accepted Wisdom
Reconsidered." Unpublished Paper.
Wildgren, J. (1971) "The Measurement of Hyperfractionalization,"
Comparative Political Studies 4, No. 2 (July):233-243.
Wilson, D (1979) Tito's Yugoslavia. London: Cambridge University Press.
Windsor, P. (1980) Changes in Eastern Europe. London: Royal Institute of
Intenational Affairs.
Wjatr, J. (1981) "Poland's Party Politics: The Extraordinary Congress of
1981," Canadian Journal of Political Science 14, No. 4
(December):813-826.
Yugoslavia (1921) Statistički pregled izbora narodnih poslanika za
Ustavtvornu skupštinu kraljevine Srba, Hrvata i Slovenaca izvršenih na
dan 28 Novembra 1920 god. Belgrade: Narodna Skupština.
------------- (1924, 1926, 1928) Statistika izbora narodnih poslanika
Kraljevine Srba, Hrvata, i Slovenaca 1923, 1925, 1927.
------------- (1932) Popis Stanovništva od 31 Januana 1921. God. Sarajevo:
Državna Stamparija.
------------- (1935) Statistički izbor narodnih poslanika za prvu
Jugoslovenskih narodnu skupštinu 1931. Belgrade: Narodna Skupština.
------------- (1938) Statistika izbora narodnih poslanika za Narodnu
Skupštinu 1935. Belgrade: Narodna Skupština.
------------- (1959, 1967, 1972) Popis Stanovništva, 1953, 1961, 1971.
Belgrade: Savezni Zavod za Statistiku.
------------- (1963) Šema Stalnih Rejona za Demografska Istrazivanja.
Belgrade: Institut Društvenih Nauka.
------------- (1964, 1965, 1967, 1969) "Predstavnička Tela Društveno
- Političkih Zajednica," Statistički Bilten, Savezni Zavod za Statistiku,
266, 372, 491, 590.
------------- (1967-1979) Statistički Godišnjak Jugoslavije. Belgrade:
Savezni Zavod za Statistiku.
------------- (1968) Demographic Movements and Projections in Yugoslavia.
Belgrade: Institute of Social Sciences.
------------- (1971) Migracije Stanovništva Jugoslavije. Belgrade: Institut
Društvenih Nauka.
------------- (1976) Yugoslavia Thirty Years After Liberation and Victory
over Fascism 1945-1975. Belgrade: Federal Statistical Office, 1976.
------------- (1980) "Borci, Vojni invalidi i porodice palih boraca,"

194

Statistički Bilten, Savezni Zavod za Statistiku, 1174 (April).
--------------- (1982) "Nacionalni sastav stanovništva po opštinama, konačni
rezultati," Statistički Bilten, Savezni Zavod za Statistiku, 1295 (May).
Zalar, C. (1961) Yugoslav Communism: A Critical Study. Washington:
Government Printing Office.
Zaninovich, G. (1970) "Party and Non-Party Attitudes on Societal Change,
in R.B. Farrell (ed.) Political Leadership in Eastern Europe. Chicago:
Aldine.
Zimmerman, W. (1977) "The Tito Legacy and Yugoslavia's Future," Problems
of Communism (May-June):33-49.

OTHER PUBLICATIONS

Borba. Belgrade.
Danas. Zagreb.
FBIS (Foreign Broadcast Information Service) Daily Report, Eastern
Europe. Springfield Virginia.
Komunist. Belgrade.
NIN (Nedeljne Informative Novine). Belgrade.
Narodne Novine-Hrvatska. Zagreb.
Službeni Vesnik-Makedonija. Skopje.
Službeni list-Bosna i Hercegovina. Sarajevo.
Službeni list-Jugoslavija. Belgrade
Službeni list-Vojvodina. Novi Sad.
Uradni list-Slovenija. Ljubljana.
Vjesnik. Zagreb.

Index

198

political crime in, 152-154
repression of Albanians in, 77
See also Appendix A; Republic,
definition of

League of Yugoslav Communists
(SKJ/LYC)
See Communist Party of
Yugoslavia
Legislative system
See Assembly system
Lenin, V.I., 13
Liberal democracy
quantitative analysis of, 27-41
Liberal-democratic regime, 139-140

Macedonia
invalidation and choice taken up
in, 133
See also Appendix A; Republic,
definition of
Macedonians
See Yugoslavia, ethnic
composition of
Management strategies
See Regime strategies
Measurement and analysis of
Political Systems (Coleman)
See Entropy
Melting-Pot Assimilation, 12
Americanization, 13
Canadianization, 13
Marxian version of, 13
See also Regime strategies;
Syncretic Amalgamation
Mihailović, Draža, 59
Modernization, 18
Communist program of, 21
Montenegrins
See Yugoslavia, ethnic
composition of
Montenegro
See Appendix A; Republic,
definition of
Moslems, 70, 94, 96
See also Yugoslavia, ethnic
composition of
Multi-candidacies
See Candidate choice
Multi-cultural societies, 18
conflict in, 18
modernization in, 18
politicization of cultural
diversity in, 18

problems of cohesion in, 9
See also Cultural diversity;
Political cohesion
Multi-culturalism
See Cultural Pluralism

National problem
See National question
National question, 1
Communist views on and
inter-party factionalism in,
51-55
(see also Communist Party of
Yugoslavia and inter-party
factionalism in)
Communist views on
(1924-1934), 54-56
Communist views on
(1935-1941), 56-57
elite studies of, 2
survey studies of, 2
workers' councils literature and, 2
See also Cultural diversity;
Regime strategies
Nationalism
and the Albanian intelligentsia,
158
and Croatian intellectuals, 144
and the intelligentsia, 144
in Croatia, 144-145
in Kosovo, 144

Partisan movement, 58-66
area of wartime operation, 60-63
ethnic composition of, 63,
71-72n.2
in Figure 4.1, 64
leadership of, 21, 58, 66, 141
social composition of, 72n.3
wartime recruitment of, 61
See also Communist Party of
Yugoslavia
Party competition
See Political parties
Per capita annual income, 21-22
in Figure 2.2, 23
Plural candidacies
See Candidate choice
Pluralism, 78, 147
and elite anxiety, 144-146
See also Pluralist Socialism;
Pluralistic Accommodation
Pluralist Socialism, 14, 77-79, 103,
129, 133, 142-146, 150, 157-159